Dear Ginie,

 I struggled for several years attempting to get my thoughts on paper. After taking your writing course, *How To Write A Book In 3 Weeks*, the words exploded onto the page.

 I finished my book a few months after completing your class and sales continue to grow. In addition to selling overseas in English, a foreign publisher just paid me a licensing fee to create a Finnish version and I am in negotiations with companies in Brazil and Turkey for additional translation rights.

 Without your help I certainly would not be enjoying these fruits of my labor. In fact, I might not have written the book at all. Thank you very much!

Ross G. H. Shott
Author of "The Dark Arts Of Immortality"

Ginie,

We just finished writing our book!

I don't know if you remember us at the UT (University of Texas) evening class. My husband knew your brother and I just signed up to find out what he needed to do to get this book OUT OF HIM!

Well, you inspired him and he went home, sat down and wrote it. It was surreal to watch. It just flowed out of him. 68,000 words.

Bill is so ready to write the next book he has been developing for years. A plastic surgeon – can you believe it? You really started something.

This past year we have felt that we are on a new path on life's journey and then we signed up for your course. We sensed your spirit immediately.

Bless you,
Sue and Bill Bailey, MD

Ginie, I had collected a lifetime of experiences and happenings knowing they had to be put in print. Thank you for presenting an instructive class that gave me the details and application to do it. My book "Angels Whisper" is now available through all major stores only months after I completed your powerful course in "getting published." Your book-writing seminar was the greatest tool. Many thanks.

"Your class helped me organize and get my book finished. I have been doing appearances, book signing, expos, workshops, radio shows, et., so I'm doing well! Thanks for putting the helpful information into your teaching class.

Sincerely,
Lou J. Free
Author of "Angels Whisper"
- in bookstores and ParadiseWest.com/loujfree

Learn how <u>YOU</u> can Write A Book In 3 Weeks - Or Less! from best-selling Author & Speaker Ginie Sayles

Whether it is Fiction - or Non-fiction - you can toss aside the tedious "Old School" methods of writing! Now, Bestselling Author GINIE SAYLES teaches her own unique and simple methods to help you become a prolific writer.

You can write faster than you think you can!

In this book you can LEARN:

- ✓ To <u>**structure a Fiction Plot**</u> *in about 30 minutes to an hour!*
- ✓ **Completely** <u>**outline a Non-fiction Book**</u> **and chapters –** *about 30 minutes to an hour!*
- ✓ **Day-by-day steps to write your book.**

Forget the foolishness of so-called 'writer's block." The book you have inside you may be the key to a whole new life – but first you have to get it from idea to completion – and now you can!

Ginie's techniques are easy, effective, and amazingly simple. You will be surprised at how much you can accomplish quickly.

Growing up in a small West Texas town where she was born, GINIE SAYLES never dreamed she would become a bestselling author.

"In fact," she says, *"I had no confidence whatsoever about being able to write a book at all. I was overwhelmed at the thought of trying. That is one reason I teach this course – to take the intimidation out of writing – and to show people how they can do it in spite of themselves.*

Students do not need a background in writing because I make it so easy to understand that anyone can follow my step-by-step methods."

Because of her books, Ginie has appeared on major talk shows and media worldwide - and she funded The Ginie Sayles Scholarship For Single Parents with the royalty from one of her books.

Books by Ginie Sayles

For Current Book Titles, DVDs, and CDs by Ginie Sayles, check with your local bookstore or various online sources, such as Amazon.com, Barnes and Noble, Borders, giniesayles.com, and popular Social Internet sites.

Writer's Block Is A Crock!

Write A Book In 3 Weeks – Or Less!

Ginie Sayles

iUniverse, Inc.
New York   Bloomington

iUniverse books may be ordered through booksellers or by contacting:

iUniverse
1663 Liberty Drive
Bloomington, IN 47403
www.iuniverse.com
1-800-Authors (1-800-288-4677)

Because of the dynamic nature of the Internet, any Web addresses or links contained in this book may have changed since publication and may no longer be valid. The views expressed in this work are solely those of the author and do not necessarily reflect the views of the publisher, and the publisher hereby disclaims any responsibility for them.

ISBN: 978-1-4401-2881-3 (sc)
ISBN: 978-1-4401-2882-0 (ebook)

Printed in the United States of America

iUniverse rev. date: 06/25/2009

Cover Graphic by Reed Sayles
www.giniesayles.com

*I dedicate this book to **you**.*

Loving Thanks
(Acknowledgements)

Thank you to God, and to my loving and devoted husband, Reed Sayles, who is my 'support system' and my 'success factor.'

Thank you to my late parents, T.R. and Vera Morris, who sacrificed for my brother and me, and to my ancestors who died long before I was born. My study of their lives inspired me to live my life more fully.

Thank you to Audrei – the sunshine of my life – and Ben Simcox: you both mean so much to me; and to Austin, Trey and Brandon Simcox.

Thank you to my Grant Scott and to my Austin Scott for joy, love, and fun we have shared. Your Gin-Gin loves you more than you can imagine.

And to Sherryl, Shannon, Stephanye, Sabrina, Skeeter and their dear children.

Thank you to Will Alexander, a young man of Special Needs, whose presence taught me that *we all have 'Special Needs'* to simply "be included" with people, and that simply being 'with' and included by people communicates more than words.

Thank you to Shawn Waggener for helping me get this book in shape!

I especially value my English professor, the late Prentiss C. Windsor of Angelo State University. He was a man of integrity and an exceptionally fine professor. So much of what he taught has been useful to me in my writing career and in public relations.

Thank you to Charles Murrell at giniesayles.com. You keep the website humming and do an exceptional job.

Thank you to Lugene Zang Recinos, a talented entrepreneur and a special friend.

Thank you to the many fine schools, organizations, and individuals throughout the USA, Canada, and England, who have sponsored my seminars on this and other subjects.

A particular thank you to the wonderful students whose desires to write books inspired my desire to write this book for them.

Certain individuals have simply given meaningful memories to me – many years ago; but just knowing them has added a sweet energy to my life – and that in itself is encouraging. So, although it is **unrelated** to *Writing A Book In 3 Weeks – Or Less*; I want to mention a few of these dear ones:

My friends who taught school with me the first year I taught school in San Antonio, Texas; or were somehow on the scene with us at that time. These friends made life more fun. I am listing them with their maiden names (and spelled as best I can remember it), as I knew them: Sarah Dennis, Voncil Barnhill, Susie McGee, Diane Henneke. I love each of you.

Love also to my cousins, Nancy Weathers Nowell, Doris Moncrief Nichols, Betsy Shuble and her sister, Diana Franklin and John and Peggy Odam – and all members of their respective families.

I also value the education I received from English teachers at Big Spring, Texas junior and senior high schools, and at North Texas State University, now known as The University of North Texas, at Angelo State University, which is part of the Texas Tech system.

English textbooks and works by Harper and Row, Harbrace, John Gardner, McDougal Little, Tom Bailey, American Heritage Dictionary, Kathryn Falk, Clement Wood.

Table of Contents

How This Seminar Became A Book

A woman in Rochester, NY, approached me after one of my *Write A Book In 3 Weeks – Or Less* seminars and said, "You could have continued to write one book after another with your great system and no one the wiser as to how you do it so fast. I am amazed that you share this secret. I would never tell anyone else how I do it."

Well, I once took a psychology test that revealed I enjoy the success of other people. I was surprised when I learned that not everybody feels that way. Perhaps that is why I love sharing the information in this book – just as I have shared various information in seminars and interviews throughout the USA, Canada, England, and many places around the world.

Thinking of the comments of the woman in Rochester, I decided that a book would get the information out to a wider audience – although I do sell DVDs of all my seminars, including this one. I also decided to add information that I share in my *Fiction Writing Workshop*.

And I encourage you to study writing from many sources. Why? Because I do not believe any one person is the 'end all and be all' of knowledge on any subject. – and frankly, I do not trust those people who think their way is the only way.

Frequently, it is the culmination of information from many sources that ignites your unique style of writing and ultimately your success as a writer. I am happy to share what I have learned – and happy to be a part of your adventure as a writer.

Welcome to the Ginie Sayles Method of what I have termed 'Speedwriting' in *Writer's Block Is A Crock! Write A Book In 3 Weeks – Or Less!*

I wrote this book for you.

Rules I Break And Make
In This Book

I mostly use my own writing as examples for my explanations rather than 'classic authors' because I believe that if I am going to tell you how to do something, I should have done it, myself. Too, many classics are not applicable to our market today; and my work functions just as well for my purposes.

As you read this book, you may also notice that I sometimes use numbers – 1st, 2nd, or just 1, 2, et cetera – instead of writing first, second, or one, two, et cetera. Yes, as an English major, I do know the difference and that it is preferred to spell out numbers within text; however, I chose not to do that in many cases to keep a measure of uniformity with my title *Write A Book In 3 Weeks* and that has simply been my choice. To make such a choice, however, I want to let my readers know that I have been deliberate in doing so.

Also, I include stories of people or situations that I have either been told or that I saw on television or read somewhere many years ago. I tried to find the source or the names of the people in the stories or situations, and when I was able to find them, I credited the source. However, when I was unable to find the source and if I felt the story or person or situation was important to the point I was making, I included it. I do state that "I once saw" or "I was told" or a similar prefacing remark to let you know. I give specific identification and credits when I can;

but I do not want to eliminate information I remember but cannot locate when I consider it related to the point I am making.

Sometimes I hyphen and capitalize the word Non-Fiction. I do that in order to be sure that anyone with reading difficulties will be able to better read it. And I capitalize a lot of words for emphasis and I know it should not be necessary; but since I talk with emphasis in my seminars, I use all caps in the same way.

Part 1

INNER SPEED

Who
Writes Books In 3 Weeks
– Or Less?

*Even during the days of quill and ink, there were
speedwriting authors. – Ginie Sayles*

There are many authors who write fast; and this has been true
historically. Before personal computers and even before the typewriter, there are authors who are noted for what I call speedwriting – which enabled them to leave behind an impressive collection of works that would be considered prolific in any era.

Below, I have listed a few noted speedwriting authors and
the number of days it took them to write their books:

Famous Speedwriting Authors

Barbara Cartland - 7 Days - Listed in the *Guinness Book
Of World Records* for writing a whopping 723 books, Barbara
Cartland is the most prolific author on record to my knowledge.
She wrote various types of books, from romance novels to health
books – and each of her books were written in 7 days. As an
interesting sideline, which has nothing to do with her speedwrit-

ing; she was related to the late Princess Diana, and many of her romance novels give an inside glimpse into British aristocratic life.

Janet Dailey - 8 Days - From what I have gleaned from Janet Dailey's style of speedwriting is that she writes a novel – start to finish – in 8 days straight. Her bestselling books are translated into various languages.

Sylvester Stallone - 3 ½ Weeks - Movie star/writer/producer "Sly" Stallone, worked his way into the crowded landscape of Hollywood Hopefuls by using his stand-out good looks and athletic physique. He put bread on the table for his family by taking parts in low budget movies, and it also enabled him to make important film connections.

He submitted one screenplay after another to producers who continuously turned down his offers until he submitted *Rocky*, which he wrote in three and a half weeks (Although one source cites he wrote it in 3 days). *Rocky* was a movie of record-breaking success that spawned numerous sequels.

Terry McMillan – How Stella Got Her Groove Back – 30 Days – A single mom in New York City, Terry McMillan has written several bestsellers. She is listed as having written her bestselling book, *How Stella Got Her Groove Back* in a measly 30 days.

The Starr Report – 72 Hours– *The Starr Report* was a tabloid-style report with a political agenda of questionable merit. It contained more than 500 pages and reportedly was written in 72 hours. One million books were on the stands in one week (*USA Today*).

Agatha Christie - 1 to 4 Weeks - Her classic mysteries are made into television series and even a few major movies. This popular mystery writer is supposed to have written many of them in only one week and usually no more than four weeks.

Robert Louis Stevenson - Mere Days - Notoriously prolific in an era that predates most typewriters and certainly computers, we can only marvel at the swift penmanship of this man. He allegedly wrote *Treasure Island* in just a matter of days. Apparently, when an idea gripped him, he wrote feverishly, following his line of thought to the end.

George Sand – 30 days – *Rose Et Blanche.* This controversial woman, who seemed to thrive on scandal, became a prolific author. Although the time it took her to write other books varied; her first novel, written in collaboration, took only 30 days.

Alexandre Dumas The Younger (Junior) - 3 Weeks – His talent triumphed over illegitimacy and racial prejudice, neither of which is an issue today in France; but apparently they were at that time. He was the illegitimate son of a seamstress and the famous author Alexandre Dumas The Elder (Senior), who wrote *The Three Musketeers, The Count Of Monte Cristo,* and *The Man In The Iron Mask.* And his great-grandparents were a French nobleman who married a black Haitian slave girl.

The Younger (Junior) is famous for a novel he wrote in 3 weeks, *Lady Of The Camellias,* that immortalized his love for a French courtesan who died of Tuberculosis. The title refers to her profession as a courtesan: prostitutes advertised their availability for sex by carrying white flowers if available (not having a menstrual period) or red flowers if unavailable (menstrual).

Whereas most courtesans carried roses or other more common flowers; the courtesan young Dumas loved carried white or red camellias.

Widely known as *Camille,* his three week, partly fictionalized account of their love still lives on as a classic two centuries later.

Lady Of The Camellias (*Camille*) by Alexandre Dumas The Younger – written in 3 weeks – has been made into:

- 2 operas
- A ballet
- 4 movies to date:
    - *Moulin Rouge,* starring Nicole Kidman
    - *Camille,* starring Greta Garbo and Robert Taylor, the great classic black and white movie which you may see on Turner Classic Movies (TCM.com)
    - *Camille,* starring Rudolph Valentino, love god of the 1920s silent screen era – which you may also view on TCM.
    - *Camille 2000 (*a quasi-porn movie of 1969)

Mickey Spillane – 19 Days – *I, the Jury,* his first novel, which sold more than 6 ½ million copies just in the USA.

A Famous Clergyman – 1 Night - A number of years ago, I watched a television show about the life of a minister who was a published author of several successful books. One day, he turned the page of his desk calendar and saw that a book manuscript he had forgotten about was due at his publisher's the next day. He sat down and wrote all night long and sent his manuscript by courier to the publisher by the end of the next day, when it was due. I suspect he may have drawn information from some of his past sermons that he had on file; but that is just my supposition.

I could go on and on listing authors who have written books fast – even in three weeks – or less – including an author who had an idea for a book while traveling overseas and finished writing it before arriving at the destination.

As you can see, these speedwriters never heard of so-called writer's block – or simply disregarded it or did not believe it – which was to their benefit.

WHY
Write Books In 3 Weeks
– Or Less?

What's the rush? Is it really so important to write fast?

Why bother? Is it really so important to write fast? Depending on
your goals as a writer, yes, it is important.

In fact, there are six important reasons why you should
learn to write fast:

1. Maintaining Your Flow of Creative Energy
2. The Holy Grail Of Publishing
3. The Reading Market Changes
4. Your Life Changes
5. Speedwriting Forges Bestselling Authors, More Money
6. You Achieve More

Reason # 1: Maintaining Your Flow Of Creative Energy

The most important reason of all for writing fast is YOU.
Maintaining a flow of Creative Energy that gets you from start to
finish on a creative high is the ultimate key for productivity. Most

prolific writers understand the importance of maintaining their initial Creative Flow.

When you have a great idea for a book, you feel excited about it. Ideas flow freely – and you ride a creative high as you sit down and start writing.

Alas, daily duties cut into your time and you may find yourself thinking those activities have priority over your Creative Flow of writing a book. Demands of family and friends can run roughshod over your free time. Suddenly, major seasonal holidays pop up and you stack gift-wrapping materials on top of your desk, covering your fledgling manuscript. You promise yourself that you will get on it after the winter holidays – and you may even make it one of your New Year's Resolutions.

True to your resolution, you dig out your manuscript, look at it, and, instead of the exhilaration of the Creative Energy you felt when you began it; you feel the heaviness of "dead energy."

Creative Energy is momentum. Dead energy is self-explanatory: no momentum.

I heard a radio interview with a bestselling author who writes enchanting Asian ethnic books. In paraphrase, she said that if she leaves a writing project for a time, that when she returns to it, she has to start all over because she does not have the same impetus for it and it does not speak to her in the same way it did, initially. The inspiration she felt at the time she stopped has evaporated.

And she is right. After a long hiatus, the book you started writing becomes a stranger to you and you end up writing a different version from the one that first spoke to your heart, or not writing it at all. All too often, interrupted writing evolves into abandoning the book idea that once filled you with excitement.

Keeping yourself in the flow of your Creative Energy until your book is finished *is the key to writing fast* – faster than you can imagine possible – and surprising yourself with a complete book – even in three weeks or less.

Learn the proper speed skills and learn how to 'create time,' especially if you have a job and family – and you can keep yourself in the flow of Creative Energy and write straight through

– every single day, refusing delays and interruptions – until your first draft is finished.

And I am going to show you how to do that in upcoming chapters that teach speed skills – but you first need to know the other reasons why it is important to write fast.

Reason # 2: The Holy Grail Of Publishing

Many people think publishers are the sacred guardians of great literature – and that an author is 'knighted' by the publisher's scepter of acceptance because the book is magnificently written. There is also the belief that once published, the author will be hailed by fame and fortune and by posterity ad infinitum.

The truth is that publishers are not sacred guardians of anything; and that they do not accept a book because it is 'worthy' in a literary sense. Publishers care more about whether or not a book will 'sell' than they do about how great it is. The 'Holy Grail' is money.

Publisher's are not in the business of publishing books; *they are in the business of making money*. The sooner you accept this truth, the less confusion you will have about writing books. In fact, memorize it, right now: Publishers are not in the business of publishing books; they are in the business of making money.

Naturally, you see your book as *"a Book! –* an important writing for now and for all time." Yes, you should feel that way.

But publishers see your book as just a product and they value it only on the merit of whether or not they think it can make money for them.

A book can be brilliantly written but if publishers think it will not sell at a profit, then it will not get published, no matter how beautifully written it is.

Conversely, a mediocre manuscript – or even a trite one – that has a good market (people to read it) ready and waiting – will be published immediately. That is because publishing houses have a staff of editors who can whip a mediocre manuscript into shape in no time and sell it.

9

This knowledge should make you feel better! Why? Because it means that you do not have to write a masterpiece – which means you can stop pre- judging your work as "not good enough" – because it does not have to be "good enough" – just *MARKETABLE*.

Like any other business, a publishing house must make money from the books it publishes – otherwise, the publisher will go broke – and out of business. They are not being 'mean' or callous; they are just watching the bottom line in order to survive.

All this brings us to the fact that the 'almighty publisher' is the most sensitive of all to market changes when it comes to publishing an author. Whether or not they choose to publish you depends also the "current" reading market at the time they receive your manuscript.

YOU do not have to be a perfect writer; but fast? – Yes!

Why? Because the reading market is ever changing.

Reason # 3: The Reading Market Changes

The great classics, which were the bestselling books of their era, are now "required reading" – i.e. 'forced' – on high school and college students, who would otherwise never pick up the Classics on their own. Furthermore, today's publisher would not accept many great Classics, if the Classics were submitted as virgin manuscripts for today's market. Money follows the reading market – meaning 'what the readers want.' Publishers mirror the market.

Readers are fickle and greedy. Their interests change from book type to book type, and whatever they want, they want *now*. Reading markets change from two to five to ten year increments.

Scanning the landscape of the reading market over a select 20-year period from 1980–2000, we can see many changes in reading tastes.

At the beginning of that time period, the hottest selling novels were **Contemporary Novels** of the era– a chatty, sexy, glitzy, gossipy style of book that gave readers a titillating glimpse inside the fictional lives of rich, powerful people.

Steeped with bed-swapping scandals and lurid secrets, with casual pill-popping and a social drug-scene set against a glamorous background from Dallas to Aspen, Monte Carlo, Hollywood, Manhattan – all the glamour hotspots of the day, snow skiing champions, snow bunnies (non-skiing female groupies who hang out at the expensive ski lodges during 'season') and business moguls betting their souls on a business merger – the glamour of money set the scene and power motivated the Characters.

New writers jumped aboard the Contemporary Novel phase; but over time, the market changed and contemporary novels of that era began to lose money for publishers.

Now, readers wanted books by Celebrities – Ivana Trump, Joan Collins – although the books were usually written by a ghostwriter or edited by the publisher to give it a professional finish. **Celebrity books** that seemed to give readers an inside glimpse into the glamorous lives of famous icons only lasted a couple of years or so in public popularity before the market changed again.

Memoirs became the bestselling book rage. A literary agent explained it to me this way – that *The Wall Street Journal* wrote about the memoirs of an eighty-year-old woman – and the reading market fell in love with it. There was an intimacy and sincerity about memoirs.

Even writers of fiction, whether on purpose or not, found the memoir-style of writing successful during this time. The stirring book, *Bridges Over Madison County* by Robert James Waller had that same haunting intimacy of a woman's diary that catapulted the book to fame during that time period. The memoir effect of the book may have been coincidental to the times; but it was compelling in the memoir style and just as effective when made into a movie.

Once again, other writers saw sales climb in this genre and jumped on the bandwagon. Of course, when the market gets flooded in a genre; that is exactly when the reading market changes again.

This time, books that topped the charts were the **"Feel-Good" books,** such as *Chicken Soup For The Soul* by Jack

Canfield and Mark Victor Hansen. This led to a series of success-ful Chicken Soup books for everyone from Moms to Teens to Business people – and it was a gravy train for publishing that had many authors coming up with a similar format.

Novels based on **Secret Codes**, such as Dan Brown's pow-erhouse book, *The DaVinci Code* entered the market with a bang. Other writers naturally jumped on the bandwagon of breaking secret codes of the government or organizations.

The expanding media relationship with the Internet has greatly influenced non-fiction books that mirror current stories – murders discussed in the media, or political parties covered by the media, or political figures covered by the media, and political issues covered by the media.

Publishers are also aware of the influence of the media on readership and they are more inclined to scoop up writers or per-sonalities who are current and hot in the media.

If a publisher turns on a television and sees a person or views an article about that person on the Internet; the publisher or an agent or television or movie producers will all run wild, scrambling on top of each other in bids to sign the media-popular personality with their firm. Why? Because they know readers/viewers are interested in this person and/or the subject this person represents and that translates into money.

If you like topics in the media and if you are also a fast writer, you may be able to make money with media-based topics.

How can you know what is the current market trend? Visit your local bookstores such as Barnes & Noble and find the "Best-seller" rack. They are typically located in the front of a bookstore near the register where you pay for books.

What if your book is not current? Write your book, anyway because there will still be plenty of fans who favor that market trend even now. My grandmother, Eva Addron Carroll used to say, "Almost everything comes back in style" or 'everything old is new again,' which is true. Sometimes there will be an update to an old style; but the pendulum of time swings both ways.

What if you do not know if your book even has a market? Write it anyway. If you like it, most likely there will be others who will like it, too. And be sure to read *Chapter 12, Target Audience – Know Who Your Readers Are*, for ways to zero in on your market for greater success in writing your book and in selling it.

Reason # 4: Your Life Changes

I know a woman who wrote an entire book in her leisurely pace – and it took her ten years. When she started writing her book, she was in her fifties; but when she finished writing her book, she was in her sixties. No sooner was her book published than her husband began having health problems of such a serious nature that prevented her traveling to promote her book.

Which is scarier to you – writing at a leisurely pace and getting your book written in ten years (if you live long enough); or writing 3 hours and 40 minutes on weekdays and 9-12 hours a day on week-ends for 3 weeks and getting your book written in 3 weeks?

Study the suggested 3 Week Schedule in *Chapter 11 on Creating Time for speedwriting*; or *Chapter44 – Write a Book in 6 Months – 1 Year – Less than 2 years* – Taking Your Time, Finding Your Pace - for leisurely writing.

Reason # 5: Speed Writing Forges Bestselling Authors, More Money

Popular authors, who can meet the demand of publishers by producing books with regular frequency, often become bestselling authors over time. So writing reasonably well is only half the equation of becoming a bestselling author: being 'prolific' is the other half of the equation.

Therefore, publishers like to have good authors who are also prolific. In today's high-tech world, there is little excuse not to be prolific!

Money is made when an author creates a readership of people who like the author's books so well that they impatiently snatch up new titles by that author as quickly as the new books come out.

Read my Chapter 50 on e-books for more information about the developing trends in books and the rising influence of the Internet on writing and on publishing.

Reason # 6: You Achieve More – And That Is The Point

Even if you do not think of yourself as an achiever; something inside you would like to think of yourself that way. And you are – you just may not know how to release the achiever inside you, yet.

By learning how to write fast, you finally achieve your dream of writing a book. No two ways about it, when you learn how to get your ideas down – from beginning to end – you are an achiever.

Chapter 3

Can *You*
Write A Book In 3 Weeks
– Or Less?

Does writing a book – and writing it fast – really apply to you?

I know a lot about you. Over the years of giving this seminar in 25 major cities throughout the United States and Canada, I have found there are three categories of people who attend my seminars and buy my DVDs and Books on *Writer's Block Is A Crock! Write A Book In 3 Weeks – Or Less!* Apart from educators and those who claim they are 'simply curious' you will fit into one of the following three categories:

You are:
1. A published author, with books in bookstores
2. A newspaper or magazine journalist (freelance or staff)
3. A frightened hopeful – scared that you cannot really write a book at all – and wishing with all your heart that you could.

Surprise! Whichever one you are, you can write a book in three weeks – or less!

Published Author

A Harvard Physician with several books already to his credit attended my New York seminar on this subject. He thanked me quite vigorously for giving him exactly the tools he needed to speed-up his writing – BECAUSE in medical writing, 'whoever-gets-published-first' on a breakthrough or theory can bask in the acclaim and may get rich from licensing it.

If you are a published author, you already know that money is the name of the game in publishing and since time is money, learning how to speedwrite is a key to increasing your success. As a published author, you are looking for new techniques to shorten your writing time – and in today's competitive market, you are wise to do so.

Journalist

If you are a journalist, you already have a lot going for you because you have been published, which shows you have good writing skills. And you are probably pretty fast at stringing sentences together with a punch.

You also know how to gather and to condense information into the most important elements and to put it together quickly.

But every journalist I have ever known secretly nurses a book idea. Most want to write a novel they have been thinking about. Others want to tackle an issue in a non-fiction book.

The thorn-in-the-flesh for most journalists is that while nursing a book idea for years, they think they cannot take time away from their bread and butter writing as a journalist. They think they don't have time.

So, if you are a journalist, wishing you could write a book as quickly as you write an article, you will learn in the Speed Skills chapters how to do it in a simple, easy way.

Scared Hopeful

Don't worry, if you fit into this category of being a scared hopeful, rest assured, you can find help in these pages – because – **I began exactly that way. I was a scared hopeful, too!**

I know what it is like to have a dream that you don't even have the confidence to call hope…that is just a tiny wish, filled with longing…a wish you are afraid to acknowledge because it does not seem possible that you can really write a book.

So, if you are scared to even hope…to even wish…to even imagine being a writer…let me point out that because you are reading this book, right now – that something inside you *knows* that you have ideas of value to share in writing.

Isn't that great?

Something inside you 'believes in you' or you would not be reading this book now.

There are a lot of other activities you could be doing this very minute – but you are not doing any of them. You are reading this book at this moment – and that means a mustard seed or a tiny spark of interest (which is all it takes) believes or wants to believe that you can write a book.

And, my writer friend, that is ALL you need. Just the teeniest, tiniest sort-of-wish, or scared hope – *plus speedwriting skills*, which I will teach you – and the key factors given in this book – and that is all you need to take you from reading this book to writing a book of your very own.

I know, because I started where you are, as a scared hopeful. I know, because no one – not you, not anyone – could have had less confidence, less faith, and more doubt and fear than I had. You cannot start lower than I did – so wherever you are; you are starting at a better point – which is great.

Can *you* write a book in 3 weeks – or less?

A resounding 'Yes!'

Chapter 4

My Story

Can a first time author really write a book in only three weeks or less?

I never believed I could write a book. Never. My level of confidence about achieving anything has always been close to zero; and the prospect of writing a book was completely out of the ballpark of my self-expectations.

And yet…all my life, I wanted to be an author. Before I could read and write, I drew stick figures and, pointing at them, related a story about the stick figures to Mother. I spent hours studying my big brother's comic books and tried to figure out the action going on.

In grade school, I wrote poetry and songs and in junior high and high school, I wrote short stories and a play.

Beginning at age ten, all the way through high school, I kept a daily diary, which became my best friend. I wrote my observations, opinions, hopes, teenage problems with my parents, activities with my friends, crushes on boys and my favorite movie stars and the latest songs I liked. Writing kept me grounded and developed my writing skills, although I did not think of it that way at the time. I simply loved my diary.

In my senior year of high school, my English teacher assigned my class to write an essay on what we wanted to do in life. I wrote that I wanted to be an author.

But a high school counselor who also asked me what I wanted to achieve in life squelched that desire. I told him I would like to write books, to be an author.

The counselor shook his head and said I was unrealistic. Such ideas were just daydreams, he said and emphasized that I should be realistic.

I was crestfallen. He was an authority figure and I was just a teenager. He knew best, I thought. Such dreams were way over my head. Hope was gone.

Years later, after my books - and I - had been hailed around the world on television, in magazines and newspapers, I returned to my high school to be inducted into the Hall Of Fame for my achievements as an author and as a public personality.

Surely enough, attending the induction ceremony was the high school counselor who, years before, had said my dreams of being an author were unrealistic. Of course, I was friendly with him, and I never mentioned the destructive impact of his words.

I did not have to. There is an old saying that "success is the best revenge;" but I did not feel revenge. I simply felt vindicated and, frankly, saved – and most of all, grateful to God.

However, at the time he spoke the discouraging words to me, I was an impressionable teenager. And for years, the desire of my heart to be a writer was outweighed by the fear that what I most wanted was unrealistic as he had said – that it was way over my head, out of my league, and just plain impossible.

Your 'Heart's Desire Is Sacred'

To this day I believe any life affirming 'heart's desire' of a person is 'sacred' – perhaps it is God's blueprint or roadmap for our lives, if we are true to it. One of the greatest crimes any person – teacher, parent, sibling, friend, analysts or counselors – can commit is to kill the healthy dreams of another person, no matter how impossible the dreams may appear at the time. It may be that when the Scripture warns us not to call someone a liar or a fool, it is because in doing so, we may kill the Sacred Seed of a life-affirming Heart's Desire that God, Himself, implanted.

And I believe **the right to success belongs to all of us.** Maybe that is why I share everything I can in seminars and books to help people achieve their dreams. My cousin, Betsy Shuble, who is a photographic artist, not only takes stunning photographs; but she is also involved in Bible study groups. She sent an email to me a few years ago, and referred to me as "Barnabas, the Encourager." I had not been aware of Barnabas before her email; and it is an honor; and true that I want to encourage people to pursue their healthy dreams. Encouragement lifts up the encourager as well as the one who needs to be encouraged to succeed. *Discouragement is vanity on the part of the discourager.*

It is exciting to see people achieve their life affirming dreams. Consider me your cheering section, because that is exactly what I am.

Hiding Out

When we are afraid to pursue our secret desires, we "hide out' from ourselves. We hide out in jobs that are not really who we are and that are not fulfilling. Oh, we may fill up our lives with a lot of interesting 'activities' and interesting people and we may enjoy all of them on some level; but by and large, a deeper 'core' satisfaction is missing.

I did that. I pursued classes and careers and relationships that all had merit; but they were not 'me.' I was not drawing from the wellspring of my own soul to be true to my interests, to my desires, to my fulfillment. I was busy, yes. But I was busy hiding out.

The funny thing about it is that the ways we 'hide out' from ourselves end up being more complicated, complex, and in the end, more difficult than pursuing the desires of our hearts in the first place!

And so, we play it 'safe' by living life the way we are told is best for us, in ways that are acceptable in mainstream society. We often live 'other people's prescriptions' for our lives, not our own.

When we hide out from ourselves and live the life we think is best and safe, we abdicate our dreams and live a half-life – wondering why we are not quite happy, a little empty inside. No risk, no danger, no failure…that is how we are operating.

Ah, but not taking a risk is dangerous because we risk never knowing the joy of fulfillment – and yes, perhaps after experiencing hard failure many times. Hiding out from ourselves deprives us – and in the end **not taking a risk to be who we are *is* the only true risk, the only failure**. A former editor of *Parade* magazine, Walter Anderson, wrote a book *The Greatest Risk Of All* (1988), telling stories of people whose lives were changed when they dared take a risk – and that the greatest risk of all is not taking the risk that can change our lives.

For half my life, I hid out and I was marginally happy. My happiness was in helping my daughter succeed in her goals. I kept thinking fulfillment would 'happen' *someday* for me; but I was looking for fulfillment 'outside myself.'

Looking back, I now see my hiding out from myself as very complicated and much, much harder than pursuing the secret dreams I thought were completely out of my reach.

I think of those years of hiding-out as emotionally draining.

How did I hide out from myself?

1. I hid out from myself by living my life the way family members told me to or to please their expectations of me.

2. I hid out from myself in two ridiculously wrong marriages– because "being a wife was supposed to be a solution."

3. I hid out from myself in a series of complicated romances that allowed me to focus on romance as my primary source of excitement rather than focusing on my own achievements as my primary source of excitement.

4. I hid out from myself in meaningless social activities in the name of friendship.

5. I hid out from myself in jobs that were impressive, interesting and far more complicated and less satisfying than pursuing my heart's desire.

6. I hid out from myself by living vicariously through my daughter's successes instead of creating my own success.

All these methods of 'hiding out' kept me busy, busy, busy and allowed me to keep myself distracted from the inner unrest of 'soul dissatisfaction' that came from not fulfilling my true heart's desire – which is the birthright of every person.

My solution? Get even busier, of course, in non-achieving ways! Stay distracted! Focus on something else. Keep hiding out from myself.

What I Did RIGHT In Spite Of Myself - While Hiding Out

Having a baby was a good reality-check for me, though; because I had to face the fact that my little girl was dependent solely on me for financial support. This fact motivated me to go back to college when she was three months old, and to go year-round until I finished.

As a divorced mom, I went through college on Welfare and a student loan – and *my college education has made the single biggest impact toward being able to support my daughter without child support.*

Through Welfare and Student Loans, **my government invested in me and made me a better citizen.** I could not have made it without both programs. Some people may be able to do so; but no one can fairly measure the abilities of other people by their own abilities. I know my situation at the time and that if my government had not had faith in a down and out citizen and proved it by investing in me, I could not have made it – therefore, I hope it is always available to all who may need it, as I did.

Upon graduating, I telephoned Welfare Services and told them I had a job teaching school waiting for me and I would no longer need their help. And I thanked them.

My parents also invested in me as best they could. My parents, T. R. and Vera Morris, lived a hundred miles away from my baby and me. They did not have much money; but they did what they could afford to do. Dad bought me a second hand car for $200 and got it fixed when it broke down (many times). Mother came to watch my baby when I had to cram for final exams.

My parents knew, first hand, how hard it was to make a living with little education.

Dad completed the eighth grade and attended the ninth grade. Mother completed the fifth grade. I am extremely proud of my parents for the good, decent lives they lived, paying their bills on time, paying their taxes (and feeling honored to do so) and bringing up two children. Dad had a decent but low paying government job and Mother was a meticulous homemaker. They did not have much money, but they managed to make ends meet.

Daddy took extra jobs painting houses on week-ends so I could take classical piano and classical voice lessons, tap dancing and ballet, and to pay for me to wear braces. He did the same for my older brother so he could go to scout camp, study piano, violin, and guitar.

My parents very much wanted my left-handed brother, Lefty, and me to get a college education. Lefty had a paper route from grade school through high school. In college, he took student loans and worked 3 jobs simultaneously; but we both owe a great deal to our parents who contributed every cent they could afford to help us attain a college degree We were the first in our family to graduate from high school and also from college.

My brother, Charles Edward 'Lefty' Morris became a highly successful attorney, authored a law book, served as President of the Trial Lawyers Association, established a respected law firm, Morris, Craven, and Sulak in Austin, Texas – and he was on television, informing people about the law. It is no surprise he was listed in *The Best Lawyers In America.*

Like Dad, Lefty considered it an honor to pay taxes – even in the highest tax rate – to benefit our country and its citizens. Lefty was a wealthy man who did not try to find ways to reduce his taxes. He used to say, "A country cannot be great if it does not help the disabled, the mentally retarded, the disenfranchised, the elderly, the impoverished children, veterans, or its citizens in times of need even as it provides opportunities. This is a great country and it gave me the opportunity to be successful; so if paying 40% or more in taxes is the price of living in this wonderful country and repaying it for my opportunities and to help others; then it is an honor for me to pay taxes."

My brother knew how hard it had been for me to go to college with a baby, and Lefty attended my college graduation. My parents, of course, were there. Mom and Dad took money out of their savings to buy me a college ring, which I now wear on a chain around my neck.

On **Graduation Day**, as I stood on the risers, wearing my cap and gown and waiting to hear my name called, I flashed back on how difficult it had been to get a college education as a single mother.

"If ever I have disposable income," I thought, "I would like to create a scholarship for single parents of small children."

Little did I dream that I would one day assign my entire author's royalty on my second book to create *The Ginie Sayles Scholarship For Single Parents* of small children.

But on graduation day, when my name was called and I stepped forward to receive my diploma, I never fathomed writing a book. Even though I was receiving a university Bachelor of Arts degree in English and speech, I still did not think I could write a book. I knew I could teach students grammar and how to value literature and to write reports and essays; but I did not believe I could write a book.

Job Hide Outs

Teaching school was a good job for a single mom; and for those men and women who have teaching as their heart's desire, it is a wonderful profession. The highlight for me was when I was voted Teacher Of The Year by a student body of about 750 students.

Then, for almost a year I was a **Public Relations** executive for Houston Grand Opera and editor of the in-house Opera Magazine. This involved writing, yes; but mostly short pieces or brief press releases.

In retrospect, I do believe Public Relations – or "PR" as it is called - was my most natural talent. I was lucky to have had a stunningly bright mentor named Beth Murfee. The skills I learned in PR ended up being an important key to my later success when I finally wrote my books.

My final hideout – and a turning point for me – was entering the world of high finance as a **Stockbroker** for E.F. Hutton & Co, Inc. – one of the top two brokerage houses at that time. It was quite an honor and the most demanding achievement for me.

I will always be glad for having had the experience in all the above professions, even though I was definitely hiding out from myself.

A Turning Point

When I returned from advanced training in New York, I was the first woman stockbroker at the E. F. Hutton and Company, Inc. office in Lubbock, Texas.

The men who worked there were encouraging and nice to me. At noon, most of us ate lunch at our desks and watched the ticker – a large electronic screen that stretched across the top of a wall and constantly ran stock symbols of the Exchange with the current prices of those stocks.

Munching our sandwiches and watching the ticker, one day, the young male brokers began discussing Miss America. Later one of them referred to her as Miss USA.

I interrupted, "Sorry, guys; but Miss America and Miss USA are two different pageant systems – and very different from each other.

"Miss America is *not* a beauty pageant. Miss America is the single largest scholarship in the world for women. And whereas women contestants are expected to take care of themselves and to be fit and firm; each woman is considered to have her own unique beauty. We have had handicapped Miss Americas. It is a pageant; but not a 'beauty' pageant."

I paused, glancing at the movement of the stocks on the ticker and then looked back at them, "The Miss USA Pageant, on the other hand, is a true 'beauty pageant' and contestants are judged on their physical beauty of face and figure."

The men asked me a few questions about the two pageants and a lively discussion ensued about women and pageant systems. I shared with them that most pageants are a public relations arm for a community or an industry – that the Rose Bowl Queen is chosen in a type of pageant, and so is the Kentucky Derby Queen, and on and on. The winner is chosen to be the image and spokesperson who will communicate the message of the community or industry to the public and bring attention to that industry or community.

When lunch was over, we went back to work – and a turning point in my life.

"You Should Write A Book"

"You should write a book about it, Ginie," said one of the young stock brokers after lunch ended.

We had all refocused our attention on making telephone cold calls to the next name on our lists, when he stopped and made the comment to me.

His words brought my attention back to his face as he said, again, "You really should write a book about it, Ginie. I don't think many people know the difference in pageants."

His words struck a chord that reverberated through me until the old dream stirred with longing. I *wanted* to write a book.

And I wanted to write a how-to book about pageants. I knew from prowling libraries and bookstores that there simply were no books readily available at that time on how the major pageant systems chose a winner or the judges, trainers, and top winners telling contestants how to win the crown.

I knew there were many young people and their parents who wanted the information, especially with so much money and opportunities at stake for winners. I wanted to write a book that could arm contestants with knowledge that gave them an even chance of winning. Yes, I wanted to write such a book – but … no…not me…I couldn't write a book!

And yet, the young broker before me now verbalized my secret desire. "You should write a book,"

His words echoed over and over in my head and with every echo, the desire in my heart grew more intense.

The Doorbell Of Your Dreams

Do you want to know something funny? Looking back, I realize now the young man did not 'literally' mean that I should go home and write a book. He was just complimenting my knowledge about it and emphasizing it with his comment.

But when someone rings the doorbell of your dreams, you swing-wide the door of your heart and believe this person has the Gift Of Prophecy for you!

And I am glad I was naïve and gullible. I am glad *I believed* that he literally meant I should write a book and I am glad I believed his words were meant for me.

With all the enticement of a snake charmer, his words moved in and out of my thoughts all day between cold calls I made to prospective clients.

But – and there is always a 'but' when faith is not quite strong enough – I did not have a typewriter. Personal computers – PCs – were not standard equipment in every home at that time. They were far too expensive – at least five thousand dollars for a primitive version – and the average person who made a good living did not have them; much less a person in my situation.

Writing a book by hand would have been all right; but I write in scribbles and scratches, curving up at the bottom corners of a page, with arrows pointing to something. So, even if I wrote it by long hand, I would never be able to sort it out for someone to type, eventually.

Nope. I really, really needed a typewriter.

But…I could not afford to buy one.

The Buck Stops…Where?

When I run out of answers for my life and keep tripping over my limitations, I say a prayer. I am not advocating you do it if it is not your nature or if you do not believe in God, which is your right. I am simply telling the way it happened for me.

The facts were that I was broke, divorced with no child support, my credit was shot, and I was a new broker with no income to speak of. And now I had a dream in my heart that required a typewriter. I did not have a typewriter and I could not afford to buy a typewriter.

So, I passed the buck to God in a prayer, asking for a typewriter.

Once you pass the buck to someone else, you feel relieved because you think it's not your problem, anymore. You have an "out."

And after I said the prayer, I felt more peaceful in the acceptance that I probably would not have a typewriter and so writing a book was not right for me. I thought nothing more about it when I went to work the next morning.

No sooner had I arrived in the office than the new office manager sent me on an errand upstairs in the storage room to bring down particular investment leaflets.

I told myself that a new broker is also an office 'go-fer' in some ways and I went upstairs to the stock room and browsed through the stacks of muck until I found the leaflets. Gathering them in my arms, I turned around.

My eyes fell on an IBM Selectric typewriter. Now, this might not be peculiar, except that I spent every day for three months up there, studying for my Series 7 exam for my stockbrokerage license, but I never saw the typewriter before that moment.

I stopped, put down the leaflets, and looked it over. It seemed to be in good shape. I went downstairs and handed the leaflets to the new branch office manager.

Hesitantly, I said, "There is an electric typewriter upstairs that seems not to be needed. I really would like to have a typewriter. Is there any way I can buy or rent it from the office with payments deducted from my paychecks?"

Like me, the manager had obviously spent time upstairs in the storage room or he would not have known where the leaflets were.

But he looked surprised. "I didn't know there was a typewriter up there." He paused in thought and then shook his head. "But I can't do that, Ginie. I'll have it checked out for repairs in case we need it in the future."

As I left his office, I thought, "Well, that is my answer. I am not supposed to write a book." And I dropped the idea.

A few days later, one of the brokers told me the manager wanted me to report to his office. As I walked to his office, I worried about whether or not I had made a mistake in my work.

But as soon as I entered his office, I saw the IBM Selectric typewriter.

"Ginie," he said, "Remember the typewriter you found upstairs?"

I nodded.

"Well, I had it checked out – and there is not a lot wrong with it; but because it is electric, it would cost more to fix it than it's worth; so I am going to let you have it."

I stared at him in surprise. "Do you mean I can buy it...or rent it?"

"No," he said, "I am giving it to you. It's all yours."

I was dumbfounded. At that time, an IBM Selectric type-writer cost $500 brand new – and $300 used. *Giving* it to me? Free? I thought of the prayer.

Then I became practical. "Would you mind putting that in writing? I mean, do you mind signing something to say that you are letting me have it?"

"Not at all," he said, "I will place it on top of the typewriter for you to take with you at the end of the day."

Looking back, I wonder if he wanted to be kind and just 'said' that it would cost more to fix it than it was worth. Whatever his reason, it was a generous gesture on his part and an answer to prayer for me.

I now had an IBM Selectric typewriter – and free. At home I checked it out and it was actually in good shape. Only two keys were a little slow; but no big deal. Now I could write my book. There were no more excuses.

So...it seemed God had passed the buck back to me.

If It's To Be, It's Up to Thee...and ME

You would think that with what appeared to be an "answer from On High" that I would go home and burn up the typewriter keys writing my pageant book, wouldn't you?

After all, the only thing I needed was a typewriter! Right? And now I miraculously had one – and it was in good condition and free.

Ahh, but my writer friend, I did not even "switch on" my IBM Selectric to start writing my first book until *three years later.*

Three years! Why? Because I still did not *believe* I could write a book.

This is as true for you as it was for me. Until you believe you can write a book, you won't write it. Even if an angel appears at your bedside tonight and says, "You can write a book," **you still will not write the book until _you_ believe it!** This is why I help you learn how to believe plus the skills.

So in my case, even though I had miraculously received a first class typewriter – and free – it was time for me to accept responsibility for my part of the deal. And to do that, I needed more than a typewriter. I needed some level of 'operational faith.'

No More Hiding Out

Fast-forward three years – I had moved to Dallas, Texas (my Soul City) and the typewriter sat fallow on my desk in my tiny apartment for the whole three years.

The change in me began on a day I returned to Dallas from a trip. Unlocking my apartment door, I stepped inside and set down my luggage, and locked the door behind me.

The first thing my eyes landed on was the IBM Selectric typewriter where it had rested – undisturbed all these years – on my desk.

Guilt washed over me.

I really do want to write the book about pageants, I thought, sadly – and instantly, the same old words flashed through my head. *I can't.*

I can't. The words echoed in my thoughts again and again, *I can't write a book about pageants. I can't.*

Start Where You Are – Not Where You Want To Be

The idea of writing a book was overwhelming. It seemed way too big for little old me. *Unrealistic.* I was afraid. I was scared I couldn't do it and that if I tried I would just fail.

What I did next changed my life. *All purposeful action begins with a decision*; and I made three decisions and acted on them, then and there:

1. I *decided* to **look at my fear of failure and to see if I could deal with it**.

   I wanted to be an author; but I felt it was impossible for me! So rather than denying the feeling and pretending I would write 'someday' I respected the truth of how I felt at that moment; and then...

2. I *decided* to **start where I was, not where I wanted to be**.
   So, I posed *a new question* to myself, "Okay, if I can't write a 'book' about pageants; then what *can* I write about pageants?"
   The first and most obvious answer is "write an article about pageants for magazines."
   Sounds good, doesn't it?
   But I already knew from experience that it is difficult for unknown writers to get an article published in magazines or newspapers.
   Some people disagree with me about this – so you can try it for yourself; but my experience with being an unknown writer submitting articles to a magazine is that:
   - (1) Most magazines will send you a fact sheet of the types of articles they seek or accept.
   - (2) It takes a good bit of time for them to read it.
   - (3) They usually decline – so you have lost 'months' of time and feel even more defeated.
   - (4) If they don't decline, it can be up to two years before your article sees daylight.

Speaking with the hindsight of an author, I can tell you that – for me – it is easier to write a book, get it published, and then sell the magazine rights to magazines. When my third book, *The Seduction Mystique* first came out, national women's magazines published segments of my book every single month that year. The segments looked as if they were articles written by me and even had my name on the by-line; but if you look at the fine print at the bottom of the page, it reads: *from The Seduction Mystique by*

Ginie Sayles. Reprinted by permission of Avon Books, a division of The Hearst Corporation.

However, back to that fateful day in Dallas when I had just returned from my trip, I did not yet possess that knowledge. I just stood inside the door of my apartment, looking despondently at my lonely IBM Selectric and thinking *I can't write a book about pageants; and I can't write a magazine article about pageants..."*

I was back to **starting where I was, not where I wanted to be...so...**

3. I *decided* to find a level of success for my writing, other than a book. This time, I asked myself the following question:

    "Okay, if I cannot write a book about pageants... and...

    "...if I cannot write magazine articles about pageants...

    "...**then, what *can* I write** about pageants?"

Good old Creativity kicked in – and the **answer** was instantaneous. Suddenly, I *knew* I could write a series of brochures about pageants and sell them in *Teen Magazine*.

My whole body lit up! Happy energy surged through me – because I knew I could do this!

✓ True, I felt I could not write a 'book' about pageants; but *I knew* I could write a series of brochures about pageants.

✓ True, I felt I could not write an 'article' about pageants for magazines because the article would be at the mercy of the magazines and might never see the light of day. But *I knew* I could write a series of brochures about pageants.

✓ Yes, yes, yes! I *knew* I could write a series of brochures about pageants!

✓ *Teen* Magazine was perfect, too; because at that time, the Miss Teen Pageant was owned by *Teen* Magazine, which in turn was owned by Peterson Publishing.

With a great whoop of excitement, I grabbed a sheet of paper and a pencil and rapidly scribbled a list of all the brochures I would write. I would write a brochure on the various types of pageants. And I would write a brochure on filling out the application forms and structuring a winning pageant resume. And then I would write another brochure on wardrobe…then one on swimsuit…and one on modeling…and on and on.

As soon as I finished making my list, I slipped into my blue desk chair and – ta-da! –switched on the IBM Selectric typewriter, while feeding the first sheet of paper into it.

Thoughts were spilling out of me so fast that I was typing rapidly to keep up with my thoughts. I was not even thinking about it, anymore – I was *doing* it and completely focused on it – and all because I finally found a level of accomplishment I "believed" I could do. Faith is Action and Action is Faith – I was acting in faith that I could do it – wow.

The Little Dutch Boy Inside

For three years, I had been like the story of the little Dutch boy who kept his thumb plugging a hole in a dyke – to keep water from breaking through the dam.

But I could not type with my thumb in the dyke – and after three years – I removed my thumb from the dyke of my fears – and the dam inside me burst – releasing all the Creativity, all the imagination, all the knowledge, flooding through me – and releasing the book that had been pent-up inside my fear.

Now, I was so excited and energized that ideas came to me wherever I went. I started carrying a small spiral notepad – my sacred idea book – to jot down ideas as they came to me. Sometimes I would wake up at four o'clock in the morning and think, "Oh yes, I need to add thus and such." This happened so often that I began to sleep on the sofa next to my desk.

My list of brochure topics were beside me on the desk; and whenever I finished typing a brochure, I checked it off my list, then picked up my stack of freshly typed pages and put them in a neat pile in the center of my living room floor. I had a tiny apartment and my floor was my filing cabinet.

During that time, I met and started dating my husband and on our first date, he had to step gingerly over and around the stacks of papers on my living room floor. He did not know what they were – just that they were some project I was working on.

Finally, the day arrived that I checked off the last brochure topic on my list, picked up the stack of papers and arranged them in a neat pile on the floor next to the other stacks of papers.

I WAS FINISHED!

I had already reserved classified ad space in *Teen Magazine* for their large fall issue. All I had to do was to send in the ad, and to print up my brochures.

Settling into my blue chair behind my desk, I looked proudly at each stack of papers. I could hardly wait to get each one printed and to see the new brochures.

Substance Of Things Unseen

Suddenly alarmed, I sat upright. My room was filled with neat stacks of paper – and each stack of papers represented a brochure – but each stack was too big for a brochure. It would cost me a fortune to have them printed!

It dawned on me, then…that I had not written a series of brochures, at all. *I had written a… book!*

Slowly, I turned to my desk calendar and pinpointed the date I had arrived back in Dallas from my trip…and then I counted the days to the date I was sitting there that very moment – and I realized it had taken me exactly three weeks.

Three weeks…to write a book.

My First Book In 3 Weeks

I did not 'set out' to write a book in three weeks. I *discovered* that you can write a book in three weeks!

With only the faith to write brochures – mustard seed sized, to be sure – I now saw before me the book I had wanted so much to write. It was certainly the substance of things unseen for me.

If *YOU* have been nursing a book idea for three years or more – you have already written it – it has fermented inside your subconscious mind – and now all you have to do is to put it on paper or in your computer hard drive.

Success

I went ahead and advertised the first edition of my brand new soft cover book, *How To WIN Pageants* in *Teen Magazine* and I also sold it through pageant systems.

I had three Miss Texas' in a row who had used my book during their preparations; and after a few newspaper pictures of Miss Texas and me with my book, a publisher signed me for a first edition hard cover. I will elaborate more on that in the Chapter 12 on Target Audience, Know Who Your Readers Are.

The hard cover of *How To WIN Pageants* debuted at The Miss America Pageant and also at The Miss Canada Pageant. *The Washington Post* newspaper covered The Miss America Pageant in Atlantic City and quoted me and my new book.

A murder mystery writer, Sarah Shankman, used my book, *How To WIN Pageants,* as one of her resources in writing a suspense novel, titled *She Walks In Beauty,* about murder at the Miss America Pageant. In the front of her book, she acknowledged her sources and included mine with the words, "Thank you to Ginie Polo Sayles and *How To WIN Pageants.*"

Not only was I interviewed on television and invited to speak at the Miss Canada Pageant; but also my life experiences broadened in ways I had not expected. It was a wonderful adventure.

My point is that you, too, have no idea of the new and interesting paths that can open up because you write a book. Your new book can be the key to a whole new life – and a new, rewarding relationship with yourself.

The beautiful truth is that **when you finally stop hiding out and reach for the desires of your heart – however timidly – the desires of your heart will reach back for you**. It is a treasure of truth.

Reach for a goal – break it down to bite-sized pieces – just as I told myself I was writing brochures (because that was my small, entry-level of faith), you can tell yourself whatever you have to in order to find a level of belief that can get you started – and your goal will reach back for you.

Because reaching for a goal – breaking it down to bite-sized pieces – is Action and *ACTION IS FAITH.*

Chapter 5

WHY
Writer's Block Is A Crock

Mob beliefs in writer's block means your dreams as a writer are strung up to the nearest tree of excuses and left to die. – Ginie Sayles

The concept of writer's block is the worst lie – and the biggest joke – perpetrated on authors and would-be authors since creative writing began.

Plainly – writer's block does not exist – and it has never existed. It 'sounds good' – but it has caused more damage to the psyche of writers than the frustration of a computer on the blink.

Creativity – Key To Survival And Success

My belief is that Creativity is our ultimate survival tool. If a fire alarm went off where you are right now, would you say, "Oh, I am blocked. I don't know what to do?"

Of course not. Your Creativity would kick in automatically and instantly search for a means of survival, spurring you into action to save yourself. Creativity is you, and being you, it cannot leave you. It is impossible.

Creativity is who you are. Creativity is as much part and parcel of you as your eye color or your fingerprints – and it is just as uniquely yours as your fingerprints – *and* because it IS intertwined in your unique DNA, your creativity cannot abandon you anymore than your fingerprints or eye color can abandon you. Your Creativity *IS* you.

How Did The False Concept Of Writer's Block Occur?

The most likely scenario I can imagine that gave rise to this monstrous lie probably happened very innocently. I can see it now – perhaps a journalist (and I am a friend to journalists) had an approaching deadline to turn in an article on a subject of choice.

But much like uninspired students who, understandably, wait until the last minute to write a theme and turn it in; this particular journalist was probably depressed, tired, or just plain not motivated to write the article. However, the journalist needed to keep his/her job and needed the income.

Tough spot. I think we can all sympathize with committing to do something and later realizing we *don't want to* do it.

And we may wish we could *want to,* but wanting to 'want to' is not the same thing as truly wanting to do something. So, we keep dragging our feet and wondering what is wrong with us when the bottom line is "We don't want to do it!"

Our misery is compounded by the guilt of wondering why we cannot get going.

Back to the poor journalist, suffering dread and lack of motivation and at the same time needing the job or money. The journalist probably whined aloud to a spouse, "I can't think of anything new to write."

The spouse shrugged and said, "Sounds as if you hit a roadblock."

"Yeah," mumbled the frustrated journalist, "A writing roadblock."

Ah – at that moment, good ole Creativity kicked in and our down-in-the-mouth journalist lit up and had the Creative Idea (not all creative ideas are true; just marketable) to write about not feeling like writing and instead of calling it 'lack of motivation'– came up with the snappy sounding combination of a writing road-block and called it writer's block. Ingenious!!

See how unblocked our writer suddenly was? The journalist was finally writing about something that *felt* true for her or him and was motivated to share it. It was a brief bit of 'Creative' self-analysis without admitting lack of motivation.

Keep in mind that it was the Creativity of the journalist (*which the journalist thought was blocked but obviously was not*) that came up with the snazzy sounding slogan 'writer's block,' proving that Creativity was working all along to save the journal-ist. Creativity was helping the journalist deal with the issue and still get the work done. What a wonderful friend Creativity is.

Furthermore, it sounded so good and so new during a time of pop psychology in every bookstore and newspaper and maga-zine, that the concept hit the media with combustible speed. Suddenly, everybody was talking about writer's block or writing about it.

From that moment on, every half-hearted, half-motivat-ed, zero-motivated, or depressed writer in the world greedily snatched at a wonderful sounding excuse to hide behind. "See, you can't blame ME for not writing my book – I have writer's block!!!!"

It sounds marvelously clinical – and there is not one bit of clinical evidence for it. Just a flashy sounding excuse to put off writing….again…and it sucks you deeper and deeper into non-achievement.

The second possible scenario for the origin of this lie is that a therapist coined the expression while working with a depressed or unmotivated writer. It had a kinder sound than just calling it what it was. It sounded more authentic as something for which the therapist could offer treatment. Certainly, not all therapists would use it as a great way to make money 'treating someone for depression or lack of motivation while calling it writer's block; but some might.

In any scenario, it was a catch-all term spawned to blame something 'outside the writer' to make the patient feel better; but it has backfired.

The term – writer's block – does not offer a solution, just a fuzzy term that keeps a believer 'stuck'

The bottom line is this: Creativity cannot leave you, which means that Writer's Block is impossible. It is a crock of you-know-what!

Wisdom Of A West Coast Senator

I have clients, worldwide, who have private, one-on-one consultations with me about business or relationships.

A few years ago, a West Coast Senator had a private consultation with me in Texas; and before the consultation began, we were chatting about his trip to Texas, and the talk then branched into travel in general and ended on the subject of human gullibility.

He said, "I grew up in a family that traveled to Europe several times a year and I always felt great during my trips, throughout my stay, and I felt great when I returned. Then, after I married, my wife and our family traveled the world, as well, and going to and from each place was a pleasure."

He paused and laughed before adding, "Then, a few years ago, I read an article titled 'Jet Lag,' and, Ginie, I have had Jet Lag every since!"

What the Senator said struck a chord in me on behalf of my writing students. *The Power of Suggestion is a very real influence in our lives.*

Ideas Are Psychologically Contagious

I once took a class in advertising and learned that fortunes are made in advertising simply through the power of suggestion – i.e. the contagiousness of ideas.

Think about it. If ideas were not contagious, there would be absolutely NO television commercials. Advertising plants the seed of suggestion that our lives will be healed or better, some- how, if we have the right pill, hair color, shampoo, antiperspirant, or jeans.

When ideas are contagious 'en masse,' it is called "mob mentality;" but just because a large number of people accept something as true does not mean it is true.

Mob mentality – meaning a group of people who all think the same way or believe the same thing – has resulted in inno- cent people being strung up in a tree and hung – or persecuted as witches, such as the Salem Witch Trials or destroyed in the World Trade Center by people willing to kill innocent people because of a false idea that was psychologically contagious to an entire society.

And just because an idea has been around awhile *does not make it true*, either. By comparison, the practice of bloodletting was around for years, but it was just as dangerous a practice all those years ago as it is today.

Mob belief in writer's block means your dreams as a writer are strung up to the nearest tree of excuses and left to die. I do not care how many people 'choose' to believe the false idea of writer's block; it is no truer than the witch trials of Salem or bloodletting. And, yes, it is sad to think of the creative, talented people whose writing dreams die because they believe a lie.

If something "sounds official" and gets us off the hook at the same time, we are eager to embrace it and to claim, "It's not my fault that I can't write – I have writer's block."

In reality the concept of writer's block is just another cheap, easy "excuse" not to write and not to blame yourself.

But you do not want to hide behind excuses anymore. And because you know the idea of writer's block is a joke – and that the joke is on you if you believe it – you can laugh it off as a joke – as a crock of you-know-what!

Writer's Dread
Call It What It *IS*

The only way to get rid of a dread is to do it. – Vera Morris

"But, Ginie, I just can't seem to get going," you may lament at this point. And, if so; then you need to learn the only real reasons people temporarily feel they cannot write and what to do about it.

When you cannot write, it can be boiled down to one or more of the following legitimate reasons listed below. Identify – in specific words – the true reason you may not be writing – **identify it specifically– and you can deal with it and overcome it.**

- **Fear** – Fear of failure is a common reason for not writing. It was certainly my reason for three whole years! There are several methods for dealing with Fear, which I cover in the last Chapter 53, on Winning.

- **Priorities** – When it comes right down to it, you would rather go to the beach or to a party or to some other social activity than to spend hours sitting at a computer. If so, that's fine; but be honest about it. Realign your priorities according to your deeper Passion and be absolutely sure this is not Fear tricking you. If you are positive it is not Fear and if you are positive you have no Passion for writing the book (it was really your Dad's idea, anyway); please be honest with yourself, forget ever writing a book, and have a great time at the beach and socializing with friends!

- **Writer's Dread/Burnout** – This is very common among people who make their living writing. They know they need to write something; but they dread it. When I addressed *The National Writers Association* in Southern California on *Write A Book In 3 Weeks – Or Less*, a woman approached me, afterward and said, *"I am a published author, and I have been suffering 'burn-out' for the past two years. I thought I had writer's block, but you have convinced me I had writer's dread – which is obvious because I dreaded the long, tiresome process of writing a book. This information was just what I needed to short-cut the process that drained me so."*

This sentiment was echoed by Mimi Tanner, who wrote, *"When I finally ordered Ginie Sayles' program Write A Book In 3 Weeks – Or Less, I had already written several non-fiction books. The hardest part was always organizing the massive amount of material – then writing and rewriting until the information was explained logically and clearly. This can be overwhelming and very tedious. Forget writer's block. I had writer's dread."* She went on to say, *"I have referred back to this program many times - including when I need inspiration and motivation for a writing project...I'm grateful to Ginie Sayles for sharing this. She's proven again and again that she has a genuine desire to help others succeed."* In other words, this author called it what it was and then used the information that is in this book to help her get through a project she dreaded at that time.

You may still have writer's dread for a project, but when you truthfully call it what it is, you will eventually cope with it, dread and all. Those who latch onto the false idea of writer's block – instead of calling it dread, which it is – will not get the work done. They are blaming something outside themselves.

- **Habits** – Sometimes not writing can boil down to poor habits. Great News! You can create any habit you want just by doing it 21 days in a row, which is long enough to create the wonderful force of any habit you want to have. You are going to have habits, anyway, so why not choose the ones you want?

    For example, if you get out of bed at the last minute and think you do not have time to make your bed, you are creating a habit of not making your bed – and that is certainly up to you.

    If, on the other hand, you time yourself to see how long it takes to make your bed and discover it takes about 2 – 3 minutes, you can make up your bed as soon as you get out of it before going to the bathroom or immediately after – and when you instantly makeup your bed the minute you get out of it (not perfectly, just neatly) for 21 days, you will do it automatically from then on and never think twice about it.

    The same is true in forming a work habit. When you have a job, you have work habits imposed on you by a boss and they become automatic. When you set your own work habits at home, you are *choosing* how you want to live – and after 3 weeks, you are automatically living it.

    If you turn off your cell phone, set your digital Timer for 1 hour and sit down at your computer and work until the Timer goes off, you will be amazed at how much you accomplished in 1 little hour. After 3 weeks (21 days) of doing this at a particular time, you have created a habit that is your friend.

- **Losing the Muse** – If you make your living as a writer, it is likely your Muse (inspiration) responds well to the incentive of money. If you have been enjoying a financially flush period, your Muse may have taken a vacation. Don't worry, your Muse will show up at exactly the same time your overdue bills show up!

- **Stuck** – Read Chapter 31 for Fiction; Chapter 43 for Non-Fiction.

- **Not Enough Sex** – just kidding…but feel free to quote me, if it helps your mate be more romantic! Besides there is a strong measure of truth to it.

  A therapist told me that studies of monks in monasteries revealed that less sex produces a decline in creative interest and more lethargy. Think about it – sex creates life, itself, so sex is an ultimate creative source of energy. When sex is happy, everything else falls into place and writing is easy.

  Don't buy into the old concept that not having sex 'transmutes' energy into a different creative channel – not true. **Sex 'creates' energy!**

  Of course, you can still write, whatever your sex life. I would just like to see sex and writing complement each other for your overall happiness.

- **Grief** – Grief means '*something died in your life*.' It is true that writing can be cathartic and a healthy way to grieve for some individuals; but it is just as true that some people are temporarily immobilized by loss because their energy is drained from avoiding grief.

  o *Death of a Relationship* – Someone you love went out of your life. The person is not dead; but the relationship is. This may be the end of a love affair; of a marriage or what felt like a marriage; or the end of a friendship. You may have drifted apart or you may have been betrayed or one of you left the relationship.

o *Death of a Job* – You lost your job, possibly due to personality conflicts or office politics or bad economy or you just could not stay in the job, anymore. Part of your identity in this career has died. You are not sure what you will do next.

o *Death of a Lifestyle* – You realize you can no longer afford the house, furniture, car, and memberships you enjoyed for years. Mortgage payments, car payments and other obligations have mounted up and now you grieve the loss of a lifestyle you enjoyed.

o *Death of a Person* – The physical death of a parent, sibling, spouse, child, grandparents, cousin, or aunt, uncle, mentor, or friend - someone who was a meaningful part of your life died. The relationship may have been conflicted or loving; but you feel their loss.

When something or someone you counted on dies in your life, it is as normal to feel the pain of loss as it is for a person who has lost a limb, because you lost part of yourself and yet you know you have to 'go on somehow.'

Give yourself permission to feel the pain of grief when something dies in your life. This kind of depression is a *normal* depression that is healed by appropriate grieving, not by medication.

Grieving the death of something is **not** an abnormal depression. *Such grief is not mental illness*: it is *a normal process of mourning the loss of something dear to you.*

Grief is a composite of many feelings:
- *Sadness* (very deep sadness at times)
- *Anger* (because of the loss)

- *Guilt* (often unjustified guilt that you should have done something differently when it probably would not have changed the outcome)
- *Loss* (learning how to cope and to adjust to life without the someone or something that has died).

When you have fully dealt with your grief, you will find yourself functioning normally again and able to write to your heart's content.

Years ago, I gave this list of reasons people temporarily do not write to my class in San Francisco. After class, an older gentleman told me he now realized he had not had writer's block, as he'd thought for years – that he had years of unresolved grief.

It seems he began writing a book before he went to Viet Nam. When the war was over, he still wanted to write the book; but every time he sat down to write, he lost his will.

"As you talked tonight, Ginie, I realized I have bottled up grief for all I lost in that terrible war. Buddies standing beside me who were killed or maimed and I did not have time to grieve. And something in me died, too, in the war – the death of my innocence, the death of that trusting boy I was when I left to serve my country. Sitting here tonight, I decided to enroll in a grief therapy group and face up to it all. I want my life back and I want to finish writing my book."

You CAN WIN your dreams of writing a book – and faster than you think; but only by facing truths of why you have not been writing and by not hiding behind a false excuse.

If anyone says to you, "Sounds as if you have writer's block," immediately laugh (because writer's block is a joke) and deny it (because it is not true) and say something like this, "No, I am sorting through my own creative process," or "No, I am just working out some details," or "No, I am just examining my options," or "No, I am figuring out what I want to do next."

And immediately change the subject. You do not need to get into a discussion or into any details about your project or to draw this person into your very own uniquely creative issues. But never agree with a lie, such as writer's block, or you give it power.

Years ago, I realized that we may not always say what we believe, at first; but that over time, we end up believing what we say. Watch what you agree with.

If you temporarily cannot write, call it what it IS and not some nebulous writer's block. If you are stuck, review the chapters mentioned and get unstuck.

Chapter

7

Passion
The Antidote That Exposes
The Lie

I do not believe in discipline. I believe in Passion.
– Ginie Sayles

The antidote that exposes the lie of writer's block is Passion! No one with Passion for a project ever sings the woe-begone blues of the writer's block lie. They don't have to. They are excited, flooded with ideas, and can hardly wait to switch on their computers.

When they look up at a clock, hours later, they are shocked at the time. It flew by because they were living in a Creative time warp – a time when you are "one" with your productive Creativity, which I call 'Creative Flow,' a term I expanded from the simple 'flow' used by psychologists to describe business professionals, working in a similar state of suspended time. Flow is an absorbed interest in your work; but Creative Flow is absorbed interest in work that originates within you and you alone.

Passion ignites Creative Flow. Passion is made up of many elements working together – intense desire, personal will, deep interest, strong belief, focused concentration, forceful emotion – and it all works together to generate motivation. An idea won't let go of you. It keeps surfacing in your thoughts no matter how much time goes by.

You will know you have released fear and found your Passion when you realize one day that you are writing because it is impossible not to. You are writing because you want to. You are writing because you can't 'not' write…because you must.

Passion Fathers Discipline

When you have Passion for a project, you automatically discipline yourself to do the writing and never even think of the word 'discipline.' You simply *want* to see this to the finish – you can hardly wait to see it as a complete manuscript. And you want it so much that all the energy is there to see it through. Even on an occasional low-energy or 'down' day, you still want it enough to sit yourself down and switch on your computer.

Discipline without Passion is dead. That type of discipline is for 'jobs' – and somehow you muddle through a dreaded job and hope that something in your job will ignite even a tiny spark of interest. You need Passion to father an automatic discipline.

How do you 'get' Passion? You write what you *want to* write. That's it, that's all, and it is that simple.

The unhelpful label of writer's block means that you lack Passion for your project. If you have Passion, discipline falls into place automatically. When you have Passion, you are willing to muddle through times of feeling stuck without stopping your project. Passion does not make it 'easy;' Passion makes it satisfying, fulfilling, and 'worth it' – through up and down moments in your writing.

A Great Idea Does Not Always Ignite Passion

You may have a terrific idea that you believe will make money and you may get excited about it. You may find that as you write about it, your excitement grows and new ideas flow – ah, that my writer friend IS Passion!

On the other hand, you may get excited about it at first; but once you get underway with it, you may find yourself making every excuse imaginable to do something else. You reprimand yourself for slacking off but that does not help. You remember how lucrative a deal it could be and you force yourself to get back to work on it; but that only helps a little.

There is nothing wrong with writing for money, even if the topic is a bit sterile to you. And if you go ahead and force yourself to finish it, it can be well worth the money. I have done that myself, sometimes. If a publisher or my agent contacted me with an idea they wanted me to write, I certainly did it – even if I had to force myself to complete the task; but it was not Passion that drove me.

It was as much out of respect for the people who asked me as it was for the money, though. After all, I wanted them to be open to my real works of Passion and I was honored they thought of me for a writing project.

Even so, I contend that just writing for others and just writing because you have a good idea does not inspire the kind of Passion that fulfills your very soul as a writer – and why not? For the very reason that it did not come from your soul.

Writing without Passion is like sex without love. It may be okay; but it lacks magic!

To Write With Passion, Get In Touch With Your Soul

I want you to write with Passion! Your very own true Passion.

How do you do that? To write with Passion, you get in touch with your soul.

And how do you do *that*?

You take inventory of what is already in your soul. Your soul was most formative beginning at birth through about age 25. As a new being on this earth, you were eagerly taking in information, learning, searching, experiencing, and enjoying certain experiences more than others, loving certain stories more than others.

Every time you had a favorite 'anything' – or every time you struggled and succeeded in overcoming a problem in your life, then, just as a postmaster strikes a rubber stamp on an envelope to make an imprint of the original stamp – your favorite story or successful experience also struck an imprint onto your soul.

All your favorites are there, inside you, like precious jewels you once enjoyed that now wait for you to take them out and enjoy them again – perhaps retooling them into a new design. Yet, even the new design will be based on the experience or story that once thrilled you.

When you take the story or experience you loved or discovered and use it as a starting point to write – see Chapters 17, 18, and 19 – because you have touched the cornerstone of your Passion – and Creativity will begin to flow.

To Maintain Passion, Touch Your Own Heart

We experience our lives through our emotions. Never forget that. And our emotions are heightened by sensory awareness – sight, sound, scent, touch, taste – the 3 S's and 2 T's. Our minds enjoy inner richness with words that stimulate our emotions and our senses.

Write words that touch your own emotions and you will touch the emotions of your readers. If your writing makes you cry, they will weep. If your writing makes you laugh, they will chuckle. When you touch your own heart, you will maintain the momentum of Passion.

Readers want to experience Passion, too. Let them experience yours by touching your own heart as you write.

Personal Interest Reignites Passion

Let's pretend you have written the first three chapters of your book. The next day, you sit down before your computer, type Chapter 4 at the top of your page and….and then you stare at it for ten minutes, trying to think of what to write. Some people automatically write in consecutive order – i.e. Chapter 1, Chapter 2, Chapter 3, et cetera; and that is great; but it is just as great if you do not.

If you find yourself struggling to think of what comes next, you can stall out, like an airplane whose engine has been cut off. And that is exactly what happens when you lose your Passion.

Instead of locking yourself in to a consecutive process of writing, restart the engine of Passion and prevent a stall by allowing yourself to flow instinctively into your writing as follows:

1. ***Write The Scene That Entices You First.*** As a teenager, I read that Margaret Mitchell wrote the last scene of *Gone With The Wind* first. It must have been a scene that came to her (as they often do out of the blue) and inspired her. Once that scene was written, it gave life to her imagination about other scenes – also out of order – that could lead to this one great, final moment. As each scene was written, the power of the author's own Passion emerged.

   Eventually, she had written enough of the story that she could see the force of it. She had written enough to realize that she really could write a novel.

   Getting to this point, in turn, creates self-motivation to 'tie up loose ends,' to fill in gaps with transitional scenes, to research and verify information, to rewrite scenes she may have thought were all right before.

   Only now, it did not feel like work. The motivation was built into having followed her Passion, each day, until at last the Passion was writing the book. *Passion is motivation.*

2. ***Keep Following Your Interest Every Day And Your Creative Well Never Runs Dry.***
   I am writing this topic, first, for this book right now – although you are probably reading it several chapters into this book. But this subject is my current,

most-compelling interest. I woke up this morning, knowing that you will need this topic more than any other when you reach this step in your writing.

When you were in the ninth grade, you may have studied a poem *The Rhyme Of The Ancient Mariner,* which tells of an old seaman who was periodically overcome by a feverish compulsion to tell an experience he'd had. When he felt it come on him, he had to stop whatever he was doing and tell the story. It was his compelling focus of the moment.

That is the way to write. If the old mariner had tried to complete some other task, first, he would have found himself distracted and performing his task poorly. And you will, too, if you try to force yourself to write in sequence, rather than by Passion, or by a topic that dominates your interest that day.

Let your mind wander to the scene that you can hardly wait to write – a scene that may be out of sequence – that may belong in a different part of your book altogether. But, go ahead – write it – out of order. Do not worry about where it goes, yet, or what chapter number it is supposed to be. Just write it. Suddenly, you will find your fingers flying to keep up with a flood of emotion coursing through your veins and, yes, you are writing in the Creative Flow of Passion.

Chapter 8

7 Key Factors
The Whole Person Approach
To Writing

Putting it all together builds your speed and effectiveness in writing.

You have to deal with yourself as a "whole person" when you write a book – your moments of self-doubt, as well as your cherished goals. You are a complex human being, filled with dreams, goals, emotions, time constraints, financial considerations, job deadlines, family expectations, and secret hopes. And whereas you have ideas for a book, you may wonder if your idea has merit, who will read it, and if you really have time to write it.

Therefore writing a book in three weeks or less entails much more than just the skills for writing it – although you need those, too.

There are seven key factors that pull together all your human strengths and weaknesses to energize your will power and your abilities.

The Seven Key Factors are:

1. **Operational Faith** – believing you can write a book

2. **Equipment** – having the right equipment increases speed
3. **Time** – how to create time when you think you don't have any
4. **Target Audience/Market** – who will buy and read your book
5. **The Fire Of Your Creative Spirit** – igniting 6 stages of Creativity
6. **Purpose** – knowing why you are writing your book – which is incorporated into the chapters of Why Write Fiction and Why Write Non-Fiction
7. **What To Write** – the genre or type of writing you want to do – which is incorporated into Part 2: Fiction and Part 3: Non-Fiction

Key Factors 1 – 5 above will be addressed, individually as separate chapters that follow.

Factors 6 and 7 have been incorporated into the Skills Sections of this book.

Key Factor
Operational Faith
Ways To Create Faith
To Write A Book

Faith is an Action of risk. And Faith grows as it goes...
– Ginie Sayles

Even when you learn the skills to write faster; if you do not *believe* you can write a book, then you still will not write your book. Skills are dead without some level of faith.

Remember, I did not believe I could write a book, either! So you are not alone.

Do not feel shame if you do not have faith to write a book, yet. Faith grows as it goes – just *doing what you can* waters the little mustard seed of faith. The more you do, the stronger your faith gets. Even small Action is faith.

How can you grow your faith?

1. Learn the power of positive faith statements.
2. Inspire yourself – surround yourself with anything that encourages you.
3. Happiness, joy, enthusiasm, optimism are tools of faith.

4. Make it real with related steps.
5. Be willing to start small.
6. Do this important exercise
7. Faith we can learn from a farmer.
8. Learn a lesson from your ancestors.

Positive Faith Statements

There was a class of Illiterate adults who had signed up to learn how to read. Unfortunately, they were dropping out at an alarming rate. When they were asked why they quit the program, they shook their heads with resignation and said, "I can't read. I just can't read."

The idea of reading was as overwhelming to them as writing a book had seemed to me. They were dominated by fear. And fear had convinced them they could not read and that it was impossible for them to learn.

So the reading teachers came up with an ingenious idea: At the beginning of each class, the teachers had the illiterate adult students look at their books and say, aloud (so you can 'hear' your words), "I can read" over and over roughly ten to twenty times *before* opening their books.

Amazingly, the dropout rate was cut in half and soon a majority of the adult students learned to read. They became 'literate adults.'

You see, Fear immobilizes and Faith empowers, so the illiterate adults had to dismantle their own fears by *saying what they wanted to believe as already being true*.

We may not always say what we believe; but we eventually end up believing what we say, especially if we say it enough times.

A famous lawyer who won many cases was asked his secret for convincing a jury to vote his way. This is what he said, "Tell people what you want them to believe. Then tell them again. Tell them again. Tell them again and again and again. And then tell them again – and they will eventually believe you."

Your subconscious mind is exactly the same way. It believes you and what you say more than it does anyone else. You are the ultimate authority on you and your brain knows that. So, if you want to believe something – but you feel as if you are lying when you say it, please realize that you are not lying at all – you are *reprogramming* your belief system.

Keep saying what you want to believe as if it is already true. Keep saying it. Keep saying it. Keep saying it. Keep saying it. Refuse any doubts by shaking your head 'no' when a negative thought encroaches – and then keep saying what you want to believe again and again and again with growing pep rally conviction.

You can do the same for your writing. Build your success by building your faith. Affirm ten to twenty-one times each day – and aloud – the following positive faith statements:

"I, (your name), am now a writer. I am an author. I am Creative."

"I, (your name), now attract to me all things necessary for fulfilling my writing goal."

Positive Faith Statements are a form of prayer to me. You are not stating a prayer as a plea, which is fine, too; but in this case as a statement of faith. The Bible tells us "Faith comes *by hearing* and hearing *by the word*." You hear yourself speaking the word of faith.

It won't kill you to do it – and you don't have to believe it at first. Just keep saying it no matter what you 'think' you believe about it and let the words take root in your mind.

If you want to take the time, you can record yourself reading the positive faith statements. Say them with enthusiasm and a big smile to put energy into your words. You can go to sleep at night listening to them to let it sink into your subconscious mind. You can play them while you clean your apartment or while you relax in a bubble bath. It's up to you. Just be sure you counter any negative feelings with positive faith statements.

Many times, in my career and in my relationships, my life has changed rapidly for the better by stating 21 times for 21 days, a few positive faith statements relating to that situation. I found that positive statements built my faith and faith created expectation; and expectation caused me to behave in ways that attracted the very solutions I needed at the time.

Positive Faith Statements have absolutely worked for me. They provide a mind-set that assists me. I am *"speaking those things that are not, as if they 'are'"* and that is what it becomes. I used to say my 21 statements like a high school pep rally, building excitement in my voice more and more with each one and the 21st was joyous!

Inspire Yourself - Surround Yourself With Encouragement

Sometimes you have no one to encourage you. No one, that is, but you. And you must find every way that you can to encourage yourself. Tape encouraging posters, magazine ads, and pictures that inspire you.

When I was working on *How To WIN Pageants,* I came across two magazine ads that I tore out and taped next to my desk where I saw them several times a day.

The first ad by ARCO (Atlantic Richfield Company) showed a young man in a lonely, empty warehouse – all alone – practicing a violin and the ad read: *It takes a lot of work to play.*

The second ad by ROCKWELL INTERNATIONAL showed an opera star onstage at curtain call, taking a bow amid flowers thrown to her feet. It read: *The most difficult goals usually are the ones most worth achieving.*

When my book, *How To WIN Pageants* was being published in hardcover, I contacted both companies and received their permission to put their ads in my book. They even provided me with the actual ad graphics, which appear on pages 50 and 51 in *How To WIN Pageants* hardcover edition.

Thank you to these two companies and to others like them for encouraging faith and effort on a personal level when we may feel "I can't." Those ads kept feeding "I can" to me as I edited the book.

The Bible says, "Without a vision, my people perish." I feel that I was, indeed, dying on some level because I was afraid to have the vision I most wanted – that of writing a book. I needed encouragement; but I had no one to encourage me – but me. You can encourage you, too.

Happiness, Joy, Enthusiasm, Love, Optimism Build Faith

Happiness is not a destination, but a signpost. When you are driving on a highway, you occasionally pass highway signs that let you know you are either on the right road or the wrong road. Well, that is what happiness is – a signpost in your heart that you are on the right path for you. You may not have achieved your goal, yet; but you feel happiness because you are following your healthy Heart's Desire, which means you *are* on the right road for your life.

Joy in your work is its own reward and it comes from the word 'rejoice' – which, to me, is appropriate when you discover your healthy Heart's Desire and direct your energies into it.

Enthusiasm from old Latin meant 'possessed by a god, inspired.' When you train your mind into enthusiasm for your project, you align your Creative Spirit in harmony and receptiveness to an inspired flow of ideas.

Love your ideas, love your workspace, love your time with your work on your book, love reading it again and again and again. Love the changes you make that make it better. Love yourself for these creative moments of growth in this powerful new direction. Yes, you may feel moments of frustration or confusion; but even those are part of loving your work enough to care.

Optimism is an approach to your work that expects good. Expectancy is what sets our path each day. What do we expect? When you choose a state of happiness, joy, enthusiasm, love, and optimism, you are walking in Faith, too. As I said before, a pep rally builds excitement. Give yourself a pep rally.

All this creates a happy state of mind. A happy state of mind indicates you believe good is going to happen to you as you release your Creative energy in writing.

When people choose a fretful, grumbling mentality toward their project – complaining about how hard it is – they act as if life is too big for them!

A happy state of mind lightens the load of any work you are doing. And a happy state of mind is, at first, a conscious choice – and eventually, a habit. Choose a happy state of mind. Happiness is inside you – not outside of you.

"Don't Worry, Be Happy"

Listen only to 'Happy Music' – learn the words to up-beat, encouraging songs and turn off anything that suggests a depressed, loser state of mind. Bobby McFerrin's *Don't Worry, Be Happy* has good advice, period; and especially when you are being creative.

Instead of sad, depressing music, sing any song with upbeat messages. I once heard my aunt sing a very old song, "Accentu-ate the positive, eliminate the negative, latch onto the affirmative, and don't mess with Mr. In-between." I began singing it during those times when I needed encouragement.

An old Frank Sinatra song called "High Hopes" has a sim-ple, encouraging message that I often sang to keep me cheered up. It is a cute song, too.

And I love Michael Buble's song, *Everything* – which is about love – but fall in love with your work and the words apply.

Your Secret Garden

A charming DVD to watch is *The Secret Garden*, produced by Francis Ford Coppola of *the Godfather* fame. Based on a 1911 novel by Frances Hodgson Burnett, it demonstrates through a story how powerful your mind is in creating your happiness and fulfillment.

In the story, a walled garden is discovered. Overgrown with weeds, the pitiful looking roses are severely neglected, but not dead. By the end of the movie, you realize that your mind is your secret garden, and whatever weeds of beliefs and thoughts are growing in it can be uprooted and new ones planted to bring health, strength, achievement, love, and fulfillment. The roses of your happy thoughts may be neglected but they are not dead and can be nurtured to health.

It is a marvelous DVD and one well worth seeing. I encourage you to do so.

Make It Real – NOW – Take Related Action

If you have not yet started writing your book, get in the "now" by taking some sort of related Action. *Action makes it real.* Try one of the following methods of getting your book in motion by taking relation Action to make it real:

- *Title Your Book – A Title Makes It Real.* Write or type a temporary Working Title. Writing down a title takes your book from the nebula of thought and gives it a reality. Just as a person wants a title to define the concept of his or her job, your book title defines the concept of your book. Your final title may change later, so don't worry over it. Just give your book a good "working title." Even Hollywood does that with movie projects.

- *Carry A Spiral Notepad or PDA Just For Ideas On The Subject.* This is something you will do, anyway, as part of my method. It is your sacred idea device and do not write anything else in the notepad but ideas for your book.

Downloading Copyright Forms Makes It Real. Go to www. copyright.gov/ and download form TX. This stands for 'text.' Be sure to read Chapter 47 All-Important Copyright in this book. Be SURE to read that chapter.

Be Willing To Start Small

If your book project feels overwhelming, cut it down into bite-sized pieces.

No one really writes a book all at once. All writers write a book just *one word at a time.* And that is all you have to do… just write one word after another. Just write one sentence and let the others follow. If you can write one page, you can write two hundred pages, just one page at a time.

One of the most inspiring stories of faith is that of Alex Haley, author of *Roots.* This was a man whose Passion to learn his ancestry and to write about it became so intense that he did whatever he had to do, and learned whatever he had to learn in order to write his book.

Roots was not only a bestselling book; but it was also a dynamic television program, resulting in a sequel, *Roots II,* that tells of his journey – a powerful story of Passion and Faith.

Do What You Can – And Leave The HOW To Faith

During the time I was getting my *How To WIN Pageants* Ad ready for *Teen* magazine (see Chapter 4 My Story), my car broke down and I was unable to get to the business across town that had made the ad I designed 'camera-ready' as required by *Teen.* I was also between jobs and every cent I spent had to count.

Standing in the small living room of my apartment, I realized that my problems were looming larger and larger. I did not know how I could possibly achieve all that my heart wanted to achieve.

With no car, I decided I would walk across Dallas to the business and walk back so I could get my camera-ready ad, package it, and then walk to the post office to mail it with what was left over after paying for the camera-ready ad. For a moment I realized I was doing all this and I had no idea what kind of future my manuscript had. I did not know how I was going to make it pay off. But I suddenly said, aloud, "Well, I don't know how I am going to do it; I just know I am going to do it."

Now, I do not ask anyone to believe this because I cannot adequately explain it; but as soon as I said those words, I *physically felt* an invisible current – like an invisible wave – flow toward me – and it was a **physical** feeling, not an emotional one. My body could feel it.

I was surprised.

I have thought of that moment many times and the only way I can explain it is that when I said the words and I meant them with full and total conviction, I believe the tide of Faith turned in my favor and Life began to sweep toward me and with me, into fulfilling my Heart's Desire.

I have deliberately said the words since then because I wanted to feel that wave again; but it only happened that day – and I think it must have been because in a moment when everything seemed against me, I wanted my goal so much that I was willing to take the hard steps I had to take and not know 'how' and not to worry about 'how' – just to know that *somehow* I was going to do it. I did not feel strong, I just felt willing to take the next step as if everything would work out. Without knowing it, I was doing what I could and leaving the HOW to Faith.

Do This Important Exercise

Your relationship with yourself as a writer is one of the most important keys to keeping going and living your faith. So do this important exercise to nourish your self-concept as a writer: Either on your computer or with a pen and paper, write a scenario containing the following:

1. Write your ideal writing day as an author. Be sure to describe your ideal setting, equipment, and everything just the way you want it.
2. What happens to you when you write?
3. How do you feel when you write?
4. How do you feel after you finish for the day?

5. Do you feel stronger?
6. Do you feel happier?
7. What do you like about writing?
8. How would you describe your relationship with yourself as a writer?
9. Does it bring you closer to yourself?
10. Does your own writing enlighten you as well as express you?

You may not have the ideal circumstances – yet – but you have a mental target. One famous author who now lives in a mansion was quoted by an ex-husband that before she was famous, she told him she wanted to live in a mansion and write books; and that she had the most important tools to get her there – her typewriter, paper, and quiet time after the kids were in bed. In the meantime, she could escape their dreary environment and live in her mental mansion in her writing. It is interesting that she eventually brought her ideal circumstances into reality.

The Faith We Can Learn From Farmers

Think of this: farmers would not waste their time plowing the land and planting seeds and tending the land – if they did not *believe* their work would pay off – if they did not think the seeds would grow into crops they could harvest.

The farmers may watch the crops wash away in flood, die from drought, or be destroyed by pestilence. All the days and nights of hard work and aching muscles seem to be for nothing.

There is no guarantee. They risk failure every year.

But every year, in spite of the risk, farmers will buy seed and set out to plant it.

Why? Because the farmers *believe* the seeds will grow, in spite of past failures. If they did not think crops would grow, they would not plant the seeds. And yet, because of their Faith they take Action and enough of it pays off to feed all the rest of us.

Farmers act in faith by planting seeds and tending them… Faith is Action.

The Faith We Can Learn From Babies

A baby pulls itself up and tries to walk, tumbling to the floor. What if the baby thought, "Heck, I can't walk. I'll just get by with crawling" and never tried again? Right – we would all still be moving around on our all-fours.

Babies do not 'judge' themselves as right or wrong, good or bad, stupid or smart, capable or incapable; they just keep pulling themselves up off the floor – again and again and again – after every fall until one day, they are able to take a couple of steps before falling. Finally, they are walking. I sometimes think God had babies to learn how to walk before they could understand language so they would not be discouraged by criticism.

Think like a baby. Real wisdom lies in their non-judgmental efforts, over and over to keep going for what they want. Now, that is Faith.

Learn This Most Valuable Lesson From Your Ancestors

Years later, while working on my family tree, my husband and I were standing in a cemetery one beautiful morning in Comanche, Texas, searching for graves of some of my ancestors. A few graves that were listed in a cemetery book had disappeared and no one knew where they were. Naturally, we wondered if other people were now buried on top of them. No one knew.

A number of headstones were bare markers with nothing on them. Most had names and dates, some were inscribed "Father" or "Mother" or "Beloved Son" or "Gone But Not Forgotten."

But they had been forgotten in spite of the inscribed words that promised they would not be – and in some cases, even their graves were lost.

And then, I wondered what dreams were lost with my ancestors....

- What talent had returned to dust?

- What secret desire lay buried forever beneath a mound of dirt?
- What gifts died unborn because of simple fear?

Life has a deadline. We know it but we often lose sight of it.

I wondered if being made in the image of God also meant that we are given a Creative Spirit to fulfill our lives.

I am not saying that is how it is. I am saying that is the thought that went through my mind as I gazed upon the graves of my forgotten ancestors.

It struck me again that...life has a deadline.

Standing in the cemetery that day, I realized that even though I had written four books by that time, that I still had a number of writing goals I had not pursued. So I asked God to help me stay aware of delays and to help me to stay on course to complete my work before I die.

My work may or may not have eternal longevity; but it is a written record of my overcoming fear and a lasting record of my Creative self...something that may encourage and be of value to others, and perhaps to my descendents...a story behind the picture of me...a story behind the headstone.

This is true for you, too. Life is your opportunity to leave your unique imprint on this world during your time here.

Latch onto the tiniest coattails of Faith and take Action so that you do not let your dreams crumble, unborn, into dust with your body when this golden moment of life is over.

Chapter 10

Key Factor

Equipment

Having the right tools increases your speed.

If you want to write a book – especially in three weeks – you will do better if you have the right tools. It does not require a lot of tools; but it does help to have certain elemental ones.

Digital Timer

The single most-important equipment for writing a book in three weeks or less – second to your mind/body and computer – is a digital timer. Most kitchen departments of household goods and also electronics stores have easily affordable timers. Most come with batteries; but if not, it is a small expense to buy them.

The main reason for a digital Timer is because you don't want the old loud ticking timers that are distracting. Also, I prefer timers that do not have a 5-minute warning – but if that is all you can get, so be it. Radio Shack timers cost a little more but they have the ones that do not have a 5-minute warning beep.

Why is a Timer important in writing a book? Because a Timer is about time – and that is what writing fast is all about – time – when you are writing a book in three weeks or less. You create tiny deadlines with your Timer that keep you moving forward. Time is not wasted when you use a Timer as you work.

A Timer is your Super Big Secret to Creativity. By the end of this book, you will better understand the way Creativity, itself, works – and your Timer is Creativity's best friend.

A Computer – As Current As Possible

You need equipment that can "haul paragraphs" around for fast editing. Yes, I know Danielle Steele writes all her books on an old manual typewriter (not electric) – but the only book I ever wrote on the IBM Selectric typewriter was my Original First Edition of *How To WIN Pageants*.

The publisher of the Second Edition – or First Edition Hardcover – insisted I learn how to use a computer and to submit my final manuscript that way. I am very grateful to the publisher for insisting I learn to use a computer, because it is without a doubt superior to a typewriter in quality and timesaving – which is valuable for speedwriting authors.

Your Sacred Idea Device

The great Russian playwright, Anton Chekhov, always carried small writing utensils in his pocket so he could immediately capture any idea that came to him for any reason and at any moment – that he might later utilize in a play.

Having some sort of reliable 'idea device' is important – because once you begin, you will find ideas flowing out of you at the weirdest times – and you must 'catch them' as they are flowing.

It is tempting to tell yourself that you will remember your idea and write it down later; but so often, you later forgot what it was and may be upset because the idea was so good.

Stop whatever you are doing and make a note of your ideas as you get them. If you are driving, please pull off the road to a safe location and write it down, then carefully resume driving. If you have a digital voice recorder, you can click it on and talk while you go.

If you are in the middle of a conversation with someone and you suddenly have an idea, say, "Excuse me, I have to go to the bathroom. Hold that thought because I will be back in a minute." Then, go to the restroom and write down your ideas. Go back to the conversation and ask the person to finish his/her tale. It won't hurt a thing. And you will be glad, later. You do not lose ideas and you do not lose…time – which is the most important gift you can give yourself.

Choose whichever method is easiest and most comfortable for you to take notes – PDA, cell phone with PDA capabilities, spiral notepad and pen that fits in your jeans pocket, or voice recorder – but choose only one method as your 'Sacred Idea Device' so you don't get scattered and end up losing some ideas that you forgot were on another device.

- *Digital Voice Recorder* - Some digital voice recorders can be transcribed by matching voice recognition systems so that you just plug it in and your computer transcribes your notes for you. Nice. I have not used voice recognition systems yet. There is another plus to a voice-recognition system computer – and that is for individuals who have debilitating dyslexia but wonderful book ideas.

  If you do not have a voice recognition system, you must transcribe your tapes or notepad or PDA notes, daily. You must. Make it an easy ritual, so that before you begin writing each day, take out your note-taking device and transcribe the notes you have.

- *Pocket-sized Spiral Notepad and Pen* - If you do not want to use a PDA then at least get a pen and pocket-sized spiral notepad that fits into your jeans, briefcase, breast pocket, coat pocket, or handbag — just for your three week period. If you are using a notepad and pen – keep it sacred – don't use it for grocery lists or you will use it up and not have room when a great idea hits you.

- *Personal Digital Assistant – PDA – Most Cell phones have PDA and digital voice recording capability, too.*

Just be sure you have a Sacred Idea Device so you can capture those wonderful, elusive ideas that can make your book outstanding.

Key Factor
Time
How To Create Writing Time

This little slot of time is mine. It is not much time, no matter how long it may turn out to be; but it is mine and perhaps the only thing I really possess after all.
– Ginie Sayles

There are a number of "Sacreds" during your three-week period – and Time is one of them. You DO have to make your work time sacred.

That means for three weeks you must not let other people control your so-called free time (as if anyone has such a thing). In fact, *you must create time* out of thin air – and I have a few suggestions for ways you can do that. But first…

How Much Time Is Needed To Write A Book In 3 Weeks?

200-220 pages (60,000 words) is the length to target for your book. How many pages do you need to write per day in order to write 200 pages in 3 weeks – or less?

Week-Days: For three weeks, you will target writing at least **3 hrs and 40 minutes per weekday** – approximately **6 pages per day** (a total of 30 pages per week) on your weekdays.

Week-Ends: On each weekend – Saturday and Sunday – set aside **9 – 12 hours per day** and write **18.3 pages per day** = 36.6 **total pages for each weekend**.

Total Time and Pages: By the end of **3 weeks**, you have written a total of **90 pages** on weekdays and **110 pages** on the weekends – which equal **200 pages** – hoorah!

Now, let's break it down into a do-able time period that fits into your daily life.

How To Create Time On Week Days And With A Job

How do you stuff three hours and forty minutes into your weekday, when you also hold down a job, have a spouse and children? You *create* the time. It may not be easy; but you do it.

For Example:
1. *Speedwriting (and Billionaire) Habit #1: Rise one hour earlier* than anyone else in your family each weekday. **Set your Timer for 1 hour and write for at least that hour**. Stop when your family wakes up.

   Why get up early? Well, when I researched men and women entrepreneurs who created a financial fortune from nothing; I learned that the majority of them – not all of them but most of them – had formed a habit of rising an hour before anyone else in their households and working for that 'sacred' hour.

A cosmetics entrepreneur who took a single moisturizing cream and turned it into a Cosmetic Empire attributes much of her success to forming a habit of rising at 5:30 every morning and working an hour before anyone else woke up. She said she felt she got a whole day's work done in that hour.

This was echoed by all the entrepreneurs who practiced this habit. They claimed to get more accomplished during that one hour each day than all day long at the office.

They had no interruptions, no distractions. Think of it this way – your mind is fresh from the Creative world of dreaming and able to reach those Creative areas of thought before harsher realities of the day intrude.

2. *Speedwriting (and Billionaire) Habit # 2: Pack a lunch* and take it to work with you. I read that billionaire Warren Buffett (my favorite financial hero) always takes a brown paper sack lunch to work.

   For just three weeks, you can do it, too. You are not going to lunch with your pals at work. You are going to quietly munch your sandwich by yourself – wherever you have to go to be alone – and **write for 40 minutes**.

   Oh, and when co-workers inevitably ask, "Why aren't you going to lunch with us?" just say, "I have to catch up on a lot of little things. I figure it will take a few weeks, but I promise, the minute I am caught up with myself, I will be back on track with lunch." *Something* like that! But PROMISE YOURSELF YOU WILL NOT TELL THEM YOU ARE WRITING A BOOK.

You will understand the importance of this when you read the first – and most important – secret in Chapter 14, The Secrets To Success.

3. *Speedwriting (and Billionaire)Habit # 3: Write again after dinner.* High-powered executives often get a little extra work accomplished after dinner.

    You can do this for a mere three weeks. When you and your family converge on the house each evening, do not even think about writing until everyone (including you) gets fed – or you will all end up eating each other in tired, hungry, end-of-the-day insults or an out and out fight. Eat first. It soothes the savage beast inside us all.

    Get everybody fed and then give the Ultimate Control – which is the TV remote control to your mate and disappear into another room, set your Timer for 2 hours and immediately **write for 2 hours.**

    If you are a single parent, have your TV remote control set on the Parent Control so you know what the kids can watch. You can also have the children work on their homework for an hour and then watch television.

    Whether married or single, make sure the kids are bathed and in bed by 9:00 p.m. Studies show that children do much, much better in school if they go to bed regularly and early. Their brains are growing, not just their bodies. They really do need the rest and you need peace and quiet from their running around the house, too.

    For your own sake, try to be in bed by 10 or 11 p.m. if possible – because tomorrow you are getting up an hour early, again.

How To Create Time On Weekends

The days you have the most hours to write are weekends. Reserve *12 hours* on *Saturday and Sunday, each,* for writing. You will probably write about 9 or so hours each week-end day– but absolutely reserve 12 hours. People often find they actually use all the time.

You may say, "Ginie, I can't write for twelve *straight* hours!" and I will smile and say, "I can't either."

The key is to work and rest alternately with mini-breaks every so often during long work stretches. But min-breaks should not be empty time of doing nothing. Mini-breaks are just brief twenty-minute changes of activity that let you keep thinking.

For example, my marathon days work something like this: I wake up around daybreak, fill up our teakettle and turn on the heat under it. While it is heating, my husband and I say our dedi-cation to each other (1 minute) and our prayers (1-2 minutes). Then we do a 2-minute work-out (given later).

When our teakettle whistles, I stop to brew tea, drink a half glass of milk, fill up my teacup and head to the computer. I set my Timer for 10 minutes, turn on my computer and check email but I do not allow myself to get distracted by email or anything else during that time.

I decide what I want to work on that day. Always, always, always, I choose my strongest interest in what I want to write that day. It does not have to be in order.

Then, I set my Timer for 2 hours. Immediately, I dive into my manuscript and work for about two hours.

When my Timer beeps that the two hours have passed; I take 20 minutes to shower and shampoo, towel down, clean my shower, sink, and clean the potty with a disposable cleaner: it makes such a difference in my mental attitude about my environ-ment and personal pride.

Then, I return to my computer.

I set my Timer for 2 hours and start writing. When my Timer goes off, I am usually so deeply involved in my writing that I set it for another hour.

After two or sometimes three hours, I am hungry. Taking another twenty minutes, I make something easy and fast to eat. It can be anything from cheese and an apple with half a glass of milk to a handful of walnuts with milk or my favorite left-over muffins (recipe in Cook Book section) with milk, or maybe slice and bake cookies with milk or a ½ bowl of original Familia cereal. Fast, easy, satisfying. That is all I need.

Back at my computer, I set my Timer for 2 hours again. When the time is up and if I am deeply focused on my work, I set it for another hour. I usually work about three hours this time.

At that point, it is time to get out of the house! So, I slip on something appropriate for the weather, add lipstick, a touch of powder, and go for a brisk walk – sometimes, I will jog (trot) and walk alternately. It is a gentle exercise to stretch my legs and body; not a serious 'run.'

During this 20 minute time period, I do stop to smell the roses or to pick up a pretty fallen leaf or to study the cloud patterns – because it refreshes me…bathes my soul. If it is raining outside or if the weather is too cold; I set my Timer and jog indoors for about 5 or 10 minutes while getting an update on CNN – but I do not allow myself to keep watching, no matter how interesting it may be. Then, I chat with my husband for a few minutes.

When I return to my desk, I work until I am finished for the day. When I stop this time, I do not go back to my computer unless I suddenly have an idea that must be added.

This is my writing pattern for two week-end days during my 3-week book writing.

When you are doing something you **want to do** – something you love – you do not feel as if you are working. You are thriving, and often you gain energy. After 9 to 12 hours of writing from your soul, even exhaustion has an electric energy to it.

Basic Rules For Your Work Time – Every Day for 3 Weeks

- Skip Happy Hour for 3 weeks. All your time counts.

- For 3 weekends, turn down any and all social activities with friends. It is just for 3 weeks, after all – and you can certainly give up those weekends for your very serious and personal project of writing a book.

- Turn off the sound of your telephone and cell phone – so that while you are working, you never hear it ring and never hear messages that are left by callers and never hear the signal that you have a text message.

- Do not work in the room with your television or radio playing. If a certain kind of music fits a section of your writing, you can play that type of music in the background on your ipod, mp3 player or on your computer while you are working on that particular segment of your book.

- Tell your children and spouse that you have to be undisturbed during the time you are working on your project – and that if they do not disturb you, you will all have ice cream (or whatever you know is their favorite food or beverage) together when the time is over. Keep this reward! If they are good, have the food or beverage with them, faithfully. Reward is your best friend for good behavior from everyone. And, just as you practice behavior modification on yourself, be sure to use it on your children and spouse by not having that particular food or beverage at any other time except after your work time.

- Even if you do not feel like writing, set your Timer for 2 hours, sit down and open your manuscript whether or not you feel in the Mood. Start reading your work and inserting notes. And most important of all, if you have an idea for another segment of the book WORK ON THAT – because that thought is your inspiration and by working on what interests you most at the moment, you will reignite your interest.

Two Single-Moms Who CREATED Time – AND Bestsellers

- **Terry McMillan** – Author of *Waiting To Exhale* and *How Stella Got Her Groove Back* (both books were made into movies) was a single working mother who rose before dawn, sometimes around 4 a.m., and worked until her son woke up. After getting him fed, dressed, and off to school, she took her writing with her and edited it on the subway to and from work.

- **Mary Higgins Clark** – Author of numerous mystery novels that have been made into television movies, was a widowed mother of 5 children. She had a full-time job; and when she decided to write novels, she got up at 5 AM every morning and wrote two hours until 7 AM.

Use Behavior Modification – Integrate Your Mind And Body

Integrate your mind and body with what I call *sensory behavior modification.*

Behavior modification is based on the Nobel Prize winning Russian scientist, Ivan Pavlov, and his experiment with dogs. His study showed that a mind can be trained to anticipate an experience and that the body simultaneously responds to the anticipation with predictable behavior.

For example, to summon his dogs for dinner, Pavlov would ring a bell. They would arrive, see and smell the food and salivate. Eventually, he tested the dogs and found that just by ringing the bell; the dogs would salivate in anticipation of the meal.

Pavlov referred to this as 'conditioned reflex.'

All people - including you, including me – have conditioned reflexes. We slow our cars to a stop when we see a traffic signal turning red – or we gun the accelerator to rush through it. Either way, our reflexes have been conditioned to respond to the color and position of the signal light.

Children mentally anticipate and physically respond to the ring of a school bell. Office workers do the same thing at five o'clock for Happy Hour or dinnertime or watching television.

Your mind is your ultimate equipment. I have already discussed at length the ways you can build enthusiasm and faith in your work through specific attention to your belief-system with mental exercises of Faith Statements and reinforcing posters.

Recondition Your Mind And Body Reflexes For Writing

Danielle Steele is said to have written her novels while wearing the same flannel nightshirt and while typing on the same very old manual (not electric) typewriter.

There may be an element of superstition involved – and, if so, good for her. But, I strongly suspect that the strongest element is that *once she puts on her same flannel nightshirt and sits down at her same typewriter, that her mind and body have been "conditioned" to let the creative juices flow*...much as Pavlov's dogs' digestive juices and salivary glands began to flow at the sound of the dinner bell.

You can do this, too. And you will accelerate the process if you utilize every sensory perception your body has!

Sensory Behavior Modification

Every item that you utilize for reconditioning yourself must be used *only* when you are writing – and never at any other time – until the conditioning is complete.

Sense of Touch: Choose clothing to write in that is made of a fabric that is very comfortable, non-restrictive – and very tactile – such as a nubby textured sweater that you can put on to get going and, once underway, peel off if you get too warm.

I now write in a variety of clothes; but until I trained my Creative reflexes, I used the same white undershirt (muscle shirt style) and a pair of shorts – also sandals my feet could slip in and out of under my desk.

If the weather is cold, I still wear my white undershirt with an unbuttoned flannel shirt as a 'jacket,' snuggly sweatpants, and thick, cozy socks – no shoes.

My now-tattered white undershirt is the kingpin of the operation; but the summer shorts and sandals and the winter sweats and socks are just as magical. I didn't wear any of them for other activities, so they still retain their 'creative glow' for me.

To have just one outfit – á la Daniel Steele – is even better. Underwear and a robe – or just a robe – that you do not wear for bed or bath but only for writing can work fine.

If neatness inspires your creative juices more, succumb to that and have a clean, neatly-pressed outfit or outfits *in the same fabric* that you can put on when it is time to write.

Keep your 'Creative Clothes' on the back of your chair. Sometimes, like Pavlov's puppies at the sound of the bell, your creative juices will start flowing when you simply look at your writing togs.

Sense of Smell: The smell of bacon and coffee can pull you out from under your bed covers and stir a growl of hunger in your stomach. The smell of evergreens, peppermint and apple cider can have you in the Christmas spirit and longing to hear old songs about chestnuts roasting on an open fire. A fresh soap and water smell is recognized as a desirable fragrance of cleanliness and it makes us look forward to our morning bubble baths or showers.

We associate fragrances with activities; therefore, fragrance can be effectively used to anchor our writing behavior. It may be that you are writing a romance novel. Fresh flowers are ideal; but they can be expensive. A potted plant of sweet-smelling Gardenias only requires minor care and it can dress up your desk while the scent inspires you to write. And do take time to smell it several times during your writing.

Potpourri – either in a bowl or in a spray – can sometimes work better. You spray your work area just before you sit down with your 'writing fragrance'.

Sense of Taste: You can often combine fragrance and taste for anchoring the pleasure of writing. They make a great duo, for example, with coffee. If you are using potpourri or a plant as your fragrance, then use your sense of taste, separately.

But, it must be a fragrant and delicious coffee blend that you never drink any other time, except when you are writing. This is especially true if you drink coffee all the time – find a delicious, fragrant blend 'only' for writing time.

The same is true for teas. You may love English Breakfast tea; but I save fragrant, tasty Earl Gray or light, sensuous Darjeeling teas just for writing.

You can have some variety. For instance, I drink Darjeeling tea, Black Magic Coffee, or hot Ovaltine as my main 'anchors' in the mornings – and those are only for writing. But on summer afternoons, I like cold Southern Grace Farms Blackberry 100% juice to sip while I am in thought.

As an aside, I got hooked on blackberry juice when I was in college. I was very ill and nothing the doctors gave me could stop the intestinal problems that plagued me. A middle-aged woman, from Sterling City, Texas, who sat next to me in my English class said to me, "My grandfather is full-blood American Indian (the term Native American was not in use at that time); and he taught me to drink blackberry juice – but *not* to eat the blackberries, just drink the juice – for any form of dysentery or upset stomach and it always works for my family."

Desperate to try anything, I finally found a health food store that had blackberry juice and it absolutely worked. After all the pills and shots and suppositories prescribed to me that did not work; the blackberry juice did.

I have since read that a number of chemotherapy patients use it to help alleviate nausea; and that people with IBS do, too. It is very difficult to find; but you can either juice your own fresh blackberries or search online. A wineglass of blackberry juice is part of my summertime writing routine.

Another food reward can be fresh fruits and berries (which look sensuous and stimulating in a ceramic, wooden, or crystal bowl on your desk) accompanied by purified mineral water or juice as a delicious reward of foods that are good for you.

Whatever foods you use as your writing anchor must be foods you only enjoy while you are writing. It has a great 'Pavlov's Puppy' effect to train you to look forward to writing time.

Sense of Sound: This is the most difficult to control and eventually; you learn to identify certain sounds of the day with your work. It may be the background sounds of your kids playing closely at hand. It may be an indistinguishable buzz of the television behind the closed door where your spouse is watching television. It may be intermittent, meaningless neighborhood sounds of lawn mowers, dogs barking, cars starting or an occasional honk or neighbors calling to one another. But, sooner or later, as you anchor yourself with other senses, the sense of sound will adapt to usual sounds that are typical for that time of day.

There is some sound control you can utilize. If you really need to do it, you can buy inexpensive earplugs at the pharmacy or a headset that gives a bland 'white sound' of nothing to override noises. I do not use ear plugs or white noise because if an emergency alarm goes off, I want to hear it!

You can play very soft music indicative of the type of book you are writing. When I was writing a scene that took place in

Vienna, Austria, I had a Strauss Viennese Waltz playing in the background in order to pick up the cadence of emotion in my Characters to match the lush, romantic flow of the music.

The time of day you work has a lot to do with the sounds around you. Pre-dawn and after-midnight will be the quietest. Week-day mid-mornings or mid-afternoons at home, will have a sane normalcy.

Feeding times, such as rushed breakfasts, 'go-to-work' or 'get-the-kids-off-to-school,' exhausted and out of-sorts dinner preparations, or 'get-the-kids-bathed-and-ready-for-bed' times are the noisiest. Choose accordingly.

Sense of Sight: Your workplace should be a welcoming sight – one that has texture and warmth, comfort and inspiration. I think of a writer's workplace as sacred. It can be the corner of a room; or it can be a whole room; or a kitchen table cleaned off right after dinner; or a TV tray with a laptop on it. Just a cozy, comforting area that you use again and again can entice you to write.

Whenever it is transformed into your workplace, keep it the same place every single day, initially, so that your workplace, too, becomes a creative reflex for writing.

I like a second floor location filled with windows shaded by treetops to filter a flood of sunshine or to frame a drizzling rain. Even when it is night-time and the curtains are drawn, I still have the feeling of windows and treetops.

Combine Sensory Conditioning

Sensory Behavior Modification integrates mind, body and ritual into effective performance. You can see that one sensory perception flows into another. Smell conjures up related sounds and sights. The smell of lemonade (smell) can give rise to images (sight) of a lazy summer afternoon, the hot sun (touch) causing you to perspire and the crickets (sound) as you drink the tart sweetness (taste) of the lemonade, itself.

Put this powerful association of the senses to work for you as a writer. Not only will it turn on the ignition of your creativity more quickly, but it will also reinforce your creative sensitivity and make you a more creative writer, overall. I utilize all sensory perceptions as a conditioning reflex to keep my writing juices flowing faster.

Create A Ritual

Rituals set you free. A writing ritual lets you take care of simple but important tasks, while you think about other things. Rituals put you on automatic.

Example of Ritual:
- 5:30 a.m. – wake up
- Brew favorite tea or special coffee
- Slip into writing clothes
- 2 minute neck, eye, and body stretches (My Easy 2-Minute Writer's Work out below)
- Say positive Faith Statements for 1 minute
- Transcribe any notes of book ideas – 10 minutes
- Write for 1 hour
- Straighten desk
- Wake up family, make an easy breakfast, pack a lunch, dress for work

Put It All Together For You, Now

See yourself now putting on your comfy socks and tee-shirt, pouring your fragrant Black Magic coffee into your favorite mug (also an anchor when just used for writing time). Take pleasure in the welcome of your workplace (slight disarray or sharp neatness), and settle into your chair, enjoying its usual squeak and the buzzing sound of your computer as you switch it on. Already, your mind is engaged – eagerly sorting ideas of where you want to start, today. Go get 'em, Tiger!

Take Care OF Your Health: Listen To Your Body

Carpal Tunnel Syndrome *can result in discomfort, loss of time on your book project, and extra expense.* Your body sends signals that, if ignored, can slow you down and eventually result in physical problems. So, when you are working hard, you must stay aware of your body's needs. Carpal tunnel syndrome affects parts of your body that are 'stressed' when they maintain a single position for long periods of time.

The two body parts I have found to be most stressed during a 3-week writing marathon are my wrists and my neck. Here is how I effectively take care of it:

- *Wrist* - I used to joke that I had 'computer wrist' in the same way tennis players complain of 'tennis elbow.' I bought a Microsoft ergonomic keyboard that solved my problem; however, there are other ergonomic keyboards that may be just as effective.

- *Neck* - The large spinal bone at the base of my neck used to give me so much pain that it would eventually get numb – which seemed scary to me. I thought about the fact that the ergonomic keyboard solves the problem with my wrist by forcing my hand to keep changing positions.

So, I decided to change the angle of my monitor by raising or lowering it every single day – and it works for me! I use four large telephone directories. One day, I will use none. Another day, I will use all four. Another day, I will use two, then change it to none; then to three. I never have the neck strain and pain I used to have.

I believe there is now a 'lift' system you can buy at office product shops that attach to your monitor and you simply move it up and down when needed; and there is an adjustable frame you can buy for a laptop.

Or you can accomplish the same thing with an office chair that you can raise or lower – which changes the angle of your neck as you view your monitor.

And finally, you may want to consider a glare screen to protect your eyes.

Take care of yourself, my writer friend; and you should certainly see a physician if any part of your body continues to give pain or consistent discomfort when you work.

My Easy 2-Minute Writer's Workout. Every morning before I write, I do the following (and it only takes 2 little bitty minutes):

- Reach up toward the ceiling with each arm 4 times
- Touch my toes 4 times
- Twist from side to side 4 times
- Stretch one arm over my head and bend to the side 4 times – then stretch my other arm over my head and bend the opposite direction 4 times
- Roll my shoulders forward 4 times
- Roll my shoulders back 4 times
- Tilt my head sideways so that my right ear goes toward my right shoulder 4 times – then reverse tilting my head toward my left shoulder 4 times.
- Turn my head as if nodding an exaggerated 'no' 4 times
- Nod an exaggerated yes 4 times
- Roll my head in a circle – 2 times – reverse direction 2 times
- Standing still, exercise my eyes – look rapidly up and down 4 times
- Eyes side-to-side 4 times
- Roll my eyes in a circle fast 4 times – reverse direction 4 times
- Eyes dart from upper right to lower left - back and forth 4 times – reverse direction 4 times
- Deep knee bends – 4 each (I hold onto the back of a chair)
- Elevate my right foot on a barstool, touch elevated toes 4 times – Reverse with left foot 4 times
- Jog indoors throughout several rooms 4 times
- Deliberately walk with good posture (shoulders back and relaxed) around the house 4 times.

This exercise routine keeps my **neck, shoulders, and eyes 'loosened up**.' Without it, I would sit almost all day staring straight ahead at my computer screen and possibly causing eyestrain, neck and shoulder strain, and hunched shoulders.

Sometimes, when I am putting in long hours at the computer, I take an 'exercise break' and go through the routine again. It feels so good to my neck and shoulders and back. It helps me a lot.

This exercise routine will never get me ready for the Olympics; but by allocating only 4 times to each step, and since it only takes 2 minutes, I know I will do it – and it keeps me flexible.

I have found that the number of times you execute a motion is not as important as the *consistency* of doing it daily that makes it most effective.

Try to come up with an easy routine that your doctor approves to take the kinks out – and use it to give your body relief from long hours of writing.

Chapter
12

Key Factor
Target Audience
Know Who Your Readers Are

One key to getting published by traditional publishers is to know who your readers are. – Ginie Sayles

An old but good book about writing romance novels described the romance market of that era as primarily young housewives living in a trailer park, curled up on an inexpensive overstuffed chair, and escaping into a thrilling romance. The book pointed out that these young women readers (target audience) would probably never experience the kinds of luxury they could enjoy for the price of a romance novel.

I discovered how true the demographics were when my husband and I returned from one of our many trips to Canada, one very cold winter night. The USA customs officer was a man in his late twenties who asked the usual questions of where you live, why you visited Canada, what is your profession, and so on. Most custom agents are very nice; but this man seemed to have had a bad day and fired the questions at us belligerently.

When my husband answered his question about my profession that I was a writer, he looked at me suspiciously and with a chip on his shoulder, asked, "Oh yeah? What kind of stuff do you write?"

I tried to explain that most of my books were relationship how-to books when he interrupted roughly "Pull over and let me examine your car."

My husband and I looked at each other, knowing it would mean standing outside in the cold wind late at night while he made an unnecessary car check – and it would delay us up to 30 or more minutes.

Suddenly the man said, "Wait a minute. You said relationships. Do you write those romance novels for women – like those Harlequin books?"

As a matter of fact, I had recently finished writing *Her Secret Life,* which is a romance novel, so I truthfully said, "Well, I am not published by Harlequin, but yes, I do write romance."

His face lit up, and his entire attitude changed. "My wife is crazy about those romance books. All the housewives in our trailer park trade back and forth. She reads one after the other."

With a broad smile, he said, "You can go on!" and waved us through.

As we entered the USA, my husband said, "Good old Harlequin saved us a lot of time!"

My point is, the man's wife exactly fit one segment of the romance market described in the old romance-writers book – a segment of women who love their husbands and enjoy being housewives even in limited circumstances while expanding their emotional/sensual range in romance novels.

I rather suspect that his wife may have read aloud to him some of the sizzling scenes in the Harlequin novels – and that, in turn, probably led to some sizzling scenes with his wife! He was just so delighted by romance novels that he must have benefited from them, personally.

Romance novel demographics have expanded to include almost all segments of modern women – married or single, rich or poor, housewives and career women – because, ultimately, who doesn't enjoy a good love story?

Knowing Your Market Can Get You Published

A friend who worked for a publisher asked if it would be all right to show a sample of my copyrighted book to the publisher. Of course I agreed and made an appointment for my husband and me to meet with the publisher at a later date.

Some time before our appointment with the publisher, *USA Today* ran a front-page story about the subject in their newspaper. In the article, it stated that "5 million" people are involved in that industry every year.

I quickly clipped out the article, highlighted that particular sentence in yellow, and tucked it inside my purse and forgot about it.

The day of our appointment, my husband and I – dressed to the nines – arrived exactly on time.

We waited outside the publisher's office for quite a long time. The secretary asked us several times if we would like to come back another time; but I gave a big smile said we had scheduled it quite awhile back and we would wait.

And, indeed, we did wait...and wait...and wait.

That is not a good sign. It usually means a publisher does not think the book is marketable, but is kind enough not to want to tell you so.

Eventually, however, we were invited into the publisher's office; but we were not asked to sit down. The publisher remained standing – and, of course, you do not sit down in someone's office unless (1) the person whose office it is sits down first (2) you are invited to sit down.

So – the publisher remained standing next to the desk as if our visit would be *extremely* brief. And we remained standing, too. This is not a good sign, either. Again, it typically means the publisher dreads hurting your feelings.

On top of the publisher's desk was my book. The publisher leafed through it and slowly said, "I have looked through your book..."

We waited.

The publisher continued, slowly "and it is very nice...well organized...nicely written..."

I was beginning to feel like a five year old showing her coloring book to an adult who is trying to be nice about it – and by the tone of his voice, I expected any minute to hear the word, "but..."

And the publisher did say 'but.'

"...but, Mrs. Sayles, I really don't think many people are interested in this subject."

What did that mean? It meant that the publisher thought a book on the subject would not sell (publishers are in the business of making money, remember?)

I thought of the *USA Today* article in my purse, quickly extracted it and handed it to the publisher (still standing, of course).

The publisher's eyes went instantly to the yellow highlighted sentence that read *"there are 5 million"* people involved in that industry every year.

KA-CHING!!

The publisher punched the intercom and said to the secretary, "Bring me a standard author's contract."

Then graciously gesturing, said, "Mr. and Mrs. Sayles, please have a seat."

We spent several hours going over every line of the contract out loud with the publisher, negotiating a few terms – and even though I was not completely happy with the final terms; I signed the contract.

Why? Because no other publisher would have had an inkling of my market for my book, either, and as my brother used to say, "a bird in hand is worth two in the bush."

If I had not clipped out the article in *USA Today,* I would not have gotten a contract with anyone.

Never presume publishers are god-like know-it-alls in the publishing market. Most of them know they are not and that is why they ask you who will read your book. And even if they think they know a market, you must know more about *your* market to be sure they publish you.

If you want to sell an unproven book idea, you must be able to tell a potential publisher the market for your book. Remember this – the size of the market (readers) for your book is the REASON why the publisher should take your book.

The first question a publisher will ask you is "Who is going to read your book?" Be sure you know your answer in *specific demographics*.

Let me remind you that publishers are not in the business of publishing great books; they are in the business of making money. Their definition of a great book is a book that is a moneymaker.

A moneymaking book has a clear-cut market. Your key to getting published is to know your market – meaning who will pay money to buy your book.

A Magazine Taught Me More About Target Audience

When a national woman's magazine published a cover story article about my work, the assignments editor called me to schedule one of their writers to interview me.

Once I agreed to the interview and after we set a date, the assignment editor went on to tell me that readers of the magazine are single, working women, between 25 to 34 years old. She said they are the faithful buyers and articles must deal with issues that touch their lives.

She mentioned that 35 is the beginning of middle-age when women are not 'girls' in the traditional sense. Their interests begin changing and issues that touch their lives also change; so they drop off as faithful buyers.

She was telling me this information because she wanted me to give answers in my interview that would apply to women in the magazine's demographics – meaning the women who buy (ka-ching!) the magazine. How very smart! No wonder it was, as I understand it, the bestselling magazine in the world at that time – so I think we can learn from that.

All successful publishers – of books or magazines or Internet or any other form of publication – know exactly who their market is if they plan to make money – and they direct all their articles and advertising to that market.

Your Market Wants Your Book

The owner of a store that specializes in selling formal evening gowns asked to sell my *How To WIN Pageants* book and so did the owner of an out-of-state bookstore that heard of the book from girls who had ordered it through *Teen* magazine.

I also sold my book directly to pageant contestants – and ended up with three Miss Texas' winners in a row who had used my book – and letters from contestants all over the country who were winning or placing in pageants when they had not before.

Several newspapers ran a picture of a newly crowned Miss Texas holding the *How to WIN Pageants* book with me and an article telling how she had used my book.

Make a list of businesses who might like to sell your book. Most of them will love the idea of offering it to their customers who qualify as your – and their – market.

Writing To Your Market

Targeting your market makes you a better, cleaner writer. It also helps you build your audience once they read you and share with others how perfectly you appeal to them. And you are more easily published and better able to sell your work. When you know who is going to read it, you also know who to target for sales.

How do you target your audience and then write to it? You ask yourself each of the following questions and be sure to answer them as you go:

- Who will read your book?
- If it is a how-to or informational book, then who needs it?
- Who will like it?

After answering the general questions, get more specific:

- What 10-year age range is your average reader?
- What is the probable educational range for your reader?
- What is the marital status of your reader?
- How large is your reader's household?
- What is the average income range of your reader?

If you feel you cannot define your audience, then let me tell you who your audience really is. It is you. That is fine, too. Just be sure you can clearly define "which you" is your audience.

- Is it *you*…as a child?
- Is it you as you are today?
- Is it you as you were a few years ago?
- Is it you as you would LIKE to be?
- Is it you the way you fear you could be, if…

If so, answer all the previous questions for you. Specificity makes you a more focused writer with a more marketable manuscript.

Finding Your Market Demographics

Let's say your book is about horses. You already know you will probably have the interest of some equestrian groups, horse breeders, riding equipment companies, riders, and cowboys. Those are all "categories" of readers. But you want a clearer breakdown of actual demographics of people most likely to buy your book.

How do you find it?

Magazines that cater to those very same categories have already broken down the demographic specifics – and you can get that information from them.

There are two ways to go about it.

First, go online and Google "horse magazines" – or whatever subject matter fits your book topic. Then visit each magazine website, one at a time, and see if it has an "Advertising" category. Study their advertising page. See if the magazine breaks down their readership into specific demographics. If not, click onto their Contact Us link and send an email that reads something like this:

"I may have an interest in advertising in your magazine but I did not find specific demographics of your readership on your website. Please send me a complete breakdown of your market so that I can determine a possible advertising budget that is best for me."

Second, browse the magazine rack at your favorite bookstore and, again, find any magazines you did not see online. Look in the index and get the email or telephone number of the Ad department. Email or call and request advertising demographic information be sent to you.

Some magazines may be secretive about their demographics – but this is rare if they really want business. If they have a strong readership, they will quickly use their bragging rights to supply specific information that will garner more advertising revenue from people who want to sell a related product.

The magazine publishers have already done all the nitty-gritty work of finding who the readers are, what their education level is, their income level, et cetera – be smart enough to cull the facts from them – several of them – so that you have a fuller extent of your market at your fingertips.

Narrow It Down To One Person

At one time, a former television evangelist was considered one of the most effective personalities in the media. His television show mushroomed beyond those who had preceded him and became a virtual empire in the world of television.

He was asked what made him so successful and effective and I will paraphrase what I heard him say, "When I look into the television camera, I don't think of a faceless millions of viewers. I think of one man…and I can see his face and I know what his life is like and what his needs are at that moment. And when I speak into the camera, I speak directly to the heart and needs and life of that one person – and because I do – people know I am sincere. And by speaking to him, I speak to them."

Personally, I think that is brilliant, as well as caring and genuine in its intent.

That is the way to write with power, too.

Chapter 13

Key Factor
The Fire
Of Your Creative Spirit

Michelangelo said of his masterpiece, The David,
"He was already inside the stone. All I did was chip
away the excess."

Since Time began, people have tried to understand the seemingly mystical power of Creativity – where it comes from, how it works, how to tap into it.

In ancient Greek and Roman mythology, Creativity was said to be a goddess, known as a Muse, whose visit to a person inspired that person in one of the creative arts. Our word 'music' comes from the Greek 'muse' goddess who inspires Creativity.

Renaissance Italians also gave Creativity a godlike status in a theory called Disegno (design). Disegno implies that a design already exists inside the art medium – stone, clay, canvas, tablet – just as the human soul exists inside the body; and a true artist works to release the design, to allow it to reveal itself to him/her through their Creative act.

Sculptor Michelangelo believed in Disegno and worked from the concept that the likeness of the Biblical David already existed in the marble and he only had to reveal it.

The word 'inspiration' that is attributed to Creativity was originally used to describe divine or supernatural experiences – with French and Latin meanings of "to breathe" – "breath" as if a breath of living Creativity was breathed into the artist.

The Bible speaks of God breathing the breath of Life into his Creation of humanity. Is Creativity the Image of God that we have in His likeness?

I believe there is some truth to all concepts in the sense that Creativity is not only a force of life through reproduction; but I also believe Creativity is the greatest 'survival tool' of mankind that enables us to change, to adapt, and to shape our lives. We have survived in large part because of our Creativity.

And Creativity is a power that carries us to greater expression beyond our ordinary selves, and perhaps it is divine in the sense of connecting us to that source, force, breath, energy, flow – of expression beyond our comprehension.

Your Creative Spirit takes that which is unseen – an invisible idea – and transforms it through your Action (which is faith) into that which is seen – a tangible manuscript or book.

Passion Lights The Fire Of Your Creative Spirit

The Fire of your Creative Spirit operates much like a Pilot Light in the daily life of a home. A pilot light is a *constantly burning* control light for gas energy.

From the moment you have an idea for a book – an idea that fills you with Passion to see it to the finish; the Fire of your Creative Spirit will glow as the "Pilot Light" in your mind, incubating the idea and developing it in your thoughts throughout your writing. And it glows brightly as you edit.

When you have an idea, it will not only function on the forefront of your mind; but it will also 'Gestate' on the backburner of you mind. Gestation – or 'mulling' – in the front or back of your mind, is one of the important processes of Creativity and it operates throughout each step – and also on its own.

Passion will light the fire of your Creative Spirit and fan the flames through 7 phases of writing. You will find the 7 phases alternate back and forth – from having an idea and mentally mulling, writing, and mulling again, to having another idea to add, and mulling, editing parts, deleting, fleshing out, and on and on and on. Your Creative Spirit is burning brightly as these phases weave in and out of your writing.

These 7 phases of writing interweaving in the passionate fire of your Creative Spirit are:

1. Creative Idea
2. Creative Incubation
3. Creative Writing
4. Creative Editing
5. Creative Fermentation
6. Creative Glazing
7. Closing A Creative Cycle

1. Your Creative Idea
- *The Invisible Creates The Visible* -

Think of it: All that we take for granted today – automobiles, paved roads, electricity, indoor plumbing, indoor cooking, radio, airplanes, space flight, television, mobile phones, DVDs, CDs, computers, Internet, email, iPods, holograms – all began with an *invisible idea* in somebody's thought process.

Wow. And wow, again.

The power of invisible ideas! *The invisible creates the visible.*

Your ideas are who you are. Your ideas are you to the nth degree. Your ideas can take you into worlds and lives you never imagined.

Many wonderful ideas have died with people who never pursued an idea that could have liberated their own lives. If you have an idea, my writer friend, I encourage you to follow it, to bring it to life. In giving an idea life, you give yourself life, too. You attain fulfillment in ways not possible in any other way.

An idea can come from anywhere – even as an idea to another idea. Occasionally, you may see a movie or read a book and realize that it would have been more interesting if it had taken a different path.

Whereas you cannot violate the copyright of another; you can create a different story and take it in a totally different direction – but your inspiration simply came from the movie or story.

One way to nurture ideas is to follow your healthy curiosities in life. I have often said – and fully believe – that if there is a voice of God we can listen to and follow, it speaks in many ways – and most often in our healthy curiosities – sometimes they are mild threads of interest and at other times they are a 'calling.'

How do I define a healthy curiosity, a healthy goal, a healthy heart's desire? Simply, a curiosity, goal, or ***heart's desire is healthy if it does no harm to anyone, including yourself***. Whenever I have followed my healthy curiosities, my life has taken a new path, I have met new people, and had new ideas to develop.

Many people, who view Creativity as a spiritual connection, also use it in business. Conrad Hilton, who created the hotel empire of Hilton hotels, was a deeply spiritual man. He attended Catholic Mass every single morning before going to work and he credited his achievements to answered prayer for ideas to solve problems that came up in his life. He said that when he prayed to God for an idea, he fully expected to receive an answer. Furthermore, he said he would intently 'listen' throughout the day for God's answer which sometimes came by giving him an idea. *Ideas are our connection with the Creative Source.*

Ideas are alive. Ideas are swirling all around you. Never judge them as "this won't work or cannot be done" – just enjoy their possibilities.

And when you feel the inspiration of an idea, capture it immediately. Like little fireflies on a cool summer evening, catch your ideas in a net of thought – let them breathe and sparkle into a blazing light.

Your ideas are precious, sacred, my dear writer friend. Ideas are *not* something you 'buy' – they are something living inside you.

2. Creative Incubation
- Release Your Ideas And Your Work Into The Fire Of Your Creative Spirit -

When you have an idea, it will not only function on the forefront of your mind; but it will also 'Gestate' on the backburner of you mind. Gestation – or 'mulling' – in the front or back of your mind, is one of the important processes of Creativity and it operates throughout each step – and also on its own. Finally, your idea will begin to flow into words that you want to write.

3. Creative Writing
- Willingness To Make Creative Mud -

My favorite comparison for a writer is to think of yourself as a potter because there are so many similarities between a potter and a writer.

For example, to make a beautiful pot or vase, a potter must first "make mud" of sorts from the clay by moistening it, in order to have something to work with. Now mud is not a beautiful pot. It is messy and without order – but it is the stuff pots are made of. And the potter can only make his/her beautiful pot from the soft mud of clay.

That is exactly the first step a writer must take – to make mud – a Creative mud of sentences piled together into the basic idea – a rough first draft. It is in that wild, free form writing that you, like a potter, create mud – and mud is very important because you cannot have a book without first creating the 'Creative mud' of your first draft to then shape into a book.

A first draft may be poorly written – muddy – but BE WILLING TO WRITE POORLY, in order to create a First Draft. Say these words, "I am willing to write poorly, if necessary to get down my ideas. I am willing to make Creative Mud."

Throughout this 2nd step of Creative Writing, your work will form and reform in the Creative Gestation process in the back of your mind. Let this flow and make notes, but do not get sidetracked into perfectly editing a particular chapter until you have finished writing your first draft. Stay in the mud stage. Shaping the pot/book comes later, after the mud is made.

The reason I do not let you stop and get too artistic on each chapter as you write your first draft is because you may never complete a manuscript that way – or at least not for years. I suggest you write your entire first draft without editing at all until you are finished.

4. Creative Editing – Turns You Into An Author
- Ultimate Creativity –

Editing is Creativity at its best. The true **ART of writing** is editing.

Many people mistakenly think – and are mistakenly *taught* – that when you are writing ninety miles an hour with ideas pouring from you that you are in the 'Creative mode' and that when you begin to edit, you must leave the Creative mode and get stern and serious. You are taught to think that editing is no fun because you are not in the Creative mode, anymore.

Wrong. The so-called 'Creative mode' is Creative Mud – and it is only the first layer of the four layers of writing.

In the end, anybody can make mud (First Draft – the important first step); but it takes Creative Artistry to shape the mud into a beautiful pot or vase (or book).

As a writer, this is where you cut away the excess mud and trim down chapters and paragraphs or descriptions into a smooth flowing picture in words. That is what turns a writer into an author. The editor inside you is the literary artist. Editing turns you into an author.

If the word "Edit" sounds unsympathetic or uncreative, think of Editing as Shaping. That is all it is. Editing is shaping your words and sentences. Shaping means deleting excess and tightening the design of your meaning – just as you do with mud to make a pot.

Think of how many times an inventor has to tinker and retinker and tinker again to make an invention work like the idea the inventor has.

Think of how many times a carpenter has to measure and remeasure, cut the wood, plane the edges, and maybe even start over with a fresh plank before the project takes the shape of the idea the carpenter has in mind.

Think of how many times a potter has to add water or add clay to get the consistency of mud just right and to spin it on a potter's wheel to shape the clay into the idea inside the potter's head.

Think of how many times an Artist brushes over a canvas, changing and rechanging the color or texture or size or shapes within the painting to make it fit the idea in the artist's mind.

Think of how many times a sculptor has to work with a chisel on many stones before the idea in the sculptor's mind can guide the chisel on the best quality of stone.

And think of how many times a writer has to delete words or sentences and even entire paragraphs – or chapters – in order to tighten the writing into the idea the author has for a book.

Reworking an invention, smoothing and refining furniture out of wood, making a pot out of mud, making art out of swirls of paint, making sculpture out of stone, and making a book out of words requires editing. Editing is the ultimate "Art" of all.

The average bestselling author edits a manuscript 14 times. What this means is that the bestselling book started out as a muddy first draft, too! Now, that should make you feel better.

Let's understand what a re-write is. It does NOT mean that you completely re-write the entire book 14 different times. No indeed. It only means that you read through your manuscript 14 times and each time, you 'edit' your manuscript – hence 14 rewrites/edits.

That is easy, because your own curiosity, concern, and personal pride will have you prowling through your manuscript at least that many times, if not more.

5. Creative Fermentation
- Before Your Final Draft – Release It For a time -

Fermentation is a state of change or development. It is a natural process we rely on to make bread, wine, cheese, yogurt, beer, cooking – and books! And the one ingredient required in Fermentation is 'time free from tampering' – *REST.*

Once all the necessary ingredients are combined – idea, incubation, writing, editing – then there is still another ingredient required to make it all work together – time away from it.

Much like a chef who combines all the right ingredients into a pot, stirs it well and then covers it to simmer on the backburner, the same will be true for you.

Remember, the Pilot Light in the back of your mind has been burning from the moment you had your book idea. It has burned through the writing process and in the editing process. Now, it must have some time alone with your book before you go further.

So, put your manuscript away for several days before writing the final draft. Go somewhere else. Do other things. Create a mental distance from your writing. A minimum of three days or longer is all right. Do not read your manuscript during "Creative Fermentation" – do not touch it – and try not to think about it, at all.

As you stay away from your work and let it simmer on the backburner of your mind, your Creativity is still working…and reworking… in your subconscious mind.

Even a potter must transform the clay that has been carefully worked into a pot by releasing it into the fire, release your manuscript to the Fire of your Creative Spirit.

A chef learns to keep the ingredients from burning and the vintner and food makers know the wine and foodstuffs have fermented, and the potter there is a time to remove it for glazing.

Distance and time are required for this all-important stage in writing – but not 'too' long. You will know when you have been away long enough to have an objective detachment for final proofing that it is time for Creative Glazing.

6. Creative Glazing

When you come back to your manuscript and read it again, you will immediately see what is wonderful about it and what can be improved.

At this point, your job is to polish and make final 'reworks' that are clearly better than they were before. Polishing, adding finishing touches. Making it look good, sound good and a good read.

7. Closing A Creative Cycle - Deadlines
- Not Perfect – Just Time To Stop -

I use the word 'closing' rather than 'finishing' because I don't think any author truly 'finishes' a book. There is always another type-o to find, another sentence to delete or to rearrange. Wordsmithing can become a compulsion – and sometimes a handy excuse for 'Fear' to lie to us and to say, "It's not good enough, yet."

Maybe it is and maybe it isn't; but the important end result is that **your job now** is to get your book – for better or for worse – out to an audience who will love reading your how-to book or your novel or your poetry, or your textbook or your photo journal.

You could spend another year or fifty years nit-picking over your manuscript – mostly out of fear that it is not good enough – or from self-esteem insecurities that it is not good enough.

Publishers have deadlines; so follow their example for yourself. They set a printing date and the manuscript goes to press with misspelled words and faulty punctuation. Warts and all, it is a book. Remember, a book is better as a finished product with flaws than an unfinished product being perfected.

So, you must set a date that you simply STOP adding or correcting. Stop. Your Creative process on this project has brought you to the good sense that you "choose to end" the cycle – not 'finish' but to end the cycle. At this point, you decide if you want to sell it or just keep it.

Let me remind you that styles change in books; so at some point, you have to get it on the market while there is a market for it. If you decide to work on your manuscript after the initial three weeks, mark a calendar for 2 important dates – (1) to mail or upload your manuscript to the Library of Congress for copyright protection; and (2) to mail or upload your manuscript (after it has been filed for copyright) to an agent or publisher. Do it – warts and all.

Write your final draft. Final means **stop**. It does not mean perfect.

And remember, just having written your final draft is AUTHOR SUCCESS, a success that no one can ever take away from you – and a success that you cannot even take away from yourself. And it is a success that adds to your stature and self-esteem simply because you DID it. You tapped into your Creative Spirit and let it lead you through all the steps to fulfill yourself and your very own success.

Good Job!

Chapter 14

Secrets
To Success

The Secret to Success is the word 'Secret.' – Ginie Sayles

The first and most important secret to writing a book in three weeks or less - is *silence*. Do not tell anybody! Say it aloud, right now – the secret to success is the word 'secret' because it is!

1st Secret – The Secret To Success Is The Word 'Secret'

If you do not tell people you are writing a book, they cannot scoff or criticize or kill your new spirit. They cannot steal your idea – and they cannot secretly gloat if you do not finish writing your book for any reason. They cannot 'dig' you about not finishing. They cannot remind you for the rest of your life that you did not finish…because they never knew you were writing a book in the first place.

And if you do not finish, so what? Who knows? Nobody! You do not position yourself as a failure if no one knows your plans.

Do not give other people the power to hurt you – and if you tell them your plans, that is exactly what you are doing – giving them the power to hurt you. Don't do it! Keep your own power.

Some people do not want you to achieve more than they do – or even as much as they do. Take a vow with yourself right now that writing the book is part of your private relationship with yourself. Adhere to a fine integrity with yourself and tell no one – no matter how excited you become about it.

When you tell someone your 'plans' you are actually(1) seeking that person's approval in some way to affirm the worth of your plans; or (2) trying to impress them.

If your writing project is real, then you do not need their approval or their reaction. If your plan is real, then you do not need to tell them. *Your only need is to write*.

If people ask what you are doing or how you are spending your time, just downplay it by saying, "Oh, I am just catching up on several tasks I have put off for a long time" (several tasks being chapters), or "Just finishing a small personal project." If pressed, just say, "Oh, it is too much work to talk about now. When I get caught up, I will have a clearer head to tell you all about it." Refuse, refuse, *refuse* to tell what you are doing. Do not breathe your intentions of writing a book to anyone.

First, write your book and then tell them – and that will impress the hell out of them!

Author Helen Gurley Brown wrote *Sex And The Single Girl*, a bestselling how-to book for single women that led to her becoming Editor In Chief of a failing magazine called *Cosmopolitan*. She patterned the magazine after her bestselling how-to book and took the magazine to world-wide success.

This phenomenally successful woman, Helen Gurley Brown, once wrote: "I think how successful you can become is probably in direct proportion to how much you shut *up* about it."

I agree! Don't tell anybody.

Even A Spouse?

Well, I know a woman whose husband was so controlling that he always took over whatever she did and then tried to tell her how to do it better. She was a talented actress and she received wonderful reviews, but when I asked her husband's whereabouts at one of her performances, she said, "Ginie, I do not want my husband to attend the plays I'm in. I lose all confidence in myself because I know he will think I could have done it better." She shook her head, "We now have an agreement that he will not attend."

If your spouse kills your confidence or belittles your hopes, and yet you love your spouse and want to stay married; you really must keep your writing a secret and I mean it. Do not let your spouse sabotage your dreams. When you DO write your book and get it published, your astonished spouse will shape up. I have seen it many times.

All people in your life will be ten times more impressed when you say "I just wrote a book," than if you say, "I am writing a book." The proof to other people is in the finishing.

The secret to success is the word secret.

2ⁿᵈ Secret – Identify With Yourself As A Writer

One day, I took my daughter to an acting audition that was videotaped for preliminary judging. Finalists would be selected from the videos, and those finalists would then perform live for top television talent agents.

After my daughter had given a wonderful taping, the woman in charge said to me, "Ginie, why don't you audition, too?"

"But, I'm not an actor," I protested, "Besides, I'm not dressed up. I only have on jeans."

But the woman continued to press and I wavered. Sensing my indecision, the woman handed me some scripts. I glanced through them, and then shook my head.

"Can I read anything I want to?" I asked.

When she nodded, I went outside to my car, brought in a small Bible and opened it to the book of Job. Then, sitting cross-legged on the floor, I read a segment that had meant a great deal to me, personally.

A few weeks later, my daughter and I both were notified we had made the finals. And after our separate live performances several weeks later, I was signed with an agent (my daughter already had one), who was one of the judges.

On the day I signed the contract, I kept marveling, "…but I'm not an actor."

The agent said, "That is the first thing you have to stop saying, if you intend to succeed in this business. You must begin saying, 'I am an actor' and identify with the profession. It does not matter if you have had any acting jobs, yet; you cannot be what you do not identify with."

This is just as true in writing. You can have all the talent in the world, but unless you think of yourself as being in a profession, you remain an outsider. This is why I urge you to say, "I am a writer. I am an author." as part of your positive faith statements. I did this, myself, when I realized I truly wanted to be an author. You become the profession you choose as your identity. But say it only to yourself until your book is finished.

3rd Secret – What Is The Single Most Important Thing I Can Accomplish TODAY?

Remember that you cannot be Creative 'yesterday' and you cannot be Creative 'tomorrow' because yesterday is dead and tomorrow is imagined.

You can only be Creative TODAY. Today is all that is alive. You can only live one day at a time – and you can only write one day at a time.

The moment you wake up, if you ask yourself "What is the single most important thing I can accomplish today? and then cheerfully pursue it, you are on exactly the right path for achieving your Heart's Desire. Yes, yes, I know it would be better put "what is the single most important accomplishment I can achieve today?' but I like it better the other way.

As a writer, you maximize your time if you sit down at your desk and ask the question about your writing. Then, set your Timer and focus on accomplishing it.

I scribbled "What is the single most important thing I can accomplish today?" by hand on a scrap of paper and taped it to the top of my computer a long time ago. It helps me stay on course, each day.

Chapter 15

Fiction
Or
Non-Fiction?

Why limit yourself? You are a writer, period.
– Ginie Sayles

You may be convinced you are only a fiction writer – or you may be adamant that only non-fiction rules your interest.

Why limit yourself? You are a writer, period. Keep yourself open for change – and open for opportunity in either writing realm.

You can write novels AND how-to books or health books or textbooks – just open yourself up to the myriad opportunities that await you if you do not put your writing talent into a box.

I teach my seminars – and offer this book – on both fiction and non-fiction for this very reason. And I am so glad I have done that because you may be thinking of yourself in one dimension and through reading this book or watching my instructional DVDs or by attending my seminar on this subject, you may realize you can do both – and at some point in your life, you may need these skills in order to do it. And you will have the skills.

At the close of one of my *Writer's Block Is A Crock – How To Write A Book In 3 Weeks – Or Less!* seminars in Houston a few months back, a woman approached me. Her voice was excited as she said, "I came here tonight to learn how to write fiction faster and I did – and then by the end of class I had a great idea for a how-to and now I know how to write it, too."

Look at it both ways: You may be in the middle of writing a great non-fiction book and suddenly have an idea for a novel based on the same information. Or, you may be in the middle of writing a great novel and suddenly realize you can write a great non-fiction book on the same subject.

My method of outlining Non-Fiction will also work great for you if you are in school and need to write a report or if you are working on a Masters or Doctorate degree and need to write a Thesis.

So make up your mind to learn how to write both Fiction and Non-Fiction! Be sure you finish the one you are on before you begin the other – or it may be a trick of fear to derail you. But do stay open to writing both Fiction and Non-Fiction.

I will say this more than once; but it is important – write Fiction the way you *feel* it, the way you see it, the way you hear it in your heart.

Write Non-Fiction the way you talk.

Part 2

SPEED SKILLS

Fiction

Chapter

16

Why
Write Fiction?

What do you hope to achieve by writing a novel?

There is no right or wrong reason to write a book, as long as it harms no one, including you. If you want to write a book, that is all that matters. Perhaps you want fame or fortune or maybe you just enjoy writing.

Creative Pleasure

Even if no one reads your book, you would still want to write it, for the pure joy of writing. There is a love of words, of ideas, of limitless possibilities in imagination that impels many writers into the sanctuary of Creative pleasure in writing.

Writing becomes a thoroughly emotional, if not sensuous experience in and of itself. The writer can go anywhere the writer wants to go, do anything, be anything, and create anything.

If you are one of these writers, you love everything about words. You can virtually taste words, smell words, touch words, see the world they create, hear them resonating in your head.

Oh, the emotional satisfaction words can bring through writing! The truth is, you would want to write books if no one ever paid you for it…and if no one ever saw it. Even so, you may long to share your love for writing with others and to bring readers joy with your words.

Without a doubt, the Creative pleasure of writing is one of the best reasons of all to write fiction.

Explore Other Lives Or The Road Not Taken

Fiction allows you to explore other lives, to test your beliefs and to learn from it. I have always learned from my writing. When I wrote *Her Secret Life*, which is a story of a young woman who loves two men and through a series of circumstances ends up married to them both at the same time; I began writing the book with an open curiosity and no prejudgment about bigamy. I was surprised at the lesson the experience taught me.

Through this vicarious adventure, I learned that you (and use the word 'you' in an impersonal sense) may be able to love two people at the same time; but you can only commit to one in the fullest definition of commitment. When you try to commit to two people at the same time; they are both the losers because they are both cheated of time you spend with someone else – and even if it is consensual by all parties, someone is eventually subservient, exploited or exploits another, even if unintentional. I never expected to learn that.

Fiction also allows you to explore 'the road not taken' in your own life. What if you had accepted the opportunity to move to another country?

What if you had married your first love?

What if you had gone to an Ivy League school? Or if you had not gone to an Ivy League school?

What if your parents had been wealthy? What if they had been poor?

What are the choices in life that changed everything for you? Fiction allows you to go back to that point in time and rewrite it to experience that 'road not taken.'

It can be interesting.

Literature

There are many categories for fiction – historical, science fiction, romance, mystery, and the list goes on and on. But fiction mostly boils down to two types – either literature or formula fiction.

Literature requires a special lineage…a bloodline of dedication. But shun elitists on this subject. It depends on what you want to write. Formula is more immediate and more lucrative. Both are viable.

Most fiction writers naturally hope to write 'literature' – a great piece of writing with the timeless quality that will endure as a classic. But, I like what Mickey Spillane, bestselling author of the 'Mike Hammer mysteries' said when he was asked how he felt about the criticism of Hemingway (Ernest Hemingway, the literary giant).

Spillane responded, "Hemingway who?" which was a great answer. After all, Hemingway may have received accolades from literary critics; but Spillane was making enormous sums of money. He used to point out that fact by saying he did not have fans of his work, he had customers.

Spillane believed that if the public likes your work, it's good. I like his moxie of sticking up for his own writing – and not letting someone else determine its value other than the people who buy it.

My point is, there is room in this world for both literature and popular fiction. Don't let anyone put down your work with a snobbish label.

Literature in the strictest sense is the most difficult to sell because literature is subject to interpretation by the most current reading audience.

You may truly write a fabulous book only to find that a publisher or several publishers consider it without merit – and yet, at a different time period, publishers hoping to get their hands on it, may have fought over the same work in bids. Taste in writing is fickle and often has nothing to do with whether or not your work is truly literature in the classic sense.

If beauty is in the eye of the beholder; then literature is likewise in the eye of the market or readership because literature is subjective.

Whenever you read of a great writer who lived penuriously and died of starvation, only to be celebrated by subsequent generations, you can put it down that here was a writer of true literature.

However, having said that, F. Scott Fitzgerald and Ernest Hemingway both lived to see their work celebrated as literature and both enjoyed the fruits of fame and fortune.

I want you to write what is in your heart to write. If writing literature is your burning desire, then you must write it, no matter what. I just want to be sure you believe in it so much that no amount of rejection can stop you. And who knows, maybe your work will not be rejected at all but welcomed with open arms by the reading world.

Because publishers are in the business of making money, literature can seem 'iffy' and so they are slower to invest in it.

As I have said, writing literature requires a special lineage…a bloodline of dedication – and if that is your desire, stick with it! Stick with it no matter what.

Formula Fiction – A Prescription For A Writing Type

Most of today's writers do not want to live penuriously, die of starvation, and never know if they were celebrated authors by later generations.

No, indeed. Most of today's writers want to make money and to live well in the here and now. To do that requires many things, including turning out a number of books quickly. The easiest way to achieve that is to learn how to create a formula – template or prototype – for your writing or to use an existing formula.

There are entire publishing genres built around 'formulas' – such as romance novels or mysteries. Many publishing groups who specialize in these genres have a check list of what their books must contain to meet the standards that satisfy their readers.

The 'standards' for many of these publishers will contain certain absolutes from a formula that makes them a lot of money.

Formula fiction is the most lucrative of all fiction writing. Whether mystery or romance, formula fiction sells. Therefore, formula fiction is the easiest to write and the easiest to get published.

In the next chapter, I teach you how to create your own template/prototype to make your writing faster and focused. Also, read Chapter 19 to see just how widely spread formula fiction is used in templates even for some literature.

Fiction Is _Not_ Autobiographical

You do not have to murder someone in order to write about a murder.

There. That one initial sentence puts to rest the insinuation that all fiction is autobiographical.

What nonsense.

Fiction can be a release of emotion, true; but it does not mean that the writer has released the emotion in the way the writer expresses in a novel.

Fiction writers draw from knowledge to a limited extent – for instance a setting can be similar to a place the writer has visited or lived; but that does not make the story that is put into the setting true. Not at all.

I find it intriguing that a woman can write a romance novel about an illicit affair; and, immediately, people speculate that she is writing from a real life experience of cheating on her husband. However, if a man writes such a romance novel about a woman, most readers think he is writing about something that never happened. And, if someone writes a novel about a murder, no one even pauses to wonder if the novelist actually killed someone.

Quite often, a novelist writes about an illicit affair or some other event for the same reason the suspense writer creates mystery fiction – simply to explore that part of life without actually participating in it. Fiction is a wonderful vehicle for exploring anything without actually participating in the behavior. That is why it is called 'fiction.' The storyline is pure fantasy. It is not autobiographical – otherwise, it would be called non-fiction.

Fiction is 'Mental Play' – creative make-believe. We can write fiction **to escape** a boring period in our lives or **to expand** our experiences or just **to 'try on'** another life – or to imagine what might have happened with possibilities of The Road Not Taken – and these are all valid and wonderful reasons to write fiction.

And yes, some authors wisely choose to 'fictionalize' a true story to protect the guilty, known as roman à clef. With fiction, the authors can take a few liberties of make-believe and stretch the facts – because it is fiction. Purely autobiographical writing cannot do that.

Chapter

17

Fiction

Plot & Characters

In Just 30 Minutes to 1 Hour

A Plot is the Main Problem that the Main Character must solve by the end of the story or book. – Ginie Sayles

In my seminars and on my DVDs, I demonstrate the steps in this chapter on Fiction and the one on Non-Fiction. Be sure you follow each step exactly.

Let's say you want to write a novel, but you have no idea what to write. Or, if you are an experienced writer, let's pretend you have been offered an opportunity to write a novel and have it published. This is an opportunity you have dreamed about; only now, you find yourself stymied. You cannot seem to come up with a plot.

Don't worry, with my simple 7 Step method, you can structure a plot in about thirty minutes to one hour!

Step One
Create Your Own Template (Prototype, Formula)

1. For this basic, thirty minute to 1-hour process, you will
   need:
   A. Several sheets of blank paper
   B. Pencil or pen
   C. Digital Timer

Settle comfortably on your sofa, with a cup of coffee, if you
wish. Being comfortable accelerates the Creative process.

2. Take Inventory Of Your Soul.
   a. What were your favorite fairy tales as a child?
   b. Your favorite bedtime story?
   c. Your favorite religious story (whatever your religion)?
   d. As you got older, what were your favorite classics
      studied in school?
   e. What was your favorite writing by Shakespeare?
   f. Think of these favorites and why you loved them.

3. Choose One

4. Write the title on a sheet of paper

4. Set your Digital Timer for 10 minutes.

5. From memory, and as fast as you can, write a summary of
   the storyline.
   • Limit yourself to ¾ page; 1 page at the most.
   • **Do not write any descriptions or details** of the
     story - only the bare bones skeletal storyline.
   • Do not stop to think Just Write:
   • Do not worry about getting all the facts right. Just
     write as quickly as you can, remembering as best
     you can.

- If something stumps you, put in what you think it 'could' be – just connect the dots in some way to make the story fit or sort of fit. What you think you remember may be more important in the long run than the actual story.
- And don't worry about grammar or spelling – just write

For Example: *FAIRY TALE Summary*

Goldilocks & The 3 Bears

Goldilocks lived near a forest. Her parents warned her not to go into it; but the lure of a butterfly one day led her deeply into the woods until lost.

There were 3 bears who lived there and they went for a walk to let their food cool off. While they were gone, Goldilocks discovered their house, went inside, ate the food, broke a chair, and went to sleep upstairs.

The bears were perplexed when they returned, saw the damage, and found Goldilocks. She awoke, was frightened, and ran away, finding her way back home.

Stop timer!   Record Time: 6 mins. 4 secs. (my time)

Look again at my preceding example. Notice there is no *description* of Goldilocks. There are no *descriptions* of her parents or of the butterfly, of the forest, or of the bears' house. And there is absolutely *no dialogue* between the bears - i.e. "My porridge is too hot!" et cetera. This is a 'bare-bones' storyline and that is the way yours is supposed to be, because that is all you want – the storyline, itself.

Step Two
Divide The Story Into Thirds

All stories and novels have ONLY three parts – the Beginning, the Middle, and the End. Each part is defined by what is accomplished in that part.

I. The Beginning is made up of identifying the Main Character (Hero) and the Main Problem (Plot). *Underline the name of the Main Character and underline the Main Problem so that you know the beginning as been accomplished and it is time to examine the middle.*

II. The Middle is made up of Complicating the Main Problem with Subplots – which include Subplot (minor but important) Characters, Subplot Locations, and Subplot Action. *Underline any Subplot Characters, Subplot Locations, and Subplot Actions that complicate the main problem. At some point, the complications will beg resolution... so it is time to end it.*

III. The End of the story/novel has the Main Character solving the Main Problem, and tying up the loose ends of Subplots – all to *satisfy the reader*.

Go back through your summary and **draw a line after the task has been accomplished in each part** – Beginning, Middle, and End. This is a fairy tale so it is simple – BUT – it contains all the same important steps of a novel.

Goldilocks & The 3 Bears

I. BEGINNING: *Goldilocks lived near a forest. Her parents warned her not to go into it; but the lure of a butterfly one day led her deeply into the woods until lost.* (Note: "Goldilocks" is our Main Character; Being "Lost" is her Main Problem that she must solve by the end of the story. Both are underlined.)

II. MIDDLE: *There were <u>3 bears</u> who lived there and they went for a walk to let their food cool off. While they were gone, Goldilocks discovered <u>their house</u>, <u>went inside</u>, <u>ate the food</u>, <u>broke a chair</u>, and went to <u>sleep upstairs</u>.*

(Note 1: Subplot Character Bears, Subplot Location of their house; and Subplot Actions are all underlined)
(Note 2: At first, Goldilocks was just lost – now she is guilty of breaking and entering! Each action got her deeper and deeper.)

The <u>bears</u> were perplexed when they returned, saw the damage, and <u>found Goldilocks</u>.

(Note: Her life may be in danger; so the story begs resolution at this point.)

III. END: *She awoke, was frightened, and ran away, <u>finding her way home</u>.*
(Note: It is time for the Main Character to solve the Main Problem, tie up Subplot loose ends and to *satisfy the reader*).

Step Three
Answer Eight Key Questions

Ask yourself these questions and jot the answers on paper:

1. What is the **Time Period** of the story?
    Answer: Roughly 300 or more years ago.

2. Where does the story take **Place** – as in the Location/ Setting?
    Answer: Europe; guessing it is Germanic, maybe the Bavarian Forest.

3. Who is the **Main Character** or hero?
   Answer: Goldilocks

4. What is the **Plot**, which is the Main Problem the Main
   Character must solve by the end of the book?
   Answer: Lost – the Main Character is Lost.

5. How many **Characters** in the story?
   Answer: 7 characters are in the story.

6. **Who** are they?
   Answer:
   • Goldilocks
   • Her 2 parents
   • The Butterfly
   • The 3 Bears

7. What is the **Relationship** of each character with the
   Main Character?
   Answer:
   • Her parents are protective, but to Goldilocks
     they seem limiting.
   • The Butterfly is beautiful and leads her astray.
   • The 3 Bears may endanger her.

8. Whose **Point-Of-View** carries the story?
   Answer: Goldilocks

Step Four
Change Time, Place, Or Point-Of-View

To use a story as a template, you can ONLY change any of
three things about your story:
   • *Time Period* – Any time period you want.
   • *Location* – Any real or imagined place you want

- *Point-Of-View* – The view point of any character in the template story

For our example, we will change only the following two:
- Time Period – Today – the year you are reading this
- Location – America
- Point-Of-View – Let's keep Goldilocks' Point-Of-View to tell the story.

Step Five
Create Parallel Characters

Look over the Summary you wrote of your favorite story and count the number of characters and the part of each character in the story.

(1) Create Parallel Characters – using all the same character roles.
   Name and Describe each Character. We can update our Main Character's name to Goldie Locklear.

(2) Know each character's relationship to your Main Character.
   You have just created your very own template. Now, transpose it into a new setting and time period with parallel storyline and characters.

Step Six
Write A Parallel Summary Of Your New Novel

Write a Parallel Summary of the story with your new characters, new time, new place, and be clear whose point-of-view leads the story.

We will KEEP:
(1) The same number of characters

(2) The same relationships
(3) The same number of obstacles

See Example on the next page.

Example: *NEW NOVEL Summary*

I. BEGINNING: *A runaway teenager,* **Goldie Locklear** *believes her parents do not understand her dream (signified by the butterfly) to be a movie star. Her parents seem too limiting and harsh.*

But she follows her dream (the butterfly) and runs away from home into the forest – which is the big city of Los Angeles, California.

Goldie gets **lost** *in the big city and soon runs out of money.*

II. MIDDLE: *Goldie soon realizes she does not have the foggiest notion of how to pursue her dream now. Being a high school dropout with no work experience makes it that much harder to find a job.*

She encounters three bears who, in the story could be three men or three organizations, or three women or a mix – a man, a woman, an organization. They are her main choices or obstacles in her struggle for survival.

One bear could be **a pimp** *who offers her prostitution or a drug dealer who offers her a way of making a living selling drugs.*

The second bear could be **a nun** *who works in a ghetto Mission house and offers her kindness, a warm sweater, a hot bowl of soup and bread, a cup of coffee and a touch of friendship. Or the second bear could be another runaway girl who becomes her friend and helps her learn the ropes of survival.*

The third bear could be **the police**, *who, for the first time in her life seem as if they are now the enemy, if they catch her for stealing food or for sleeping on the street.*

...Now, your job as author, is to create a series of scenes (that is all a novel is – just a series of scenes called Chapters) *of Goldie interacting with these characters and showing action and emotion as she escapes one obstacle after another,*

III. END: . . .*until she **finds her way** home, again.*

And what is 'home?' Home is Goldie finding herself and no longer being lost. And whereas that could mean she reconciles with her parents and decides to go home and finish school and take drama classes before trying again; it could just as easily mean that you show Goldie finding her own way out of the dilemma. You could even have Goldie becoming a movie star against the odds. Create a reader-satisfying resolution.

Note: Writing with Passion means staying in touch with your soul Go back through your original template – the childhood fairytale – as many times as you need to and translate the wonder you felt as a child into your writing.

Step Seven
Fulfill YOUR JOB As Author In Each Third Of A Novel

There are 3 parts to a novel – only 3 – the beginning, middle, and end. That may seem evident; but the trick is **to know your 'mission' – which means to know what you must accomplish as a writer in each third and you will write faster.** Your job for 200 pages and each third (3rd) is:

1. The Beginning – **3 to 5 chapters** – start with the problem

   Your job is to set up the Main Problem (Plot) and to identify the Main Character (Hero) as quickly as possible in the very beginning of your new novel. Why? Because your reader needs to quickly know the character to sympathize with and to root for throughout your novel. Also, the Main Problem is the Plot of your novel and you want to "hook" your reader's interest instantly. The best way to do that is begin your book smack-dab in the middle of the Main Problem.. *Remember, a plot is the main problem that the main character must solve by the end of the book*

2. The Middle – **8 to 12 chapters** – about 8 (or so) subplot complications

   The middle is the largest third of your novel. **Your job** is to complicate the Main Problem (Plot) with Sub Plots. Subplots keep your reader from getting bored with a single theme and reveals new dimensions to your Main Character. Whatever your character is doing, ask yourself the question, "Can it get any worse than this?" If so, make it worse. Then ask the same question again, "Can it get any worse than this?" If so, go with it. Keep asking the question because that is how you create complications. Remember, Goldilocks was just lost at first; but she went into a house when the owners were away and everything she did after that was worse than what she had done before.

Always keep your Main Character getting deeper and deeper as he/she tries to solve the Main Problem. Introduce new problems that complicate the issue. The complications must build to a crescendo of intensity that begs resolution. Have a major event that is the Climax of the events.

3. The End – **about 5 chapters** – resolve problem, tie up loose ends

When the complications intensify to the point of begging resolution – **your job** is to resolve it! Have your Main Character solve the Main Problem – and wind the story down with resolved loose ends as well from the Subplots – and to satisfy the Reader.

Satisfying The Reader

One Bestselling Author had a book published that did not sell well. For years she kept trying to get published again; but to no avail.

But one day, her agent called and asked if she would take a flat $10,000 payment to write a novel according to a certain formula (Template/Prototype). She agreed and it was her first bestseller. It turns out that her first book had a "realistic" ending that did not satisfy readers; whereas the formula book had a happy ending which enormously satisfied readers. She said that she learned her lesson and every book she wrote after that had a happy ending and became bestselling books.

My point is that if you want to have 'realistic' endings, go ahead. But think about it – do you, as a reader, really like to plow through 200 pages only to find the hero has no more sense than you do? Most people don't. Most readers like to cheer the hero and feel they have experienced that victory vicariously. Still and all, write your endings the way you want to because it is your baby.

Chapter Lengths

An average chapter for a 200-220 page book is about 10 pages; but chapters can be any length from 1 page to 30 pages. However, readers like fairly brief, easy-to-read, pithy chapters.

Paragraph Lengths

The late Barbara Cartland (Guinness Book Of World Records' most prolific author) stated that she never wrote a paragraph any longer than two or three sentences because it is easier on the eyes of the reader. Looking at a page that is made up of long, fat paragraphs can create mental dread in a reader and it feels defeating – but the eye travels quickly over small paragraphs.

One Template – Limitless Books

Let's pretend your novel about the runaway teenager, Goldie Locklear, is a bestseller and now your agent and publisher want you to write another book, fast – while your new reading audience is hungry for your work.

Should you inventory your soul again and find another storyline as your prototype? Not necessarily; but you can if you want to. Yes, you can write another favorite story – fairytale, Bible story, fable, Shakespeare or other Classic – and create a whole new template/prototype for another novel. That is entirely up to you.

But if you really loved Goldilocks And The Three Bears, you have found a winning formula for your plots. You can write book after book using the same storyline; but making changes in time and place or character descriptions so that each book seems fresh and vital to your readers.

For example, we will pretend you want to write a comedy this time. Let me show you how you can turn your same formula into a winning comedy.

Repeat All Steps: Let's go back to your favorite fairytale, Goldilocks, and put it into yet another context, by just changing:

(1.) The Setting – choose a new location

(2.) The time period – choose a new time period

(3.) Point-of-view – CHANGE THE POINT-OF-VIEW to the bears' point-of-view and write a second summary. In my mind, I imagine Neil Simon writing it.

This could be...

An upstanding middle-class family whose down-and-out relative has come to stay with them. They are fairly self-righteous – in fact, rather smug – about their values and effectiveness at living their lives. They decide to take this pathetic relative under their wing and to show the person how to live life.

Or so they think! Then the fun begins. The husband and wife come home from work, planning to have a business partner for dinner, only to find their food has been thoughtlessly eaten by the dead-beat relative ("Who's been eating my porridge?!"- papa bear)

Or the family leaves for a week-end and return to find the relative has given a wild party in their absence and their furniture is smashed up ("Somebody's been sitting in my chair and sat the bottom out!" – baby bear).

They may even discover the relative having sex with a stranger in the master bedroom ("Somebody's been sleeping in my bed!" –mama bear)!

YOU ARE IN CONTROL: As fiction writer, you play God to your characters. That means you can change Goldilocks into a boy or a man or an old man or an old woman or into an animal - such as Benji. Yes, Benji is similar to the story of Goldilocks in the form of a lovable puppy, who gets lost and escapes one obstacle after another until he finds a home. Possibilities are endless!

Okay – now *you* do it! You see how easy it is – so sitting in front of your computer or with several sheets of blank paper – Create Your Own Template/Prototype:

Set Your Digital Timer
1. Create Your Template with a Summary of a Story you like
2. Divide The Story Into 3rds
3. Identify Main Character, Main Problem/Plot, Locations, Activities, Resolution
4. Ask Yourself 8 Key Questions
5. Choose Time, Place, Point-of-view; Create parallel Characters
6. Write Summary Of Your New Novel and Divide Into Thirds
7. Know Your Job As Author In Each Third Of Your Novel. This is critical for good writing

Transform it into a novel.

Writing Fiction – Write The Way You *Feel, Hear, And See* It

When you are writing a novel, there is a flow of words in the Mental Movie of your mind – a flow of thought, a flow of feelings, a flow of sight and sounds that are distinctly yours.

Readers want to step inside each scene that you are describing. They want to taste, touch, feel, smell, hear, and see all that you do.

You are producer, director, casting, wardrobe and set designer – all rolled into a single flow of Situations and events. You hear the way your characters talk, you see how they move, what they wear, where they are – and even if you pause from time to time to think it out; stay true to what you hear and see in your Creative mind.

Write dialogue the way *you* hear it in your mind. And don't even think of it as 'dialogue' because that sounds too technical and you can get formal and harshly judge your work, killing it.

No, just think of dialogue as "conversation" you can hear in your mind between the people in your novel. Some writers do not even refer to their characters as characters – they refer to them as people. That makes all of it real inside the writers' heads.

Whatever works for you in that regard, get back on the raft of your plot and ride your Creative flow of words, ideas, feelings, and moments as you hear it, as you see it.

Remember that fiction writing is mental play. You are playing make-believe in any universe you want to inhabit, with anyone you want to put into your world, with any 'road not taken' or any Situation that comes to your mind as "what if"... Enjoy writing and experiencing the fantasy of fiction.

Repeat Of An Important Process: Write In Layers

Your main goal is to get the story down as quickly as possible, with all the major parts in place. During that time, *write straight through from start to finish, without editing at all*. If you feel you must do some editing as you go; then limit any edits in a chapter to no more than twice as you work through your First Draft. Then add more **layers that bring your book to life!** Writing in layers works! And it works like this:

1. **Layer 1 – Your First Draft Layer** – your first draft is the story. Write straight through, in any order; but all the way to the finish, without editing. If you find yourself irresistibly re-reading and making changes; do not allow yourself to rework any chapter more than twice before your First Draft is finished. The Ginie Sayles Method is

to write your entire First Draft first; then go through it with the next powerful layers of writing.

2. **Layer 2 – Your Mental Paintbrush Layer**– as you read your first draft, paint a layer of description into your Character, Setting, Situation and so on, in each chapter. This is part of Creative Editing.

3. **Layer 3 – Your Sensory Layer** – be sure you have added all 5 senses in each chapter. This is part of Creative editing.

4. **Layer 4 – Your Final Editing Layer** – add to – and then take away whatever is not needed. *Do this several times.*

When you write in layers, your writing becomes better and better.

The DAY-BY-DAY CALENDAR and The MONTHLY CALENDAR THAT FOLLOW will itemize how to use these steps in a daily manner for 3 weeks. Of course, you should adapt these steps to your own life and use them as a strong guideline.

Chapter 18

Day-By-Day
Fiction Calendar

A goal is a dream with a deadline. – Napoleon Hill

I have given you the Process for Writing A FICTION Book In 3
Weeks – Or Less in the previous chapter. Now, I will set it out in
a daily calendar for you.

I have found that success starts in your mind; and success is fulfilled with a deadline on your calendar. So I am going to build a
3-week calendar to help you keep on track. Do not feel a slavish
dedication to it; but do follow it as closely as possible.

Preliminary Steps Each Day: Create 'Readiness'

✓ Copyright Forms – download TX forms or order by calling 1-202-7073000.

✓ Timer – be sure it is a Digital Timer. Have it on your
desk.

✓ Build Faith in your Creative Spirit.
You can say a brief prayer, if you like.

Affirm, aloud your positive Faith Statements –
Set your Timer for 1 minute and then say aloud the
following:

I, (your name), am a writer. I am an author. I am
creative.

I, (your name), now attract to me all things necessary for fulfilling my writing goal.

When you say these Faith Statements for 1 minute; that
is about 8 times.

✓ Surround yourself with uplifting, encouraging posters/
pictures.

Day 1: Create A Plot & Characters In About 30 Minutes

➤ Set Timer for 1-minute – Faith Statements
➤ What is the single most important thing I can accomplish today?

✓ Take Inventory of your soul to find favorite stories.
✓ Choose a favorite story.
✓ Set your Timer for 10 minutes.
✓ As quickly as you can, write a skeletal summary of your
favorite story.
  ▪ Limit yourself to ¾ page; 1 page at the most.
  ▪ Use NO descriptions; NO details: Just a bare-bones
    storyline.
  ▪ Do not worry about grammar or spelling, just write
    it down.
✓ Analyze on paper:
  1. What is the Setting – Location where is the story
     taking place?
  2. What is the Time period?
  3. Who is the Main Character?
  4. What is the Main Problem? That is the 'Plot.'
  5. How many Characters are in the story?

145

6. Who are they?
7. What is the relationship of each Character with the Main Character?
8. Whose Point-of-view drives the story?

✓ Change the Setting - Time and Place (location) only.
✓ Write a new summary of the story with your new Setting (Time and Place).
  - Keep the same number of Characters.
  - Keep their relationships with your male or female Hero.
  - Update all of them to fit your new story time and place.
✓ Divide your new summary into thirds. All novels can be divided into 3 parts:
  I. Identify the Hero and set up the Main Problem (Plot)
     3 – 5 chapters in a 200-page book
  II. Complicate the Main Problem (Plot) with Subplots
     12 – 30 chapters
     8 – 12 complications
  III. Resolve the problems and satisfy the reader
     3 – 5 chapters
✓ You have 3 weeks to write your book in thirds; however, you may write them in any order – i.e. the final third first; or the 2nd third first; or parts of any of each. It is up to you.
✓ Put your temporary Working Title and information into your computer.
✓ Begin writing your book by writing the scene that thrills you most – no matter in which third of the book it will be.
✓ Set up a Timeline for before and after that scene.

Day 2: Creative Writing

- ➢ Transcribe ideas each day from notes before continuing to write your book.
- ➢ Set Timer for 1-minute – Faith Statements
- ➢ What is the single most important thing I can accomplish today?

- ✓ Input into your computer:
  - ▪ Double-space
  - ▪ Indent paragraphs
  - ▪ List all sub-topics
  - ▪ Put your Temporary book title in a font and style that looks like a book cover title
  - ▪ Put each chapter number in bold

- ✓ Name and fully describe each of your Characters. You may use horoscope descriptions for personality. That's fine; just be sure it still parallels the characters from the original tale or myth, so you can follow the storyline.

- ✓ Create *Parallel Characters.* Remember to keep the same number of Action Characters – and to keep the relationship of each Character with your Hero basically the same as the myth or fairy tale.

Day 3: Creative Writing

- ➢ Transcribe ideas from your PDA or notepad each day before continuing to write your book.
- ➢ Set Timer for 1-minute – Faith Statements.
- ➢ What is the single most important thing I can accomplish today?

- ✓ A PLOT is the Main Problem that the Main Character must solve by the end of your book. It is the solving of the Problem by Characters that creates 'a story.' Keep in mind:

- What is the Main Problem to be solved in your story?
- Reveal the Main Problem through ACTION and INTERACTION between Characters.
- What Action or Actions will you use to show the Main Problem (Plot)?
- Develop the story through ACTION & INTERACTION.
- Resolve the Problem/s (Plot & Subplot) through ACTION & INTERACTION.

✓ What are the 3 most important (emotional and pivotal) events that must happen in your story?

✓ Create 2 Action scenes (Chapters) for each of those events – giving you a total of 6 Action scenes (Chapters) that are pivotal.

✓ All other scenes (Chapters) should build up to and support these 6 pivotal scenes.

✓ Write the way you *feel* the scenes. The way you see them, hear them in your head.

Day 4: Creative Writing

➢ Transcribe ideas from your PDA or notepad each day before continuing to write your book.
➢ Set Timer for 1-minute – Faith Statements.
➢ What is the single most important thing I can accomplish today?

1. **Review the 3 most important (emotional & pivotal) events that must happen.**

2. **Keep working on the 2 Action scenes for each of the 3 important events.**

Note: You can have more than 3 important events; but you should have at least 3 such scenes.

✓ SCENES (Chapter). Chapters are nothing more than a series of scenes. The Main Problem (Plot) is resolved through a series Situations described in scenes. The scenes flow together as Chapters and create your book.
  • What is the Setting (Time and Place/Location) where you will establish the 'Main' Problem (Plot)?
  • Describe your Setting and Characters involved as you reveal the Main Problem through Action and interaction among the Characters. Write the way you mentally see it – write the way you feel it.
  • Re-read it, and flesh out descriptions. Is the problem clearly described through the Action and interaction of the character? Is the Setting clear? Is the scene (Chapter) clear?

✓ What is the purpose of each Chapter?
✓ Does each Chapter or scene accomplish its purpose?

Day 5: Creative Writing

➤ Transcribe ideas from your PDA or notepad each day before continuing to write your book.
➤ Set Timer for 1-minute – Faith Statements.
➤ What is the single most important thing I can accomplish today?

✓ SUBPLOTS. In the process of solving the Main Problem, your Main Characters must overcome a series of other obstacles that prevent or delay solving the Main Problem. ***These obstacles are subplots*** and they add to the interest and respect for your characters.

- Some subplots will come to you as you write – almost automatically.
- If you think of a few obstacles to solving the Main Problem that your Hero must overcome, but you are not at that point, yet, go ahead and jot them down.
- Create the Subplot problems through ACTION & REACTION.
- Resolve the Subplot problem/s through ACTION & INTERACTION.

✓ Review again what are the 3 most important (most emotional & pivotal) events that must happen in your story to fulfill your theme?

In our Goldilocks example, they were;
1) Realizing she is lost
2) Breaking into the bears' house
3) Being discovered by the bears
– and of course, that she gets home safely, which is the resolution.

✓ Create the 2 main scenes for *each* important event that must happen. That means you will have 6 scenes that are pivotal. All other scenes will be supportive of those 6 scenes.
1) Realizing she is lost
   - enchanted by the butterfly
   - loses butterfly and realizes she is in the forest
2) Breaking into the bears' house
   - looking for help
   - hungry and tired
3) Being discovered by the bears
   - wakes, disoriented and frightened
   - gets away safely
   – and of course, that she found her way safely home, which is the resolution.

✓ *Write your first draft without stopping to edit as you go. Edit after you finish your first rough draft.* This is a concept I originated for my students in the early days of teaching this course; and they found it helpful. However, if you find yourself re-reading your work as you write it and automatically making corrections, be sure you do not seriously edit any chapter more than two read-throughs before you finish writing your manuscript.

Day 6: Creative Writing

➢ Transcribe ideas from your PDA or notepad each day before continuing to write your book.
➢ Set Timer for 1-minute – Faith Statements.
➢ What is the single most important thing I can accomplish today?

1. **Review the 3 most important (most emotional & pivotal) events that must happen.**
2. **Keep working on the 2 Action scenes for each of the 3 important events**

Note: You can have more than 3 important turning-point events; but you should have at least 3.

✓ What is the SITUATION in each scene (Chapter)?

✓ Describe each scene (Chapter) more fully – weather, location, immediate surroundings, and characters.

✓ Give each scene (Chapter) a clear *purpose* through interactions of Characters. All scenes are either about the Main Problem, deepen the problem, introduce a new Subplot problem, resolve or further resolve a Subplot problem while striving to resolve the Main Problem (Plot). That is basically it.

✓ Write the way you think and feel and hear and see and sense and emotionally experience each scene.

Day 7– Day 13: Creative Writing

➢ Transcribe ideas from your PDA or notepad each day before continuing to write your book.

➢ Set Timer for 1-minute – Faith Statements.

➢ What is the single most important thing I can accomplish today?

Note: You can have more than 3 most important events; but you should have at least 3.

✓ Check your 6 pivotal scenes for plenty of Action, again. Even introspection can be described at times with Action verbs.

✓ Scenes create a Mood for the Action by describing details of how things feel, smell, taste, look, sound in the Setting. Try to match them – or contrast them – to the emotions of your Hero at the time.

✓ Action verbs and adjectives (which describe people, places or things) are the key to keeping your readers' interest. Fill out descriptions to make a scene vivid – but do not overdo it or it can be boring.

✓ Put a question mark (?) next to anything technical or historical that you question in your usage of it.

✓ Put an asterisk (*) next to anything you need to research.

Day 14: Research

- ➤ Transcribe ideas each day before continuing to write your book.
- ➤ Set Timer for 1-minute – Faith Statements.
- ➤ What is the single most important thing I can accomplish today?

- ✓ Global your asterisks throughout your new book – Control F (find).

- ✓ As each asterisk comes up on your screen, jot down on a notepad what you need to find.

- ✓ Go online and look for each item you noted.

- ✓ If you are not able to find what you want online; visit your library and search for it.

- ✓ When you return, global again and incorporate new information or corrections at each asterisk in your manuscript, and then remove the asterisk.

- ✓ Do not violate copyrights of others. Do not paraphrase. Understand the information and then explain it in your own way.

- ✓ Credit your sources.

Day 15: Creative Editing

> ➤ Transcribe ideas each day before continuing to write your book.
> ➤ Set Timer for 1-minute – Faith Statements.
> ➤ What is the single most important thing I can accomplish today?

1. Now that your Main Action scenes are underway, go back through and analyze the development of each Main Character.
2. On a separate page, identify if your purpose for each Main Character has changed.
3. Are looks, mannerisms, and motives evident in each Character's Actions?

✓ Continue to make corrections from your research, if you did not finish yesterday.

✓ Organize Chapters. Re-read your story and decide if your Chapters flow together well or in what order they most effectively belong. Change them, accordingly, in your computer.

✓ Write and rewrite the first Chapter – to 'hook' the reader instantly into your Hero's Main Problem (Plot). Start the first Chapter with your Hero in the middle of the Main Problem. For example, with Goldilocks, the story should open with the little girl suddenly aware of a change of temperature and shadows, glancing around to realize she is in the forest, looking back for the butterfly she had been following and realizing it is gone – and, shivering with fear and falling temperature, knowing she is lost. After that, you have her flashback to the words of her parents telling her not to go into the forest…of the lure of the beautiful butterfly…et cetera.

✓ Write and rewrite the last chapter – to end the book with power. Give full satisfaction to the reader.

✓ Write and rewrite the 6 most important, pivotal (and most emotional) scenes.

✓ Print it out. Use light pink paper.

Note: Using different colors of paper on your drafts keep you from going crazy if you get them mixed up. You know instantly by paper color which draft is which. Some people can edit entirely within their computers and that is fine; but if you like to read and mark changes on paper and then correct your computer file, that is fine, too.

Day 16: Creative Editing

➤ Transcribe ideas each day before continuing to write your book.
➤ Set Timer for 1-minute – Faith Statements.
➤ What is the single most important thing I can accomplish today?

✓ Read your First Draft.

✓ Make corrections as you go.

✓ Make notes in the margins for new ideas you get or for changes.

✓ After each Chapter ask, "Have I made the Action clear in this scene? Does it inspire the reader to wonder what will happen next?"

✓ Re-read parts that interest you and those that bother you.

✓ Work on them.

✓ Re-read parts that make you feel especially proud – and enjoy that feeling.

Day 17: Creative Editing

➢ Transcribe ideas each day before continuing to write your book.
➢ Set Timer for 1-minute – Faith Statements.
➢ What is the single most important thing I can accomplish today?

✓ Clean it up!
  ▪ Make revisions.
  ▪ Can you make a scene sharper?

✓ Read the purpose you had for each scene.
  ▪ Does it fulfill the purpose?
  ▪ Is the Action clear?

✓ Is there an emotional response to your work?

✓ Run your spell-check.

Day 18 - Day 20: Creative Editing

➢ Transcribe ideas each day before continuing to write your book.
➢ Set Timer for 1-minute – Faith Statements.
➢ What is the single most important thing I can accomplish today?

✓ Keep cleaning up your manuscript,

Day 21: Creative Editing

➢ Transcribe any remaining or last minute ideas.
➢ Set Timer for 1-minute – Faith Statements.
➢ What is the single most important thing I can accomplish today?

✓ Print revised draft on light yellow paper.
✓ Read it. Is it clear?
✓ Make revisions. Finalize it.

Hooray!

You have finished your basic manuscript.

You are now an author!

Day 22-Day 24: <u>*Release it*</u> *– to the Backburner of your Creative Spirit*

➢ Leave your PDA or notepad at home.
➢ For 3 days – or 3 weeks if you wish:

✓ Release your work mentally!

✓ Put your manuscript away – and do NOT look at it – no matter what. Do not sneak a peek. Do not add a great new idea to it. If you have an idea write it in your notebook when you get home, but do not touch your manuscript.

✓ Have a good time. Enjoy restful, fun activities.

✓ Go out with friends – but do NOT tell them about your new book.

✓ Let everything steep on the back-burner of your Creative Spirit by forgetting about it, dismissing it from your conscious mind.

Day 25: Final Decisions

➢ Set Timer for 1-minute.
➢ Faith Statements.
➢ What is the single most important thing I can accomplish today?

✓ Print out your manuscript on light blue paper.

✓ Read it again.

✓ Make final revisions.

✓ Use spell-check.

✓ Use word-count.

✓ Re-think the name of your book from a working title to a marketing title. The title sells the book initially. Try several titles. Choose one.

✓ Print out final draft on white paper.

✓ Fill out your copyright form *immediately. Either*

- *Upload your manuscript and payment to the Library of Congress*
- *Mail it to the Library of Congress Copyright office by Certified Mail with your copyright form, payment and required copies of manuscript.*

Monthly Calendar

Fiction

Sun	Mon	Tue	Wed	Thu	Fri	Sat
LEGEND H = hours of writing CS= Creative Spirit FD=Final Decisions The first 11 days are structural & creative Carry small spiral notebook.	**Positive Faith Statements:** "I (your name) am a writer. I am an author. I am creative." "I, (your name), now have a writing awareness. I now attract to me all things necessary for fulfilling my writing goal." Enjoy your special Creative Time!	**POINTS TO REMEMBER** As you write, put a Star * next to anything you think you need more research on or information about. But keep writing. Limit Editing to twice for each chapter until finished. Follow your interest each day	**1** 3¾-H 1. Set Timer. 2. Summarize favorite Fairytale. 3. Analyze plot 4. Change time & place. 5. New Summary 6. Temporary Title for book 7. Input computer	**2** 3¾-H 1. Name & describe parallel characters 2. Write the scene that interests you the most 3. Set up time-line before & after scene 4. Target readers.	**3** 3¾-H 1. What are 3 most important things that must happen in your story? 2. Create 2 action scenes for each of those – giving 6 action scenes that are pivotal.	**4** 12 H 1. Review the 3 most important things that must happen. 2. Keep working on the 2 action scenes for each of the 3 important things that must happen.
5 12 H 1. Review the 3 most important things that must happen. 2. Keep writing on the 2 action scenes for each of the 3 most important things that must happen.	**6** 3¾-H 1. Review the 3 most important things that must happen. 2. Keep writing on the 2 action scenes for each of the 3 most important things that must happen.	**7** 3¾-H 1. Now you're main action scenes are underway, analyze each character 2. On separate page, list your purpose for each character. 3. Describe looks, & mannerisms, & motives of each.	**8** 3¾-H 1. Go back through the 6 pivotal scenes & flesh out each character according to your analysis.	**9** 3¾-H 1. Finish work on characters. 2. Review the 6 pivotal scenes & analyze settings. 3. What is the 'mood' of each? 4. Accentuate the mood with weather, emotion, colors, landscape, interiors.	**10** 3¾H 1. Read everything you have written so far. 2. Fill out descriptions – i.e. instead of "sat on a chair" make it "sunk tiredly into the soft cushions of a pink, floral wing-back chair."	**11** 12 H 1. Review the 3 most important things that must happen. 2. Go back to writing on the 2 scenes for each of the 3 most important things that must happen.
12 12 H Free-form Writing Follow interest	**13** 3¾H Free-form Writing Follow interest	**14** 3¾H Research Visit Library	**15** 3¾H Corrections from Research	**16** 3¾H Edit & Free-form Writing	**17** 3¾H Edit & Free-form Writing	**18** 12 H Edit
19 12 H Edit	**20** 3¾H Edit	**21** 3¾H 1. Spell-check 2. Print-out End of 3 Weeks ♥	**22** CS 1. Put your copy away. 2. Have fun – rest & relax!.	**23** CS Have fun – do unrelated activities.	**24** CS No peeking! Keep it on the backburner	**25** FD Send 1ˢᵗ draft to Copyright office by certified mail.
26 CS Have fun –	**27** Read manuscript	**28** Make Decisions	**29**	**30**	**31**	**1Month**

159

Chapter 19

Great Works
Written From Templates

32 Screenplays REJECTED – Until A Fairy Tale Was His Winning Template.

If you wrote 32 screenplays and all of them were rejected, how motivated would you be to write your 33rd screenplay?

Me either!

But my favorite story is of a young man who did just that. He wrote 32 screenplays and they were all rejected. But then, consciously or not, he used a famous fairly tale called **Cinderella** as a template for his next screenplay – *which he wrote in 3 ½ weeks!*

This young man made movie history with 10 Academy Award nominations and winning Best Picture for his Mohammad Ali-inspired Cinderella story called **Rocky**. Sylvester Stallone is one of the greatest success stories in movie history. And remember, in the movie, *Rocky,* Stallone has one of his characters say, "This is a Cinderella story."

Let's see how a man or woman can use the Cinderella story to write a bestseller. First of all: **Characters have *NO GENDER* – Each character represents a specific energy**. To use a Fairy Tale as your Template, ask yourself what energy each character represents:

1. Cinderella – represents an *Energy of **Oppression***. It is "non-gender" energy. Thus, it can be used to tell the story of an oppressed person – such as Rocky Balboa living in Hell's Kitchen. An Energy of Oppression can be an orphaned child, a race of people, a senior citizen, an animal. Learn to *transpose* concepts of energy into characters of any gender, any age, any species of your own choosing.

2. Fairy Godmother – represents a ***Transformational** Energy*. Do not limit your thought to a Disney elf who waves a wand. Recognize the 'energy' and what it represents.

In *Rocky*, the fairy godmother is the tough little trainer who tells Rocky he doesn't like him because he is wasted talent, and then he climbs several flights of stairs to encourage Rocky to take the opportunity to fight the champ – and offers to be his trainer - the transformational energy.

3. Stepmother & Stepsisters – represent the *Energy of the Status Quo* – those currently in power. This energy is not necessarily evil – although it can be; but the Status Quo (meaning whoever is in power) does not want change in the power structure they currently control. This is actually normal (we see it every election, no matter who is in power, they don't want to lose it or to share it, so they demonize the other party and candidates).

The Status Quo may or may not grant opportunities to others; but, like any of us, the status quo does not want to lose its own power in the process.

In *Rocky*, the Champ represents the Energy of the Status Quo of boxing championship – the one in power (current champion). In the story, he is a good person and he is the one who offers the opportunity to an unknown fighter for publicity; but, naturally, like anyone at the top, he does not want to lose control of his own title or power.

4. The Ball –represents the *Energy of **Opportunity*** that if an oppressed character has taken advantage of the Transformational

Energy and is willing to take a risk and seize the moment of opportunity, it can lift the character up, over, and out of oppression – but it is a risk.

In the fairy tale, Cinderella did not wait for her prince to come along – she had the moxie to crash the hottest party in town and won the prize. In *Rocky,* the main character, Rocky Balboa, had the moxie to risk fighting the Champ in The Main Event. The Main Event was the Ball.

5. The Prince – represents the ***Goal-Motivating Energy Of Love.*** Love is the greatest motivator of all. In the fairy tale, the ball is being held so the Prince can choose a wife. Cinderella is motivated by the hopes of love and marriage to undergo transformation, to take a risk and to go to the ball.

What are the words Rocky calls out as he sits in the corner of the ring, his face swollen, bruised, and bloody? "Adrian! Adrian!" The name of the woman he loves. Love is not gender. Love is an energy – love is the ultimate goal-motivation.

6. Midnight – represents the *Energy of **Time Constraint*** – the *limited time of an opportunity* – the ticking of time running out. There are time limits for any opportunity, for solving a problem or for achieving a goal. Midnight is a deadline that is important to the power of the story. An opportunity does not last forever. And the Ball is the golden Window of Opportunity that closes at Midnight. Opportunity is magical but the magic has a deadline – so true of life, itself. Midnight is another key to the success of this brilliant plot.

In Rocky, *the Final Bell* that ends the fight represents the *Energy of Time Constraint* - the Midnight energy that closes the golden moment of opportunity (Moment of Opportunity is the Ball/the boxing Main Event).

7. The Glass Slipper – represents the *Energy of a **Fragile Second Chance***, if the first Moment of Opportunity (ball) was thwarted for some reason. In the fairy tale, the fragile second chance for Cinderella was the glass slipper when time ran out and she was unable to fulfill her moment of opportunity to the fullest.

In Rocky, the close or split decision of who won the boxing match leaves the potential for a second chance – or, in this case, sequels! I am half-joking when I mention the sequels; but it is up to you as a writer to *use a symbol for the energy of the fragile second chance*, if you decide to have the first opportunity interrupted or thwarted or delayed.

Powerful Template

In sum, Cinderella is a story of **Triumph over Oppression**. Cinderella is allegedly based on a story from **The Arabian Nights,** although there are many other claims to the origin of this wonderful tale of triumph over oppression.

Almost all love stories use Cinderella as the template – and publishers of romance novels will scarcely consider anything else.

When you think of it, the energy of this beloved fairy tale is the most thrilling concept of victory. It makes us cry, feel suspense, root for the underdog hero, and cheer with satisfaction at the end.

No wonder the Cinderella story is timeless. It embraces all the energies that inspire us. It is the most successful template of all. But there are many other great templates, as well.

Successful Templates From Myths, Bible Stories, and Classics

When you create a template from the works of masters, you join the ranks of other authors who have used the works of predecessors as a template or prototype for their own work that they take into a completely new mode.

You are not plagiarizing their work because your work will be different. You are just using the skeleton of their work as a springboard pattern for your own creative story.

Let's look at a sample of famous writers, producers, and playwrights whose highly successful novels, plays, or movies were *based on existing works as their templates*.

1. Children's Fairy Tale Templates

Stephen Spielberg's movie, *A.I. – Artificial Intelligence* – used **Pinocchio** as its template. Remember the little boy who is a computer said, "I'm a real boy," just exactly like the little boy who is a wooden puppet in the old fairy tale.

Robert Osborn on TCM revealed that Director Billy Wilder said his 1941 movie, **Ball Of Fire**, starring Barbara Stanwyck and Gary Cooper, used the fairy tale **Snow White And The Seven Dwarfs** as its template.

The television movie, **Homecoming**, starring Anne Bancroft, used **Hansel and Gretel** as its template.

And, as we have mentioned, **Cinderella** is used, repeatedly, in books and movies.

2. Greek Mythology Template

You know it as **My Fair Lady**; but George Bernard Shaw named it **Pygmalion**, letting the world know he created a template for his great play from Greek mythology. Briefly, the myth he chose is the story of a Greek sculptor whose name is Pygmalion. In the myth, Pygmalion sculpted his ideal woman in stone and then he fell in love with her. In time, the goddess of love converted her into a human being for his fulfillment of love.

Shaw mulled (Creative Gestation) over this favorite myth, and then created a template. Instead of his character being a sculptor of stone, his character was a sculptor of speech patterns – indeed, a speech master! And the stone or clay would be what he considered to be the worst speech pattern in England – a Cockney speech pattern. Taking a young girl who sold flowers on the streets, he transformed her Cockney speech pattern into that of an aristocrat – and, in the process, he, like the Greek Sculptor, fell in love with his own creation.

3. Classic Literature Template

A television program pointed out the great French Classic, *Madame Bovary* by Gustave Flaubert was a template for Erica Jong's book *Fear Of Flying*, which has a modern Setting and a different ending.

Moulin Rouge, the musical starring Nicole Kidman, is a retelling of *Lady Of The Camellias* by Alexandre Dumas The Younger as its prototype.

The 1990s movie, *Titanic*, was basically Shakespeare's *Romeo And Juliet* in a historical Setting with the lovers being on the wrong side of the "class-based passenger tickets." Also the musical, *West Side Story,* as well as the novel (and movie), *Love Story,* used Shakespeare's *Romeo And Juliet* as a template.

Shakespeare's *Taming Of The Shrew* also made it to Broadway and to Hollywood as the musical hit, *Kiss Me Kate.*

Shakespeare, himself, used historical events as prototypes for his great masterpieces. **Note:** *The works of William Shakespeare are very often used as Prototypes or Templates for other authors.*

4. Religious Template

East Of Eden took *The Bible* story of *Cain And Abel* in the Old Testament as its prototype of sibling rivalry caused by a parent's blatant favoritism.

Many great novels, including Herman Melville's *Billy Budd,* have unlikely characters to symbolize the Christ figure.

5. Foreign Literature Template:

Turner Classic Movies – TCM – tells us that a successful Japanese story *The Seven Samari* , was the template for an American cowboy movie *The Magnificent Seven*, which was a box-office hit.

6. Sherlock Holmes – Quintessential Mystery Template

Agatha Christie appears to have used Arthur Conan Doyle's sleuth, Sherlock Holmes, as the template for her successful thrillers. Whether it is an elderly British spinster or a Belgian investigator, she utilizes the same observation and deductive reasoning that Doyle developed in his character, Sherlock Holmes.

Over the years, similar reasoning of the Sherlock Holmes template has shown up repeatedly in almost all successful mysteries.

You can dress your sleuths in different genders, different classes, different speech patterns, different centuries, different generations, but to capture the interest of a reader, the Sherlock Holmes template of reasoning triumphs in mystery writing.

7. Edgar Allen Poe – Macabre Template For Horror

For some reason, works of horror have emerged in their own genre. Certainly, authors of this genre can tip their hats to the first known American writer of the strange dark side, Edgar Allen Poe. There is even an award named after him for writers who excel in this or related fields.

Learn Your Template/Prototype/ Formula Well

Most publishers that specialize in a specific type of writing will send you a 'Tip Sheet' or 'Fact Sheet' of the formula they want in books they publish. Check their websites to see if they are posted online; and if not, send an email, asking if they provide a tip sheet or fact sheet.

In order to write formula fiction well – and with increasing speed – you must 'internalize' the tried and true formula that you want to write.

However, after you internalize a formula or a template you create, you do not have to be a slave to either the fact sheet or the template. Use it as your springboard.

Chapter 20

No Formula
-Writing Into The Unknown -

Can you follow an idea without a plan and still write a book in 3 weeks – or less?

Sometimes you have a mental picture of a scene and you want to write it; but you have no idea where it will lead – and certainly no template that it would seem to fit.

In those moments, write your scene – the way you see it, the way you feel it, the way it flows through your heart and mind; and write it as quickly as you can get to your computer – or jot it down in a notepad or PDA or email your notes to yourself on your cell phone so that you have them when you get to your computer and can add them to your manuscript.

Trust your instincts. Trust your intuition – they are part and parcel of your Creative Spirit – they are *you*. Go with it!

As often happens, once you put down the words, new words come to you, another scene, an interchange of dialogue, and soon you are writing.

I call this writing into the unknown – because you have no idea where you are going with it, yet. You are not sure if this will be the beginning, the middle, the end – or even make your final cut.

Do not worry about it – just do the deed – write it, and write and write.

Can You Outline The Unknown?

At some point, you will begin to *feel* a possible destination for your novel. You can sense where it seems to be headed.

And at that very point, stop writing, sit down, and write a summary of where it seems to be going or what you want to do with it. I did this with a novel, after I had written about eight or nine chapters – some in sequence, most not – and I began to see the direction of the book.

By that time, I had gotten far enough along that I knew what the Main Problem was that my Main Character would have to solve by the end of the book – which meant I knew what my plot was – and ultimately that is key to where the story may be headed.

I also had gotten to know my characters *as I wrote about them* well enough to feel that I knew what 'motivated' each one.

That is all you need to know – Main Problem/Plot, Motivations of Characters – and an idea of where it is headed – and you are ready to summarize the rest of the book.

After you write your summary, divide it into thirds and follow the system – beginning with Step Six – in Chapter 17.

Template Or Unknown

Give yourself permission to write fiction both ways – using templates or to write into the unknown. But be sure you understand how writing into the unknown works – or you will find yourself lost and eventually give up – which is not acceptable since you are going to write that book if I have any say-so in the matter.

Some bestselling authors have written into the unknown and discovered their unique styles as authors.

Trust your 'gut.' See where it leads. Even if you never feel that you know the direction of your novel and even if you do not write a Summary Outline, keep following the flow of your feelings in the language of your heart. Passion can get you there even in three weeks – or less.

Let your story unfold before your eyes on your computer and discover the adventure of your work. Never be afraid to write into the unknown. Just think, this great country of America – and the great continent of North America – exist as we know it today because the courageous explorer, Christopher Columbus, had an 'idea' of finding a shortcut path to India by sailing west and he was willing to sail 'into the unknown.' He did not find India, true; but in 1492, he found a great new world.

Just imagine what uncharted *literary* territories you may discover for your own great new world of writing.

Chapter
21

Fiction Writer's
Basic Resources For Speed

Create a small collection of good reference material, inexpensively.

In addition to a good software dictionary, thesaurus, and encyclopedia, and the world-wide web as your library; you may find times when mulling over ideas (Creative Gestation) is best done with a touch and feel book, whose pages you can flip through to consider plots, to quickly check environments for possible Settings, to develop characters, to describe interiors, cars, boats, planes, and geography for the Action of their plots.

Your personal library does not have to cost a fortune. Prowl through used bookstores and you will find exceptional bargains. So, in addition to on-line resources and software basics, a Fiction Writer can benefit from having the following on hand:

Speedwriter's Reference Materials

1. **American Heritage Dictionary.** As much as I use my computer dictionary, there are times when I need a better, more comprehensive definition. As a former English teacher, I have examined a lot of dictionaries. American

Heritage Dictionary is my favorite for writing. I use a good paperback of it.

2. **Hardback Thesaurus.** I know, I know…your computer has a built-in Thesaurus; but sometimes I do not find enough choices or related choices on the computer versions. I bought a used Roget's hardcover thesaurus in beautiful condition and it gives me the variety I do not find on my computer thesaurus.

3. **Rhyming dictionary for fiction writers who also incorporate your own poetry into your work.** These books amaze me. Because I love to write poetry – even some that rhyme – I find the book invaluable.

Plot Idea Resources

When you are looking for plot ideas or want to create a template; your resource books should be simplified, abbreviated, or children's versions – because you just want the summary and nothing more.

1. **SparkNotes, Cliffs Notes, Coles Notes, York Notes, Rocketbook, Monarch Notes of your Favorite Shakespeare or other Classics.** When you are looking for a storyline, you do not need to wade through late 15th and early 16th century writing – it is too time-consuming, no matter how beautiful. You just want a refresher of the story.

2. **Children's Bible.** It should contain both Old and New Testament stories written in half or one page per story and fully illustrated.

3. **Children's Book of Holy Writings for Other Religions** Children's version of Indian Teachings, Asian Teachings, Native American Teachings, various world

religious teachings for children – the stories they learn about their culture or beliefs have interesting story plots.

4. **Bulfinch's Mythology & World Mythologies (Juvenile versions).** Mythologies are great classic plots and lessons in life. There are good mythologies from many cultures that can be used as templates for plots.

5. **Children's Book Of Fairy Tales.** You want it written for children to read, so, again, you don't waste time plodding through it. You want the main idea, that's all. Be sure these are abridged for children. Reading the unabridged *Brothers Grimm* is too grim! Bloody, in fact. I wouldn't even let a child read the unabridged versions.

6. **A Book of Opera Plots.** I fully believe Wolfgang Amadeus Mozart is the father of 'Sit-Coms' – short for Situation Comedies that rule television programming. His opera comedies, written in the mid to late 1700s are clever, hilarious, and timeless – even apart from his beautiful music. On the other hand, if you seek drama and intense passion, nothing beats an opera plot in that category, too. Many high drama operas are compelling tragedies, often based on Greek plays.

Story Setting Resources – Time and Place

1. **World Globe.** Your hero is about to escape from a foreign country...what is his/her path? What makes sense? What is do-able? A globe you can spin in your hands can be reasonably purchased from a travel store.

   However, if your novel is historical, you may not be able to afford older globes. They can cost several thousands of dollars; so, your best bet is to visit an antique map and globe shop and look (touch, gingerly, and perhaps with the sales person's assistance) for your hero's passage to safety in that day and time.

2. **Visit The Main Location If You Can.** Unless the Setting for your novel is an imaginary place or a futuristic Sci-Fi, it is best if you can visit the Setting of your novel in person.

   An author wrote a novel taking place in Colorado, complete with descriptions of Aspen trees. The only problem is that Aspen trees did not grow in the location of her story.

   Visiting a location can give you a 'truth' about it, complete with accurate descriptions of weather, flora, fauna, and general layout. Best of all, when your book is in print, these visits are tax-deductible. Take historic tours to absorb 'the culture' of a region.

   If you cannot visit, be sure to visit online and with the suggestions that follow.

3. **Travel DVDs, Travel Downloads from the Internet, Travel Magazines.** Download, rent, or buy a travel DVD of the location if you cannot visit in person. These may be reasonably available via the Internet, a library, a travel store, or a DVD rental store. These can be supplemented by travel magazines from the library stacks or online, and travel books or books about the history or culture of the location.

4. **Chamber of Commerce Literature.** In addition to the preceding research for your Setting, do not overlook the Chamber of Commerce. If their websites do not have the kinds of information you want; you can email or telephone them, requesting they send you any literature about their area that may help your understanding of the community.

5. **Tourist Bureau Literature.** Tourist Bureaus have interesting tid-bits of lore that can be woven into your novel or give you ideas for your own characters. Plus the

authenticity of houses and buildings as well as foliage that grows around them adds dimension to your novel. *The culture of a locale is the charm of your novel.* This bureau helps!

6. **Historical Society Information.** I love this wonderful resource. Once, when working on a novel, I wanted to have a storm occur in a particular Setting. I went through books on the location, called around, and nobody knew if such storms ever occurred in the area. Finally, I called The Historical Society, and a man who answered as "Bob," listened to my question. Instantly he replied, "Oh yes, that type of storm occurred here in January of 1884. There were 17 people killed." Now, *that* is valuable help!

Character Lifestyle Resources

1. **Architectural Digest.** If you write contemporary novels with affluent characters, you have ready-made rooms for them to live in. Vary the descriptions into your own words to prevent copyright violation. If you are on a budget, get at least one issue.

2. **The DuPont Registry** This publication has tons of beautiful homes for sale, world-wide, with pictures and descriptions. There may be a home for the area you want in your novel.

3. **Colonial Homes, Victorian Homes, Coastal Homes.** Go online and Google "Colonial Homes" or "Victorian Homes" or "Coastal Homes." Usually, you can find pictures of homes for your historical figures – however, be sure you describe the houses in your own words to prevent copyright violation. Look over magazine racks, too, for homes that fit the category you seek.

4. **Estate magazines.** Sotheby's and other upscale realtors publish magazines that showcase lavish estates throughout the world– some historical, some modern. You can look at one you like and describe it in your own words.

5. **The Robb Report.** Contemporary or last century historical novels with wealthy characters need this publication – at least a couple of times a year. If your rich characters are plotting diabolical excesses on a yacht, but you have never been on a yacht – this magazine has interior and exterior pictures in vivid color.

   If your wealthy heroine seduces her prey on her private jet and you have never flown in one, you will find full color pictures of private jets – interiors and exteriors – on these glossy magazine pages. And if you want your hero's disapproving father to arrive in a luxury Daimler, and you are a bit fuzzy on the details, thumb through this magazine. *The Robb Report* has luxury right down to the finest detail.

6. **Contemporary Female Clothing - Town & Country magazine.** For contemporary novels with socially elite female characters, you dress them straight out of this magazine. Another plus is that upscale vendors of carpets, crystal, china, and such advertise in it.
   a. You can describe your heroine in a dress you see on a page, wearing jewels you see advertised in another page, walking on carpet advertised on still another page, and sipping wine from crystal advertised on yet another page– all from one issue!
   b. Buy an issue for the seasons your character will be described. And do not use the copyrighted ad copy description of items you use. Describe them in your own words as you look at the items – perhaps changing the colors or other details.

7. **Contemporary Male Clothing - Esquire or GQ magazine.** For a contemporary male, these two magazines can dress him to define his character as cool aristocrat, sensual rogue, or casual man-next-door. Choose the right season of clothing for your male character.

8. **Historical Female or Male Clothing – Stage Costume Books.** For historical novels, I find costume books for the stage to be some of the best, simply because stage plays meticulously try to be accurate to the last detail. Therefore, the period costumes are usually reliable.
   a. These books can usually be found in University bookstores for drama classes.
   b. Also, I find that if you go online and Google fashions of a certain time period, you will usually find reasonably good sources. Too, doverpublications.com may help.

9. **Historical Children's Toys.** Visit doverpublications. com.

10. **Antique Car or Boat books.** Google them or find new or used books, such as an Illustrated History of Transportation.

Believable Characters

1. **Sun-Sign Astrology Book.** Students often ask how they can write believable characters. The fastest way – and this book is about speedwriting – is to find an astrology personality you like overall for each main character and major support characters. Astrology books typically list strengths and weaknesses of each personality.

   To make a hero (male or female) believable, choose 3 strengths and 1 weakness from the list and emphasize those strengths and occasionally the 1 weakness throughout your book.

To make a villain (male or female) believable, re-verse the process: choose 3 weaknesses and 1 strength to emphasize throughout the book. Why should your villain have a strength? Because if a villain is to villainous, then your hero looks a little dumb for not recognizing it. A villain should have a strength that fools people.

You do not have to believe in Astrology; but if you need a character description, nothing beats a good, sun-sign astrology book. Frequently, they even include physical characteristics.

2. **Describe Behavior Of People You See Or Know.** Be sure people you know cannot recognize themselves in your book (or you could be held liable), so after you make your descriptions, be sure to follow the general rule-of-thumb described elsewhere in this book and change at least 5+ things about the person so the person is unidentifiable.

Putting The Resources All Together

Okay, let's put all these references together in a quick (not serious) example of how to use your references for speed.

Let's say your hero invites a female to his house for dinner. **You can quickly select his house out of Architectural Digest – complete with furniture, layout, dining room, et cetera.**

She arrives, dressed for dinner in a silk Hermes dinner dress, complete with accessories **you found in Town & Country magazine.**

Over a sensuous dinner – **a menu you found on foodnet-work.com** *– the couple falls in love. They spontaneously decide to fly to Monte Carlo in his private jet. If you do not happen to have a private jet lying around, then pick up* **a Robb Report because it usually has full color pictures – interior and exterior – of private jets.** *En route to Monte Carlo, you can stage a scene in the game room of the private jet.*

*After they arrive in Monte Carlo, they decide to lease a yacht and sail the Mediterranean. Once again, if you do not have access to a private yacht, **your trusty Robb Report will usually have several yachts pictured – again in full color interior and exterior**. You can set the seduction scene in the walnut paneled stateroom with its gilded...et cetera.*

Do you see what I mean? You can quickly create a character's personality, dress the character, house the character, and put it all in a good setting in record time, just by having 'instant access' to your personal collection of the resources I have just given.

Elements
Of Good Fiction

*Elements of good fiction are traits intrinsic to a story; tools
of writing good fiction are intrinsic to the story as well; so
that tools should be treated as elements for good fiction.*
– Ginie Sayles

I list below what I consider to be the most important elements
and tools that I teach in my fiction writing workshop. I teach elements and tools together; because what is the use of knowing the
elements if you do not know how to make the best of them?

They are easy to learn, easy to understand and easy to utilize in your fiction. After you write the First Draft of your new
novel, concentrate on fleshing out each element of fiction to give
your novel the finishing touches you want.

The list of Elements and Tools of Writing Fiction are:

1. Character - Who
   - Motivation
   - Point-of-View
   - Full or Flat Characters
   - Proactive
   - Reactive

2. Situation – What is Happening
   - Chapter by Chapter
   - Action
   - Time Constraints
3. Setting – When and Where
   - Time Period (when)
   - Place/Location (where)
4. Plot – Why and How
   - The Main Problem the Main Character must solve by
     the end of the book
   - Time Span of Story
   - Subplot Complications
   - Action
5. Imagery/Description
   - Metaphor
   - Simile
   - Personification
   - Anthropomorphism
   - Symbolism
   - Onomatopoeia
6. Mood
7. Pace
8. Variety
9. What Happens Next?
10. Writing Dialogue
    - Clear Attributions
    - Punctuation
11. Author's Voice
    - Attitude/Tone
    - Style

Whereas all the elements and tools are interdependent;
some of them work together symbiotically. For example, character and point-of-view, or situation and setting – although not the
same thing at all, they reflect each other.

In the following chapters, I will explain each one and give examples – plus in some cases, I may give a small assignment that can help you develop in a specific category.

Chapter
23

Character
& Point-Of View

*Bring your natural ability to read character into
your writing. – Ginie Sayles*

You are already good at 'mentally writing' character in your day-to-day life, although you may not realize it.

Let's say a person walks in front of you. Subconsciously and without interest, you immediately know quite a lot about that person.

You probably recognize the gender. Let's say, it is a man. You have a general idea of his:

- age range
- general height
- weight range
- ethnicity
- hair length
- visible tattoos
- if he seems to belong in the environment

You may also subconsciously realize his socio-economic and possibly education levels or career and even the occasion of the moment by his clothing.

He may be wearing...

- a tuxedo
- business suit
- a uniform
  - o police
  - o military
  - o cleaning crew
  - o hospital
  - o company logo outfit
- sport coat and tie with khaki pants
- pressed jeans and short sleeved shirt
- coveralls and baseball cap
- coveralls and hard hat
- tee shirt, shorts, and sandals
- religious garb – denoting a specific religion
- jeans and cowboy boots
- jeans hanging low and belted in the middle of his hips, dragging pant hems
- jeans belted at his waistline
- message printed on his clothing

You often notice accessories, such as if he is carrying…
- briefcase
- toolbox
- a piece of cardboard with the words 'will work for food' scrawled on it
- walking cane
- gun
- cell phone
- book
- laptop bag strapped over one shoulder
- belt with his name printed on it

Jewelry can catch you eye, as well:
- earrings
- neck chains
- bracelet
- watch
  - ▪ leather band

- metal band
  - o stainless steel
  - o gold
- wedding ring
- school ring

His posture will definitely make a subliminal impact. He may be…

- erect
- slumped, hands-in-pockets
- bent

And his gait is…

- purposeful
- slow, deliberate
- aimless amble
- limp

If you are close enough, you may instantly notice his grooming details:

- wrinkled clothes
- nicely pressed clothes
- stained clothes
- dirty clothes
- smelly clothes
- clean, short fingernails
- dirty, broken fingernails
- scuffed shoes, run-down heels
- polished well-cared for shoes
- unlaced tennis shoes
- barefoot

Does he fit the surroundings (Situation)?

- no, he behaves suspiciously
- yes, he is working in construction on the sidewalk
- yes, he is selling hot dogs/other items from a portable vending station
- yes, he is on his way to an office building
- yes, he generally fits the local activity
- yes, but he seems lost, looking for an address

His attitude seems to be:
- harried, rushed
- lost in thought
- curious about his surroundings, maybe a tourist
- happy, friendly greetings to others
- minding his own business
- brooding demeanor, unhappy
- a chip on his shoulder, looking for trouble

Is there a quality that identifies regional or other identification?
- not really. He could be from just about anywhere in North America (or whatever continent you call home)
- yes, he looks rural
- yes, he looks like Small Town USA
- looks intellectual – maybe a professor
- typical middle-class guy
- homeless
- mid-American values in his style
- big city wheeler dealer type
- foreign – maybe Scandinavian (or South American or Asian or mid-eastern or other)

How does he make you feel?
- no thoughts – glance at the next person and the next as you move on – pay no conscious attention to him
- uneasy
- possibly interested in meeting him
- consider mentioning him to security

Do you see that you 'instantly know' a great deal about a person? Every single day, you make these quick, subconscious summaries of observance without thinking twice about them and just as instantly dismiss them from your mind as others cross your path. Most of the time, your mind glides on and does not linger on them as you pass on – making other passive and dismissive summaries throughout the seconds of your day.

In other words, you already 'know' the element of character. To turn this natural ability that you already have into writing, all you have to do is to bring it to the surface of your consciousness.

You will see how good you are by describing details that reveal character. And when we get to each of the other elements, you will begin to realize that you know more than you think you do and you only need to let it surface in your writing.

Note: Today, there is a trend to get away from using gender-based words, such as actor for male and actress for female – and instead just use actor to indicate either male or female.

In writing, the same trend is changing from the use of hero for male and heroine for female – simply the word hero to indicate the lead character, whether male or female. I use the new trend quite a bit; but elsewhere in this book, when speaking of my own characters, I state the word heroine to identify a main female character or hero to identify a main male character in one of my novels.

There are two methods to create your characters:
1. In-Depth Character Study
2. Fast-Track Method To Create A Character

In-Depth Character Study

Write answers to each of the following questions about a character you create – male or female of any age. At least read through the following and see what comes to your mind about your main character. You may want to use only a few of the following or find that all of them contribute to building your character.

As you answer the following questions, keep in mind that you are in control, which means you can always change your character information as you write; but this is a step in building your character so well that you will know what behaviors and choices are 'in character' or 'not in character' for the credibility of your story.

Create an imaginary male or female character of any age – historical, contemporary, or Science-Fiction (Sci-Fi) and answer the following questions:

Character: Basic Story Facts

1. Gender
2. Name
3. Age as the story opens
4. Time Period and Location of your character's life for your book – 1800s France, say.
5. Time Span of your book – an event; a season; a specific year; several years – if so, from about what age to what age; from birth to death; several generations of a family.
6. Generation of the character: child, teenager, young adult, middle-aged (35-49), senior citizen.

Character's Physical Profile

1. Appearance
   - Ethnicity
   - Height, weight, overall physical condition/fitness
   - Eye and hair color, complexion
   - Any particular striking features
   - Any physical abnormality, former Illnesses
   - Style of dress (reflect time period, culture)
   - Shirt/pant/jacket size; shoe size
   - Blouse/skirt/dress/bra size; shoe size
   - Favorite cologne, if worn, bathing preferences (shower, bubble bath…), frequency

Character's Family Profile

1. Birthplace
   - Did your character grow up in region/country of birth?
   - If not, where?
   - Where living at time of story

2. Family/Parents – general summary of each
   - Living or dead, happy or unhappy, good or bad parents
   - Ethnicity of parents – different from each other
   - Traditions
   - Expectations of their child/children
   - Other influential relations – aunts, uncles, grandparents – in the mix?
   - Siblings – general of each
   - Socio-economic level of family/childhood

Character's Social Profile

1. Education level
2. Favorite books, music, movies, television shows (if invented at time of story)
3. Social Class
   - social class speech patterns
   - social class mores
4. Sports (appropriate to the era of the story)
   - participant
   - spectator
5. Politics
   - beliefs
   - level of involvement
6. Internet savvy (if applies to time period)
   - Internet habits – chat rooms, texting, instant messages, games
7. Social life
   - Type of friends, how close?
   - Hang-outs
8. Any social exclusions, enemy/enemies
9. Trouble with the law

Character's Work/Career Profile

1. Career – success level, personal satisfaction
2. Financial level – investment savvy

Character's Inner Workings

1. Motivation – what does this character want?
2. Waiting for what – if applies?
3. Dominant personality trait – i.e. optimistic, skeptical, angry, generous, et cetera
4. Major struggle as child/now
5. Wishes people saw him/her as…/ People actually see him/her as…
6. Religion
7. Secret Longing
8. Happiest experience, most traumatic experience
9. Transformation?

Character's Intimate Relationship Profile

1. Marital status/Sex life, if adult
   - Current spouse, Previous spouse/s – types of parents they are
   - Children (general) – type of parent character is to children
   - Extra-marital affairs, Erotic predilections (general)
   - Monogamous

Character's Personality Traits (as apply)

1. Self-esteem
2. Strengths, weaknesses
3. Anxieties, fears, compulsions, phobias, obsessive patterns, if any
4. Neuroses

5. Drive or ambition, work pattern
6. Pastimes/hobbies
7. Sleep pattern
8. Favorite time of day
9. Favorite food and beverage, eating patterns/ diets
10. Extent of alcohol/ drugs – type of each, if use
11. Addictions
12. Trademark Traits

Character's Living Conditions

1. Urban/Rural/Small Town
2. Live alone, with roommates, life partner, spouse and children (love/sex above)
3. Neighborhood
4. Apartment
5. Homeless
6. House
7. Pets
8. Furnishings
9. Car (if applicable for time period)
10. Boat
11. Motorcycle, scooter, bike

Once you have identified meaningful traits from this list for your character, you have created a character. *Qualities of your character may suggest a story.*

This list is a starting point for you. Add other thoughts that come to you about your character.

Ginie Sayles' Fast Track Method To Create A Character

I do not always need an in-depth study of my characters in order to jump start my writing. And I may never plumb the depths of any of them, at all. Sometimes, yes; sometimes, no.

Even so, I still want a compelling character and I am betting you do, too.

You may have a vague idea for a main character and want to discover the character for yourself as you write, discovering how your character will react in Situations you create for him/her. That is just fine; but at some point jot down some basics about your main character so that you will not have him/her 'slip out of character' in a way incongruous with what you have already written.

For example, before I wrote **Her Secret Life**, I wrote a chapter that was in my mind for the book. Then, I stopped and jotted down a general family background of my new female hero – a child reared by her father, who is a carpenter, and helped by his two older sisters who are seamstresses, living in a nearby community. They live on a middle-class island of Martha's Vineyard in the last half of the 1800s (Martha's Vineyard was primarily middle class at that time). So with setting, time period, a father who is cold but honest and two aunts who are warm, loving and financially dependent on her father, how does all this influence the life of a young girl who grows up to be a bigamist, especially since she is already married to a fine man she cares for and lives a life of wealth and prestige in lavish Newport, Rhode Island?

To fast-track your Main Character:
1. Summarize general physical description you see in your mind's eye.
2. Summarize general family background – including time period and place.
3. Be sure he or she is a richly textured multi-dimensional Full Character.
4. Have your Main Character to have at least one Trademark Trait.
5. Make sure your Main Character is Proactive.
6. Use a Point-of-view that best pulls the reader's interest into your Main Character.

To fast-track your leading Support Characters:

1. Summarize very general descriptions of each leading support character.
2. Summarize a very general background of any leading support character.
3. As a support role, the character is Flat, less textured.
4. A leading support character should have at least one or two Trademark Traits.

Richly Textured Characters

Most fiction courses discuss Full and Flat Characters (sometimes referring to them as Round and Flat). Full characters have flaws, yet they are heroic in spite of flaws; or totally despicable because of them. They have some unpredictable or surprising qualities.

Flat Characters are fairly predictable – not complex – simple, either good or bad.

Main Characters are full. Support Characters are flat. If they are fairly important, they are usually not totally flat because they have interesting quirks or endearing qualities about them; but they are support roles to the fuller Main Characters.

In the character-rich novel, *Gone With The Wind,* Scarlett and Rhett are full characters. Scarlett is vain, scheming, and selfish; but she is also courageous, with an odd type of loyalty and family pride. Rhett is unscrupulous, almost as selfish as Scarlett, and flagrantly unfaithful; but he is also passionately in love with Scarlett, financially successful, and a devoted parent.

Melanie and Ashley are flatter characters. Both have integrity, loyalty, and honor. They defend honor for the sake of honor.

Trademark Traits

To create a Fuller Main Character, add what I call 'trademark traits' to the personality or behavior of a character. I do this with Flat or Support Characters as well.

For example, in *Her Secret Life*, I wanted a sharp delineation between the two husbands of my bigamous female hero, Kytra Bradshaw. Her husband, Thaxton Eldridge III, was elegant, and refined. He had two Trademark Traits – (1) he always replaced his cup into his saucer with silent precision; and (2) he had a quietly comical side of imitating people who annoyed him when they were gone or making a face in response to something.

By contrast, her husband, Ransom, was illiterate, savagely tempered, had a penetrating intelligence, spiritual fervor, and gifted artistry. His Trademark Trait was agoraphobia, based on a superstition that he was cursed.

As a support character, Thaxton's mother, Francine Hoskins Eldridge, was a perfect lady who also had a gentle, light-hearted personality. She had a Trademark wink which she used from time to time to 'include' someone or to make sure they got her meaning.

Create your own Trademark Traits for your characters and reinforce them from time to time, without overdoing it. Trademark Traits make your characters more believable, memorable, and distinctive.

Proactive Versus Reactive Characters

A strong Main Character is also Proactive – meaning the Character initiates Action to alter a Situation and to make it better or to change it into what he/she wants it to be. Proactive Characters exert some influence or control over their lives and environments.

If your Main Character is merely Reactive – always letting the whims of fortune determine his/her life, the story is less compelling and your Character is weaker.

Typically, as in life, Characters have a bit of both Proaction and Reaction to Situations; but Proactive should dominate for your male or female Hero.

Point-Of-View

There are three basic points-of-view for a writer to use in telling a story:

1. First Person – *Singular:* I, me, my, mine; *Plural:* we, us, our, ours
2. Second Person – *Singular or Plural:* you, yours
3. Third Person – *Singular:* She, he, it; her/hers, him/his; *Plural:* they, them their/s

When you choose a point-of-view, your writing is limited to the parameters of that point of view. Discussing point-of-view can be somewhat complicated to new writers; so I will simplify each as much as possible and then I will emphasize which point-of-view is usually the best for new writers.

First Person - Point-of-View

The **First Person Singular** has a clear, specific lens through which to tell the story. There are many good books written in first person singular; but it has drawbacks, as well.

The biggest drawback of writing in the first person singular is that you are limited to the eyes, ears, vocabulary, and perceptions of the "I" who is experiencing the story.

One special limitation of writing in first person singular is describing your character. Since your character is telling the story, all physical descriptions, if they are good, will sound vain – i.e. "I have pretty blue eyes and long, dark hair that is naturally curly. My voice is soft and melodious"…et cetera.

All such description will have to be something the "I" is relating that someone told the "I" who is telling the story – i.e. "My father says I have pretty blue eyes and long, dark hair that is naturally curly, like my mother." Or "Aunt Hattie said my voice is soft and melodious."

Instantly, you can see how limiting much of your story is, even beyond self-description.

All descriptions must be true to the education level, intellectual level, background, and speech habits that would be natural for the character. It can be difficult to limit yourself and sometimes tedious for your reader to experience a book told in social patterns of speaking that are not mainstream. Readers like to identify on some level with the main character. Speech patterns for minor characters are given leeway; but not as much for the main character throughout an entire book.

The biggest plus of first person singular is that it is easiest to write a story, feeling as if you are inside the head of the main character. In some cases, I have started a novel in first person singular to get inside the head of my main character and to feel a natural flow of that character's emotion. But once I feel a oneness with the character's life, I go back and change everything into third person, which I will discuss later.

In most instances, writing in first person will be singular.

First Person *Plural* is a style that seems overly contrived; but that does not mean it will not work. Even if attempting first person plural, it would convey a singular view because "we," must still operate as one unit, and a single lens for the story. If it is a story told from a person with schizophrenia, it might work quite well.

Second Person Point-of-View

Writing in the **Second Person** "you" – whether singular or plural – not only feels contrived throughout, but can have an awkward flow. Second person writing seems presumptuous.

Never have I felt the writer succeeded in making me feel part of the story; but always conscious that I had to deal with the author's affectation in writing, which distracts from a story that may otherwise be all right.

It only succeeds in being memorable as affectation; but, of course, being remembered at all is a type of success, even if an offbeat type of success.

Third Person Point-of-View

For your first novel, I suggest **Third Person** – i.e. he or she or they (singular and plural as applies to the situation) did X, Y, and Z. This is the easiest, most flexible, and most powerful point-of-view for any novel – and it is the point-of-view preferred by publishers.

But even this simple, direct point-of-view can be broken down into more specific third person writing.

Third Person Subjective is telling a story with the freedom of description granted in the third person – i.e. *Susan was happy that day, full of expectation* – and weaving in the point-of-view of your main character with all the lush emotion of that character.

Third Person Objective has a Hemingwayan distance between the character and emotion, which is mostly reflected in stark description – i.e. *Susan turned the calendar page. It was another day.*

So-called **Third Person Omniscient** is the most preferred point-of-view. You are the invisible 'third person' omnisciently narrating the story, knowing all the thoughts and feelings of every character. This god's-eye view is the most liberated method of writing a novel.

Your reader can experience the story from the perspective of various characters and how each character is reacting to the same stimulus – i.e. *Susan was happy that day, full of expectation. When she entered the room, Jake looked up and instantly wondered what was behind her happiness.* Your reader knows the feelings of Susan and also the suspicion of Jake.

Your writing has completeness when you use third person omniscient.

All points-of-view are fine for your writing, if it is comfortable for you and easy for your reader; but the most important thing to remember is that once you have chosen a point-of-view, be sure you use it throughout your novel – avoid switching points-of-view back and forth in your book. Yes, that can be done; but it can complicate your writing, especially if you are a first time author. If you find yourself doing that or wanting to do that; then switch to the strongest, most unfettered point-of-view, which is the third person omniscient to keep your writing clean.

Get to know your character and choose a point-of-view that seems best able to tell the story you want your character to live.

Chapter
24

Situation
& Setting

Situation drives the story. A single Situation or few Situations create a short story. A series of Situations is a novel. – Ginie Sayles

The first question to ask yourself as you begin writing each chapter is "What is the Situation?"

This is critical because *Situation is the engine of writing fiction. Situation drives the story.*

Situation is the skeleton on which every facet of a novel hangs:

- **Characters** reveal their strengths and weaknesses through *Situations*.
- **Plot** (Main Problem) is worked out through several *Situations*.
- **Settings** (Time & Place) are the Environment of a *Situation*
  - **Settings** may be influenced by *Situations*.
- **Scenes** in **Chapters** depict various *Situations*.
  - *Situation + Setting + Action = a Scene*
- **Mood** and **Pace** are by-products or stimulants of *Situations*.

I repeat: *Situation drives the story.* If there are no situations, there is no story.

Situation unveils a Character

There is a school of thought that Character drives the story; but Character and Situation have a symbiotic relationship. Even so, I see that Situation inches out as the prime driving force of the story and of each chapter.

Why? Because a Character – like a person – is 'born' into a Situation, not always of his/her choosing – and like a human being, he or she is a product of a Situation. A well-written Character is often 'molded' by the Environment/Setting of a Situation and in some respects may 'mirror' the Environment of the Setting produced by that Situation. City life can provide very different Situations from small town life and the Character will reflect that difference.

Situation can be a result of or the cause of the Setting/Environment the Character will experience – even those Settings that shape or mold the Character in many ways.

For example, if you – with the natural traits of your genetics – grew up in France, you would speak French, possibly be Catholic in religion, and express many of the values and patriotic loyalties of your French heritage.

If you – with the very same genetics – grew up in a remote tribe in New Guinea, you would speak one of the more than a thousand tribal languages, possibly adhere to spiritual teachings of a shaman or of the protestant or Catholic missionaries, wear tribal clothing, and act on the values and patriotic loyalties of your tribal heritage.

With the same genetic DNA, if you grew up in Indonesia, you would, again, express your DNA traits through the customs, heritage, and beliefs reflected in the Environment or Setting determined by the Situation in which you live.

Just as life in each of those cultures is lived in a series of situations; so, too, with characters in novels. Characters move through several Situations, creating a story. Saying it another way, Characters move with various Moods and Pace through the Settings of several Situations, while working out problems (Plot and Subplots).

Situation is the kingpin of all other elements of your writing.

No matter how strong the motivational drive of a Character, he or she must 'deal with' the Situation in order to eventually control the Situation as much as possible in the way the Character desires; but even then, the new Situation created by the Character continues to reveal the traits and essence of the Character.

(1) Choose A Situation – (2) Determine Setting – (3) Write A Scene

Open a chapter by putting your Character into a Situation that fits his/her time period. Begin writing a scene that shows your Character dealing with the Situation by DOING something. Now you have a start. *Situation +Setting+Action = a Scene. Chapters are a series of Scenes.*

When you are showing your Character in a Situation, *show only what is pertinent*. If it does not matter in this Situation that your Character likes chocolate ice cream, then there is no reason to reveal it in this Situation.

As an example of creating a Situation, I have chosen a scene from The Three Bears.

And I have:

- Transformed the bear family into **Human Beings** – a human family of mother, father, son.
- Chosen a single SITUATION of Family Dynamics in a kitchen Setting as they are **about to sit down to dinner**. Described the Situation **from the Mother's Point-Of-View**.

EXAMPLE :

Even as she laid the last fork on the table, Alice knew he would not be pleased. In the twelve years of their marriage, Sam had never once complimented her for a fine meal.

He would complain about something: it was too bland or too spicy. As always, he would suggest they take a walk or to do something else before eating dinner – as if letting the food stand on the table getting cold was the missing ingredient Alice should have magically added – that would make her cooking somehow edible.

Shoving a long black curl behind her ear, Alice paused before calling out that dinner was ready. Her reflection in the kitchen window reminded her to remove her apron. The woman looking back at her was still pretty but looked older than her thirty-four years.

Reasonably trim for a small woman, she nevertheless struggled with her weight. Sam pointed out every pound she gained but never noticed when she lost it – sometimes by purging after a meal or two.

Alice hid this secret well because she did not want their nine year old son, Sammy, to learn her bad health habits for weight loss.

At the thought of Sammy, the woman in the reflection smiled. Sammy was her reason for living.

Unlike his father, Sammy never complained about the dinner his mother prepared. As his father grumbled about the meal, Sammy stole glances at his mother and faithfully said, "It's good, Daddy. Mine is just right."

But Sam never acknowledged Sammy's opinion on the matter. To him, Alice's dinner was unfit for consumption unless they did something else before eating it and that was final.

What Does This Situation Reveal About The Character?

This Situation reveals the following about our Main Character:
- Her age and physical appearance.
- She seems to be stuck in an unhappy marriage.
- She suffers self-esteem issues revealed by Bulimic weight patterns; and tolerating emotional abuse of husband.
- She loves her son and he loves her.

Choose Your Setting For Time And Place

Setting is completely different from Situation. The woman in our story who has an unhappy marriage could exist in almost any time and place in history.

Her Situation of being unhappily married could be in Ancient Greece or 1700s France or 1939 America as we have chosen or today in any other country or in the future.

Back to our sample story: We want to make clear the Time and Place (Setting) where this Situation of our unhappily married woman takes place. We will decide the Time and Place and then write a description of it .

The Setting we describe for this unhappy marriage will be the preamble to the Action we just wrote. We have chosen America – now we need a state, city, year, and season. We can describe indoor, outdoor or both in the Setting – but we must *be sure to reveal the time period plus the time of day and season and where it is taking place* – plus details that reveal the immediate backdrop for you character, implying how it may affect your character.

Using the example of Alice, the mother, preparing dinner – I will now give two examples of the Setting that would come *just before* our scene of Alice preparing dinner.

A Setting can either:

1) **'Mirror or 'Reflect'**(foreshadow) **the Situation.**
2) **'Contrast' with the Situation.**

Both methods of writing a Setting can work.

Example of SETTING 1 – MIRROR The Situation

There was only one narrow and dusty window that squeezed light like a dried out orange into the kitchen. It was a dark kitchen and small, swallowed up by a large brown wooden table in the center of the room.

A giant cane-bottomed chair filled one end of the table, flanked on the sides by two smaller ones. Every footstep inside the kitchen echoed from the blue and white checked linoleum floor that peeled up in the corners

A bare light bulb swung slowly overhead, casting dim shadows here and there, revealing a dark grease spot on the floor that disappeared the next minute.

Heat from the oven was overbearing on this July day in Spring Hill, Arkansas; but even in the winter, the kitchen did not have welcoming warmth. It was a place where forgotten meals were served, one after the other, as seasons turned pages of the 1939 calendar that hung next to the icebox.

There was a mix of aromas – mostly of freshly baking dinner rolls, barely overriding the usual dull odor of baked-on grease that had never succumbed to a scouring pad.

Even as she laid the last fork on the table, Alice knew he would not be pleased...etc.

Example of SETTING 2 – CONTRAST with The Situation

Sunlight flowed with the scent of fresh lemons through all five of the large windows that lined her sparkling clean kitchen. The kitchen was large and bright, anchored in the center by an inviting bright blue table and matching blue chairs.

Every footstep inside the kitchen had a pristine click on the spotless blue and white tile floor that was immaculate even in the corners of the large room.

Overhead, a frosted white light globe cast a cheerful glow through the room.

Heat from the oven was made bearable on this July day in Spring Hill, Arkansas, by a slow, gentle rhythm from the ceiling fan. There was a mix of aromas – a slight tang of lemon cleanser succumbing to the inviting smell of fresh coffee, a turkey roast smothered in seasoned vegetables, yeasty dinner rolls, and a fragrant apple pie still baking in the oven.

It was a room where meals were served, one after the other, as seasons changed the menu with the 1939 calendar, which hung next to the icebox.

Even as she laid the last fork on the table, Alice knew he would not be pleased...etc.

Sometimes a Setting that Contrasts with the Situation can have more impact. Contrast can keep your reader from thinking the scene is too depressing to read.

How Long Should Your Description Of A Setting Be?

One to three or four short paragraphs tops! You can also intersperse Setting within the Action of a Character to keep the reader moving into the story and not getting bored, and revealing more and more of your Character.

Think of writing as weaving threads of Setting into threads of the Character's Actions into the pattern of a Plot (Main Problem).

Try This Exercise: In *Ginie Sayles' Fiction Writing Workshop*, I take my students outside and have them 'experience' the Setting where we are – with every sensory perception: sight, sound, smell, touch, taste – the 3 S's and 2 T's.

In one instance, we had a lovely garden with a statue, marble benches, wooden benches, a variety of trees, bushes, flowers, and lawn.

Each student was told to do the following:

1. **Look over the scene**, noting your *first overall impression*. Then note specifics - colors, shadows, light, time of day, et cetera – and think of words to describe each sight.
2. **Breathe-in the air** – and note how the air feels in your lungs, tastes in your mouths, smells – and think of words to describe each taste, each scent. Also to note

how the air feels on your skin and to find words to describe how it feels.

3. **Touch** the bark of various trees, rub the leaves between your fingers, slide your open palms over the benches, also to notice the feel of grass under your feet, and to compare all textures – and then to think of words to describe each feeling.

4. To **smell** the flowers and think of words to describe each scent.

5. To **listen** to the sounds of the environment – birds, a scamper of squirrels, of wind through leaves, of gravel or concrete underfoot, car horns or passing traffic, doors of the building being opened or closed – and to think of words to describe each sound.

After this exercise, we returned to class, and the students each created a Situation that would bring their Main Characters into a Setting similar to the garden.

The results were amazing! As each student read aloud, they realized how much richer their writing was when the Character entered the Setting we had just experienced. There was a marked difference in the writing. The listener/reader experienced it, too. The Setting was alive for each student – and the writing rang with authenticity.

For instance, an escaping prisoner somehow ends up temporarily in such a Setting for a few minutes. What would he/she think? Feel? Smell? See? Hear? Is there a taste in air? How would the prisoner's moments in this Setting affect the Situation? What would it reveal about the prisoner?

Or it could be a child at play, discovering the wonders of the world in the garden. How would the slant of sunlight dancing through tree branches seem to the child? The sound of crickets? A black-spotted red lady bug on a leaf? The perfume of a budding gardenia? A sticker in the child's bare foot?

Or it could be two lovers meeting there for the first time. Would their senses be heightened by their emotions to the lushness of the garden?

Or it could be a teenager skipping school and mulling over the consequences and whether or not the teenager cares about the consequences. What does the garden park represent to the teenager that day? How do the sensations of brushing a bit of fallen bark off a marble seat before sitting down and the feel of the marble to his hands or as he sat on it?

Or it could be a young father who has just lost his job and wanders into the park to think of how to tell his wife; and to consider how to pay the baby's doctor. He realizes he is carrying a paper sack with the lunch his wife prepared for him that morning when they thought he had a job. What does he do with it? How does the smell of it mix with the natural scents in the garden? How does it taste now? How does it look to him? Does he toss it into the green metal garbage can that blends into the Setting? Does he eat it? Does he feed it to the squirrels and birds? Does he find comfort in the garden Setting?

Or it could be an old couple, married fifty-five years, remembering the house where they lived the first year of their marriage. The house is no longer there but their garden remains. How would touching a smooth leaf from an old tree that was a sapling they planted when they moved in generate memories?

If you follow this exercise, you will sharpen your senses to the point that you will incorporate them seamlessly into your character's experience in the time and place of a Setting.

In your day-to-day life, raise your consciousness of your surroundings – because you already have this natural ability. Notice a parking lot when you park your car, the fumes of nearby traffic, the lobby of an office building, the feel of it, your sense of it, waiting for an elevator, pressing the button, people riding with you – and as you consciously think of how to describe it, your writing will become richer as you incorporate your sensory perceptions of a Setting into a Situation for Characters in your novel.

Plot

6 Ways To Outline A Plot

*A plot is the **Main Problem** that the Main Character must solve by the end of the book. – Ginie Sayles*

At some point, Plot must become the focus of your writing. The Ginie Sayles System of Plotting teaches that ***Plot must be worked out through a series of Situations***. I will provide my 6 simple methods of outlining your Plot.

1. One Sentence Summary
2. Situation List Outline
3. Story Summary Outline – such as Chapter 17
4. Situation-To- Chapters Outline* – My favorite. I use it most – it's easy and fast!
5. Chapter by Chapter Summary
6. Flow Chart Outline

Set Up Your Initial Work Page

For any outline method you choose, you can keep a clearer head if you set up your work page so that your Plot Outline is your next natural step.

For Example jot down the following notes on a sheet of paper or in your computer:

Novel type: Contemporary
General Setting: Stanford, CT (can change)
Working Title: *His Wife's Younger Lover*
Main Character: Richard Adams, a late middle-aged married man
Main Problem (Plot): Discovers his wife, Jane, is having an affair with a younger man.
Time Span for Novel: About a ten month time period.

1. One Sentence Summary

After you have made your list, take the Main Problem (Plot) and write it down again in a single sentence summary.

Plot Summary Sentence: *A middle-aged man discovers his wife of almost 30 years is having an affair with a younger man.*

With just that floating idea in your mind, sit down, open a file on your computer and begin with any Situation that strikes you – anything – you may not have any clear-cut ideas of how he is going to resolve this difficult emotional dilemma.

Even so, you must come up with a Situation for your Main Character...and then flow with the Setting or Settings in which the Situation takes place and take it from there.

Your initial Situation may be in the Setting of their wedding anniversary party that he suspects his wife is having an affair – and then have flash-backs about the other Situations that led up to it – and then the final Situation comes back to the anniversary party and his realization of the truth.

My point is, ***a Plot cannot be worked out without Situations*** – and a single Situation may be written in just one chapter – or it may take several chapters to ride out a single Situation – just like real life.

2. Situation List Outline

You can make a rough sketch of the Situations through which you will work out your Plot. This is very easy and quick to do.

Situation 1: Discovery of his wife's affair with a younger man.
Situation 2: Duties of the day interrupt and demand his attention
Situation 3: Assessment of his life.
Situation 4: Takes initial steps of action.
Situation 5: Retribution.
Situation 6: Working through the pain.
Situation 7: Decision.

As you can see, the Plot example from the Work Sheet is worked out through a series of 7 Situations. If you want to start writing your book with just a Situation Outline – a progression of what the Situations are likely to be – that is just fine.

3. Story Summary Outline

A fifty-year old man, Richard Adams, is about to leave for work one morning and looking for his business papers when he finds a love letter his forty-nine year old wife, Jane, wrote to a young college boy. Richard supposes she met him in one of her classes at the college and now he blames himself because he is the one who encouraged her to go back to school after their daughter married last year. The letter details sensual touch and she tells the boy how handsome he looks with his thick dark hair and wearing a yellow cashmere sweater.

Stunned, the discovery is complicated by the fact that he is under pressure at work and is competing with two younger workers for a promotion. He muddles through the next few months, going through the motions of work and social life. He hires a private investigator and then finds he does not want to know the details.

He analyzes himself and realizes how much he has let himself go. He considers hair transplants but decides it is too expensive. He hires a private trainer but the physical workouts are too strenuous so he quits.

His daughter calls and tells him she is four months pregnant. He and Jane will be grandparents. He evaluates Jane with new eyes, thinking of what a young man would see in her, regretting that he has not stayed aware of her sparkling qualities.

He decides to get even and soothe his aching ego by going to bed with another woman; but he is unable to consummate the effort, which makes him feel more like a failure.

Not knowing what he wants to do, yet; Richard concentrates on work and works harder than he ever has. He is often late getting home; and despite quarrels with Jane, he stays focused on the only part of his life he seems to have some control over, his work. It pays off, and he receives the promotion.

Feeling more in control of his life, Richard feels better able to deal with Jane's infidelity. Knowing Jane has arranged a party for their 30th wedding anniversary, he decides to talk to her after it is over and have her choose between him and her young lover. He is willing to let her go if she wants the young man. If she wants to stay married, then she must give up the young man.

At the party, Jane gives him a large, leather-bound book. Inside, is the first picture taken of Jane and him together when they were college students. Richard becomes emotional when he realizes the truth.

After you have written your summary, **follow the steps in Chapter 17** of this book that shows dividing your summary into thirds.

At this point, you can start writing your novel from any event that feels right to you at the moment – for example, the moment of truth could be when he is riding to work with his carpool, or when the caterer telephones, or after he goes to bed with another woman – the initial Situation is up to you.

And you are never 'locked in' to any event that you may have initially planned for your story. You are in control, which means you can revise the Situations and Settings and Action as many times as you wish while you are writing your book and working out your Plot or Main Problem for your Main Character.

4. Ginie's Situation-To-Chapters Outline

This method is a very fast way to write a novel.

After I make a Situation List of the probable Situations for my Main Character, then I write down the first Situation – Discovery of the Main Problem (Plot) that his wife's affair with a younger man.

Then I ask myself, "Okay, what Setting do I want – a time and place – where my Main Character discovers his wife is having an affair with a younger man? And what is his initial reaction to this discovery?

There are many possibilities that come to mind – but for my purpose in the story, I decide to have him discover a letter his wife wrote the young man. My Main Character is at home, alone; and he is about to leave for work in the morning.

It may require only one Chapter – or more than one Chapter – to set forth the 'discovery' moments for my Main Character. As I start writing the Situation, I find it takes me two chapters before I move him into another Situation – Situation 2 – which is that he still has to go to work.

Once again – what is the Setting (time and place) for the second Situation of having to go to work while he is still overwhelmed and feeling in a state of shock over his discovery?

It takes me four Chapters to work through the second Situation of dealing with work in a career that is already burdened with competition against younger workers for promotions – and at the same time, dealing with the discovery that his wife is in love with a younger man.

The following is an example of outlining Situations through which the Main Character works out the Plot or Main Problem in various Chapter Settings:

SITUATION 1: DISCOVERY OF HIS WIFE'S AFFAIR WITH A YOUNGER MAN

Chapter 1: *Setting: Week-day Morning in the small study of a middle-class house, middle-class neighborhood.* Richard Adams discovers his 49 year old wife's infidelity with a 19 year old college student when he finds and reads her letter to her young lover. His wife has already gone to class at a nearby college. He is alone in their study when he is rifling through business papers on his desk to take to the office. Unable to find the papers he wants, he picks up the stack of papers on Jane's side of the desk to see if it might have gotten mixed in with her papers. Midway through, he sees the letter. The letter implies sensual love making. She writes to the young man how he looked the first time she saw him, *"You were wearing a yellow cashmere sweater that matched the golden streaks in your thick, dark brown hair. That was the day our love began. How could someone so young – a boy of nineteen, so full of life, so full of promise – also know so much about loving me?"* Richard is stunned.

Chapter 2: *Setting: Wandering through the empty house, seeing Jane's half-full coffee cup where she left as she rushed out of the house just fifteen minutes ago.* Still stunned, his mind pours over the recent months. He blames himself because he was the one who suggested Jane go back to college after their daughter married last year – and now this – her young lover...a college student. She probably met him in one of her classes. But then, he realizes it is not his fault. She did not have to cheat. Clues of her infidelity flood his thoughts – all the late nights of study at the library or sudden trips to talk to a teacher, she said. Her sudden interest in going on a diet so she can get her weight down to her old college size, her exuberant behavior about school. Her comings and goings – he now sees it all in a new light.

SITUATION 2: DUTIES OF THE DAY INTERRUPT AND DEMAND HIS ATTENTION

Chapter 3: *Setting: Leaving his house, riding to work.* A car horn reminds him his carpool has arrived for work. He makes a quick photocopy of the letter on their printer and stuffs it into his briefcase. He then smoothes her original letter with his hands and places it where it belongs with her stack of homework papers on her side of the desk.

His miserable carpool ride to work with co-workers. He is nervous, distracted and upset – all of which are compounded by the trapped feeling in the car, listening to work complaints, a crude joke the driver tells, having to smile when a woman tells them about her baby taking his first steps.

Chapter 4: *Setting: Office cubicle* – barely sits down at his desk and opens his briefcase to pull out his photocopy of Jane's love letter when his boss pops in and wants to know the status of a project he was assigned. Reminds him promotions are coming up in six months. Richard is in competition with two other workers for Coordinating Manager of a new project. It is a position that Richard has wanted very much but now he wonders why he would want it.

Chapter 5: *Setting: His office environment.* He notices for the first time in a long time, the framed wedding picture on his office wall. Jane truly loved him then. She included him, no, absorbed him, into every aspect of her life.

He has a brief recollection of a few years ago, and how she had playfully pestered him with calls several times a day and sent short, funny emails throughout each day until his boss called him on the carpet about using company computers and company time for personal activity. So, Richard told Jane about it and it stopped.

He absently walks to the office break room and fills up his coffee cup, all the while searching his mind and wondering if she now sends emails to her young lover and if he sends them back. Richard makes up his mind to check Jane's in-box. Then he changes his mind and decides against it because he is not sure he can handle what he might find.

Chapter 6: Setting: *His office telephone rings as he reenters his cubicle.* It is their married daughter calling with news she is almost three months pregnant with a baby boy. She did not want to call until she had completed all early exams. Richard and Jane will be grandparents. Richard wonders maliciously how her young lover would feel knowing he was making love to a grandmother. He also wonders if the news will affect Jane's attitude toward her romance – force her to realize the age difference – and that Jane's lover is younger than her own daughter.

SITUATION 3: ASSESSMENT OF HIS LIFE

Chapter 7: Setting: *Same day. His office, standing at a file cabinet, with a file in hand.* He forces himself to research a report for a client but his mind keeps wandering. Thinking of how routine their love making had been for many years in their marriage, he now realizes he had felt it was a satisfying sex life, but apparently Jane did not. Now, he feels like a failure, abandoned.

Chapter 8: Setting: *Leaving his office at the end of the day.* Riding home in the carpool Richard makes no attempt at conversation or pleasantries. His co-workers ask if he is all right; but he waves them away with a comment about being tired. In truth, he is mentally assessing his career. He remembers Jane wrote that the young man is full of promise. Richard thinks about his small cubicle. He had been full of promise, too, once. He has ended up with a middle-management career and in desperate competition with two other people – both younger than Richard – for a promotion.

Chapter 9: Setting: *At dinner with Jane and friends in a new restaurant. Jane chats animatedly with their friends.* Richard assesses Jane with new eyes. He wonders what Jane has that a young man could desire. He recalls that over the years, she has taken steps to stay on top of the aging process. In her thirties, she had breast enhancement and then did not like it so had it removed. And a year ago when she turned forty-eight, she had her eyelids 'done' as she called it. And then she began coloring her hair and went on a diet. The thought of it makes him furious because in hindsight, he knows it was for her young lover.

Chapter 10: *Setting: At home in the bathroom, dressing for bed.* Richard assesses himself. He wonders what is lacking in him that Jane found in the young man, realizes how he has changed. Looking in the mirror, Richard sees a gray rim of hair around his balding head and thinks of the words Jane wrote about the young man's thick hair. Richard thinks about the infomercials he has seen about hair replacement and considers looking into it.

She had also described the young man as trim. Richard is not obese, but his waistline hangs over his belt, these days. He decides to visit a fitness gym near his office.

Chapter 11: *Setting: Next day, a used car lot at noon.* After another day of carpooling, Richard decides he is unable to endure yet another day of it now; so he goes to a used car lot during his lunch hour. The sales woman is friendly and easy to talk to. He buys a serviceable used car and she gives him her business card, offering to buy him lunch sometime.

SITUATION 4: INITIAL STEPS OF ACTION

Chapter 12: *Setting: A week later, breakfast at home with Jane.* Jane angrily tells him to stop snapping at her and asks why he has been touchy and moody recently. Richard wants to confront Jane, but is sure she will deny it. He needs to prove it. He wants to know the boy's name and to see him, face to face. He wants a show-down. But then he realizes that a confrontation might force Jane to choose – and Richard is suddenly sure from her letter that Jane would choose the young punk over him. At the thought of it, he feels lost. He decides to bide his time and not let Jane know he is onto her, yet. He believes he will never feel the same about Jane or their marriage; but he is determined to think it through before taking any action.

Chapter 13: *Setting: Fitness Gym.* He arrives for his first work-out appointment and feels self-conscious as he passes among members who are mostly young. He works privately then with a personal trainer; but before the end of the first session, Richard, who is drenched in perspiration and out of breath, quits due to increasing arthritic pain in his elbow, which makes him feel old.

To make matters worse, he receives a return call from the hair replacement company he called earlier that day and realizes it is too expensive and time consuming for him. He asks they remove his name from further contact. He is depressed to realize he cannot compete with his wife's young lover.

Chapter 14: *Setting: The office of a private investigator.* Richard hires the investigator to follow Jane and to take photographs of her lover.

Chapter 15: *Setting: Lunch with his closest friend at a golf club.* His best friend tells him about a business trip he took the month before and brags that he met a woman and spent the week-end with her. He seems proud of his infidelity and that his wife does not suspect anything. Richard considers confiding in his friend about Jane; but decides it is embarrassing and a blow to his ego. Too, his friend might tell his wife and it could get back to Jane and then the confrontation he dreads would probably take place. He realizes he is still not ready to face Jane with the truth he knows about her.

SITUATION 5: RETRIBUTION

Chapter 16: *Setting: Two months later, his office.* A caterer telephones, reminding him that four months earlier he and his wife met with him and planned a celebration of their thirtieth wedding anniversary next month. The caterer needs to finalize details. Richard had forgotten and the call brings surprising hurt. He cancels the appointment, ends the call, leaves his office and goes outside for a walk, battling anger and hurt.

Chapter 17: *Setting: A coffee shop.* With no particular destination, he decides to find a place to sit and think. He finds himself thinking of his best friend cheating on his wife; and Richard thinks of the opportunities he had to cheat on Jane and did not and now he is angry with himself that he did not cheat on her first. He feels foolish.

On his cell phone, he calls the sales woman who sold him his used car to invite her for drinks after work; but he is told she no longer works there. Richard does not know whether to feel foiled by fate or relieved. A woman in the coffee shop interrupts his thoughts to ask if he has change for a dollar. He fumbles in his pocket, and hands her the change. She opens her purse, drops it, and everything spills out. He helps her gather everything, and offers to buy her lunch. She is from another city, in town on business.

Chapter 18: *Setting: After lunch.* He is not ready to go back to work. He calls his office to say he is taking the afternoon off. Checking his messages, he learns the private investigator has called. Dreading the investigator's information, he does not call him back.

Chapter 19: *Setting: A nearby hotel.* The woman is responsive to him. He decides that what is good for the gander is also good for the goose. He goes to her hotel room and tries to make love with the woman but finds he can't. He is embarrassed and it makes him feel worse than ever.

Chapter 20: *Setting: Walking through their home, shadowed with twilight.* He is late getting home but finds his wife is not home, yet, either. He is sure she is with her lover. He yields to the temptation to check her emails but finds nothing. He looks for the original letter and does not find it, either. When Jane arrives home, he is careful not to ask where she was or why she was late.

Chapter 21: *Setting: The office of a private investigator.* Richard waits in the outer room at the office of the investigator, who is meeting with someone else. While waiting, Richard becomes nervous about seeing pictures of Jane and the boy. Richard leaves.

SITUATION 6: WORKING THROUGH THE PAIN

Chapter 22: *Setting: His office cubicle*: For the first time since he discovered Jane's infidelity, he finds comfort in his work. He begins to stay late, working harder than he has ever worked before.

When he arrives home each night, Jane is usually studying or already in bed. Jane quizzes him about working so late. She also asks about their love making and complains that they have not made love in months. He blames his painful arthritic arm and says he has not felt up to par lately, which is true because of his worry about her lover.

Chapter 23: *Setting: Four Months after that: An office party.* The office surprises Richard with a party to celebrate promotions. Richard's recent hard work has placed him significantly ahead of his younger competition. He moves out of the cubicle and into a private office with a window overlooking the business district. It is the first time he has felt happy about anything in months.

Chapter 24: *Setting: One week later, hospital in neighboring city*: Richard stands at the bedside of his daughter in the hospital, talking to his son-in-law and holding his new grandson, who was named Richard, after him. His daughter tells him Jane suggested the name. He is pleased but surprised that Jane suggested it and wonders if she did it out of guilt.

SITUATION 7: DECISION.

Chapter 25: *Setting:* *Two and a half weeks later, a jewelry store.* Richard's daughter reminds him to buy an anniversary gift for Jane to be presented at the party. He realizes he still loves Jane and does not want to disrupt their new role as grandparents with a divorce; but even though he wants to stay married to Jane; he decides he no longer wants to look the other way. He does not want to stand in the way of her happiness with the young man so divorce is up to her.

Their wedding anniversary is next week. He decides he will talk to her about it after the anniversary party. If she wants to stay married to him, she must not see the boy, anymore.

Chapter 26: *Setting:* *The Anniversary Party*: As Jane's invitation stipulated, everyone arrives, dressed casually. After the initial greetings, buffet, and drinks, friends surround Jane and Richard for their gift-giving. It has been ten months since Richard found the letter.

In front of everyone, Richard gives Jane his gift. He watches her face closely as she unwraps his gift and sees the gold necklace he bought for her. She gasps and reads aloud the words he had the jeweler engrave: *"After 30 years, I still love you, Richard."* Her eyes fill with tears and he wonders if they are tears of shame.

Then, Jane hands him a large package. Inside, is a leather-bound book. Across the top of the book, in gold embossed letters, it reads: Richard and Jane Adams 30th Wedding Anniversary.

Sadly, he opens the cover.

On the first page is a picture taken of Jane and him as college coeds. They were standing in front of the Science building that has since been torn down. Jane looked so beautiful – her black hair long and glossy, her blue eyes beaming. She is wearing the Madras shirt and jeans she is wearing now.

"I had to go on a diet to fit into this old Madras shirt and jeans from college days!" Jane announces to everyone and they all laugh with her. "All these years, I was too sentimental to throw them away."

But Richard is overcome with emotion and pretends to cough so no one will notice his personal struggle. With one fist, he quickly wipes his wet eyes.

In the picture, nineteen-year old Richard, with one arm wrapped around Jane's shoulder, stares back at him. A shock of thick brown hair swept across his forehead. He was tall and slender and smiling broadly…and wearing a yellow cashmere sweater.

Two spaces below the picture Jane's words were written: *My darling, I am thinking of the first time I saw you. You were wearing a yellow cashmere sweater that matched the golden streaks in your thick, dark brown hair that blew across your forehead in the wind. That was the day our love began. And soon I discovered the thrill of your touch, your lips on mine. How could someone so young – a boy of nineteen, so full of life, so full of promise – also know so much about loving me? I knew little of love until you touched me; but I know I love you as I can never love anyone else. Jane.*

Numbers Of Chapters Per Situation Can Vary

As you can see, it took me twenty-six Chapters for seven Situations. It could be an entirely different number of Chapters, depending on how I might choose to have my Main Character work out the Main Problem. You are not locked in to a specific number of Situations; and you are not locked in to a specific number of Chapters. You are in control. Situations are guidelines. And once you get into the actual writing of your novel, it may end up completely different from the outline you initially had – but the outline 'got you going.' And that is the value of an outline. It gets you going.

If you decide to follow your outline pretty closely, you will get your book written much faster. Even so, once you are writing, feel free to go with the flow in your heart, mind, and ideas, either way.

When I wrote *Her Secret Life*, I had at least twenty or so Situations that were worked out through sixty-eight chapters. Within those sixty-eight chapters, the Plot (Main Problem) was established through several Situations with various Settings; and developed through a great number of Situations and various Settings. And finally, the Subplots and the Plot (Main Problem) were resolved through a number of final Situations and various Settings – until final resolution in the last chapter.

5. Chapter-By-Chapter Summary

After you write your summary, break each main Action into a chapter. Then, summarize what will happen in each chapter.

Now, you have a **"Chapter-by-Chapter" Outline** – which is a one page summary of each chapter of your book.

Just count out 25 blank sheets of paper – and title each one – i.e. chapter 1, chapter 2, chapter 3, chapter 4…et cetera through 25. Then figure out whether the scenes you have been writing belong in one of the early chapters or in a middle chapter or near the end.

Choose one – and it can be a guess, for the time being. Summarize your scene in that chapter. Do the same with any other scenes you have written. Just summarize each scene in one of the blank chapter pages. You can always change where you have them later. This just gets you going.

Now, on your sheet of paper titled chapter 1, jot down a brief summary and any ideas about the way you think it might begin (again, this is not written in concrete, it is just an idea but it has potential).

Then, on your chapter 2 sheet, do the same thing – jot down a brief summary of what you think might happen next and any ideas you have about it.

Do this with every sheet of paper – and when you get to chapter 20, you may realize that you want to add chapters – so go ahead! Add as many chapters – and move your scenes around in these chapter pages as many times as you wish until you see where the scenes best fit.

By writing a summary of each chapter on a separate sheet of paper, you are creating a very efficient Chapter-by-Chapter outline. This is a great guideline for you as you take your writing from the unknown into a book.

You can always write into the unknown and then place it where you think it belongs – and remember, once you get into your writing, your book may end up different from your Chapter-by-Chapter outline or it may be exact. It does not matter, because at some point, you gave yourself a guideline and it got you going.

After you write the Chapter-by-Chapter outline, it is sooo easy to sit down and, using your new Chapter-by-Chapter outline, to write each chapter very quickly, even in three weeks or less.

6. Flow Chart Outline

When I was a stockbroker, I learned that businesses often use a Flow Chart to 'plot' their success as a company for an upcoming year. Flow Charts are also used in smaller projects by departments within a business; and decided that authors can use this process as well.

Flow Charts use a series of specific shapes to identify a particular activity – such as a diamond shape to indicate a decision, an oval or an ellipse shape to indicate a starting point or stopping point, a square or rectangle to indicate a process or action step– connected by a line to each other, in order of the flow of events. This has been fairly standardized; however, for a creative writer, come up with your own shapes to indicate an activity.

I find that some people 'think' like a Flow Chart. For these people, I suggest you quickly make shapes, such as a large Diamond and write a Situation inside it and then draw a line to connect one or several large Rectangles with a Chapter Idea inside each one; Ellipses for Setting.

This way, you can 'chart the flow' of your book with your own Flow Chart.

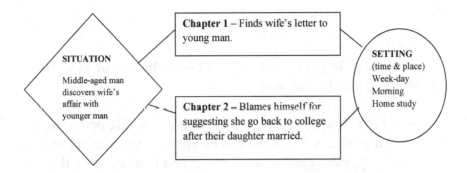

You Can Also Create A Flow Chart By Thinking Backward

Flow Charts can also be used when all you have is an idea – perhaps for an ending – and so you put that into your Diamond shape and then 'think backwards' with rectangles and other shapes, asking yourself, what are some possible ways my Characters got to this point?

In business, for example, they begin with their ultimate goal for that quarter or year. Let's pretend they state their goal as "We want to achieve greater name recognition." And they write that into a shape, perhaps a diamond.

Then they ask, "What are some ways we might be able to get to this point?"

Each idea that answers that question is put into a different shape, say a rectangle and each rectangle is connected to the diamond 'ultimate goal.'

You can do that for your book, too, if you like.

Story Boards

Story boards are graphic, scene-by-scene pictures used for some plays and movies. It is a detail of how each scene will look. To my way of thinking, the Situation-To-Chapters outline accomplishes a parallel concept – and without an art degree!

Plot Dynamics

As you write your novel, your Main Problem – or Plot – is revealed in the following way:

- **Time Span.** A specific Time Span is the life period of your plot. A time span can be virtually any time period – say, from childhood to death; or a teenage story that spans one year or seven years; or a period in history or a recent time period for the main problem to be solved by the main character. Each Situation within the Plot has built-in Time Constraints, such as a dinner that can last from a quick fifteen minutes to three or so hours. But the Plot has an overall Time Span comprised of many Situations. *Action plays out in the Time Constraints of each Situation and within the overall Time Span of a Plot.*

- **Main Character's Motivating Desire:** To have depth, your main character should "want" something – an achievement, a particular woman, power, recognition, revenge, justice, to dominate, seek forgiveness, a home, parental approval, to find his parents, liberty, the list is as endless as human beings are in their desires. But it should be *ONE major desire that motivates Action* on the part of your male or female hero.

- **Opposition/Challenge**: *Conflict Can Be Internal Or External.* As your character acts on his/her desire, there is opposition – from an inner moral struggle (Internal Conflict) – or from a specific Situation, or from another person, or an enemy, or a friend, the environment, the law, family (External Conflict) – the list is endless as to what creates the main opposition and conflict with your main character. Whereas there can be numerous conflicting situations, there should be *one major opposition –*

internal or external – that creates Action, reaction, or interaction.

- **Subplots.** Subplots add relief to your main plot. Sub-plots are minor plots within a larger plot that keep a story from being boringly one-tracked. They are the multi-tasking diversions that bring texture and dimen-sion to your story – but be sure they do not 'overtake' your Main Plot. In general, for a 60,000 word (200-220 pages) book, no more than eight to twelve subplots should work well.

- **Mounting Conflict**: It is the "interplay" of Action and reaction between the motivating desire and the opposing conflict through various Situations (set forth in chapters) that builds a rising conflict – one problem after the other – which means "the plot thickens."

- **Good Moments**: As your plot unfolds, your chapters do not have to be in constant conflict or it is too stress-ful for both the reader and for the credibility of your book. Create moments when your character feels things are falling into place…moments when your character is enjoying himself/herself. This change of Pace and Mood is necessary. But good moments cannot last too long or you lose your reader. So, the next chapter can reveal that things were not falling into place as the main character thought; or another problem (related to the main one) pops up and the conflict resumes. But there has been respite for the reader.

- **Action Turns Your Reader Into A Witness.** Once you have written your outline; then begin writing each Chapter with Action – or in the case of internal conflict – such as our example of the middle-aged man – write vivid internal reaction and make his decisive actions sharp or poignant or angry to the point your reader cheers him on.

Readers want vigorous Action, even with internal conflict – and external Action that mirrors or resolves the internal conflict. Just a thought line is okay for your summary; but not for your actual writing of each chapter. A student once read her story of a girl about to be married who walks through the neighborhood where she grew up and remembers playing as a little girl, having her first date, her father losing his job, and on and on and on – and these were great ideas – BUT – it was a synopsis of the girl's thoughts – not a clear-cut Action-brimming sequence of memories. You must 'detail and describe vigorous Action' for each forward-moving event.

There is an old saying, "Show, don't tell." I do not think the saying adequately explains the process; but it does give a general gist that means '*describe*' the Action – "She **shuddered** in **horror** at the **crack and crunch** of Jim's **shattering bones** when the mugger's **fist split Jim's face**," not just writing, "she saw the fist-fight."

Think of Action Movies – one of the most successful, money-making genres in film – and why? Because it is one **vigorous Action** after another **vigorous Action** – and you witness it.

Throughout your Plot and Subplots, you let your reader witness the Action of your story by describing the sight, sound, smell, taste, feel of an explosion, a chase, a sword fight, a forbidden kiss, et cetera… with Action.

An action-filled Plot brings satisfaction to your readers and full enjoyment to you in your writing. Even in a quieter Plot, in which the Action is internal, describing the simple external Actions contrasting with extreme internal conflict of your Characters makes your Plot a richer read.

The Ginie Sayles definition of Action is *Describe the DO!*

- **Climax/Epiphany**: This is the Armageddon or moment of truth or triumph in the final showdown between motivating desire and opposing conflict. This is the powerhouse event and it is the reason the reader has stayed with you.

- **Resolution**: The Main Problem has been resolved through the Climax and now you tie up subplot loose ends and *satisfy the reader* to close the book.

In review, a novel is the fictional story of a person solving a major problem – and working through lesser problems that pop up in the process. *Whether you develop your plot according to Chapter 17 for creating a good plot quickly from a winning template or Chapter 20 for creating a plot by writing into the unknown or from one of the outlining methods listed in this Chapter*, your plot should contain the points listed above.

Popular Plot Themes

When I was a student at the University of North Texas (then known as North Texas State University), my writing professor said there are **no new plots**. He said that all Plots (Main Problems) have been used and furthermore that there are only a certain number of plots – he said 110 but I saw a book that said there were 250.

In essence, my professor said the best a writer can do is to give a 'new twist' to an old plot theme. Plot themes mean activities built around a Main Problem (Plot).

Since I do not know exactly how many plot themes there really are; I am going to list a few popular plot themes.

1. **Adventure** – The Main Problem (Plot) will be the opposition to a quest, such as *Raiders of the Lost Ark* (sp), or the Main Problem (Plot) is a pursuit: *The French Connection, The Hunt For Red October.*

2. **Mystery** – The Main Problem (Plot) is 'who done it?' Who committed the murder or the theft. *Sherlock Holmes* books by Arthur Conan Doyle.

3. **Love** – The Main Problem (Plot) can be anything that keeps two lovers apart. It may be war or parental disapproval or social, racial or educational discrimination or the forbidden love of an affair. Contemporary romances, *Harlequin* romances.

4. **Moral Dilemma** – The Main Problem (Plot) is anything that challenges the beliefs of a person or when something believed to be wrong seems qualified as right, such as *Breaking Bad;* or the idea of killing is considered right during war. It can also be when a person has the opportunity to take something of value and needs to do so and it would never be known but the person struggles with values of right and wrong. Or a situation in which helping someone who deserves help will violate what you know is wrong, such as *Her Secret Life.*

5. **Vengeance** – The Main Problem (Plot) is that someone was wronged so severely that revenge seems to be the justifying motivation. *A Woman Of Substance.*

6. **Rivalry** – The Main Problem (Plot) is an unfair preference of one person over another that breeds a justified ill will between them: *Cain and Abel, East Of Eden.*

7. **Sacrifice** – The Main Problem (Plot) is solved by one person sacrificing for another: *Of Human Hearts* or *A Tale Of Two Cities.*

8. **Ambition/Greed** – The Main Problem (Plot) occurs as a person strives to reach the heights of success and

then discovers the pitfalls of excess: *Citizen Kane, Wall Street,* or *Mildred Pierce.*

9. **Discovery** – The Main Problem (Plot) is the revelation of something unknown or of coming of age with a teenage love affair, or self-discovery perhaps in midlife crisis or some other revelation: *His Wife's Younger Lover, On The Wings Of A Dove, Summer Of '42, American Beauty.*

10. **Transmutation** – The Main Problem (Plot) unfolds when a metamorphosis takes place changing a person with characteristics that are super human or subhuman or half-animal or magical or supernatural, such as *Carrie, Wolf man, Superman, Spiderman, and heroes found in ancient Greek myths/gods, comics, or popular horror stories.*

Use Your Plot To Hook Your Reader

Hook your reader into your plot by starting the book – the very 1st sentence of the very 1st chapter – with your Main Character smack dab in the middle of the Main Problem (which is the plot)!!

Then use a brief flashback to bring your reader up to speed as to how your hero got into this mess. From there, launch **various Situations to develop your Plot** – and enrich each Situation with a clear Setting, which includes Time and Place.

In the process, don't forget to Describe the Do.

Chapter 26

Imagery
Tools of Description

Build much of your description into the Action of the moment. – Ginie Sayles

Play with this sentence: *She walked down the street.* The sentence is not telling much. It is a basic, generic Action.

Then, take **each word** and sharpen it with description or clear identification. Choose one description for each word.

1. *She – a perky ten-year old girl with long black pigtails; a voluptuous brunette; a bent, gray-haired old woman.*
2. *Walked down– skipped happily down; strode confidently along, hobbled gingerly on*
3. *The street – the quiet lane; Fifth Avenue; the shady boulevard*

Now – repaint the sentence *"She walked down the street"* with the choices above and see what a difference it makes for your reader. Instead of *"She walked down the street,"* your reader gets a more personal and vivid experience of witnessing who 'she' is.

Example:

- *A perky ten-year-old girl with long, black pigtails skipped happily down the quiet lane.*
- *A voluptuous brunette strode confidently along Fifth Avenue.*
- *A bent, gray-haired old woman hobbled gingerly on the shady boulevard.*

And, of course, you can have a moment of fun right now by mixing them up; but not when you are writing.

Descriptions should:
a. Clarify the scene and Character.
b. Help your reader to see, hear, taste, touch, smell, and feel what you see, et cetera.
c. Bring Characters, Settings, and story to life.

How To Make Your Descriptions Blossom

Do not worry about the formal-sounding words when I say that your unique descriptions can blossom through your use of simile, metaphor, personification, anthropomorphism, onomatopoeia, and symbolism.

Really. Do not. You often use them in your writing without knowing you are doing it.

I include the formal names here so that you can:
1. Read them
2. Get the general idea
3. Internalize it
4. And then dismiss them from your mind and just write.

Anytime you are writing descriptively, you will be using these tools to some extent.

Ancient Greek philosopher and writer, Aristotle's *Poetics* was long considered a guiding force for writers; and he judged a writer's ability to use metaphor as an indication of talent. I certainly believe it is one of the striking features of a unique Author's Voice.

I do urge you to use Similes and Metaphors from time to time in your writing. In a novel, aim for every couple of Chapters, at least. These two forms build similarities between two unrelated objects or ideas so that a reader vividly understands or experiences a passage.

Most of the time, when I read a literary critic's praise for a writer, it is usually based on the writer's unique use of metaphor or simile.

All descriptive writing creates a picture in the mind of a reader; and descriptive writing can include any of the following tools of vivid writing:

- **SIMILE** – using the word 'like' or 'as' to specifically compare one thing with another. *Her eyes sparkled like morning dew.* Simile and metaphor are exactly the same, except that simile uses the words 'like' or 'as' to distinguish between the two items being compared; whereas Metaphor defines one item as the other – as follows.

- **METAPHOR** – the use of a word or phrase with parallel energy - used to make an idea, scene or personality more compelling and better understood. It does not apply literally. *Her eyes were sparkling morning dew* – This is the same comparison that was used in the example of a simile; but instead of comparing two similarities, metaphor actually defines one as the other. *Her voice was a warm hug.*

  Note: An entire story can be a metaphor: The movies, *Wall Street,* and *Citizen Kane* were each a metaphor for greed.

- **SYMBOLISM** – Concepts can be summed up in a single symbol that is easily understandable by most readers. For example, instead of having to fully explain the concepts of Christianity, you can mention the symbol of a Cross and it is instantly (and generally) understood by most readers. The same is true if you mention the Star of David as a readily understood symbol for Judaism, or you can mention a mosque to convey Muslim faith . Symbolism can also refer to a Character representing an ideal. In *Billy Budd,* the innocent title Character is considered a Christ figure.

And finally, an entire book or work can be symbolic of a belief or thought. For example, Hemingway's *The Sun Also Rises,* seems on the surface to be a story about a group of people on a drunken binge. In brief, Hemingway's book symbolizes a post World War I view that we live in a hostile universe. The hostile universe assaults humanity with an unhealing wound.

This belief is symbolized in *The Sun Also Rises,* when the hero, Jake, is made impotent from a wound in the war. The wound is exacerbated by the irony that he is in love with Britt, a woman whose nymphomania emphasizes the wound is 'unable to be healed.' They can never consummate and satisfy their love/desire. He must tolerate her affairs. Drinking and a refusal to complain are the temporary alleviations of pain and rebellion against the universe in Hemingway's symbolic tale.

For the most part, popular writers do not use an entire book for symbolism; but they do use symbols – i.e. the Cross, Star of David, Mosque – as shorthand for a concept that is *not* key to the book, only incidental to understanding elements of the Characters.

- **PERSONIFICATION** – Attributing the characteristics of a human to something not human. *Death knocked on the door.*

- **ANTHROPOMORPHISM** – Attributing human characteristics or behavior to a god, animal, or object. George Orwell's *Animal Farm* or Aesop's Fables are good examples, as are ancient mythologies that often had gods with half-animal bodies.

- **ONOMATOPOEIA** – Words that sound like the meaning of the word – and sometimes used repetitively to emphasize the Action. *Sizzling* is a word that sounds like the meaning; or a ***repetitive use of such a word emphasizes the Action***, *The tick, tick, tick of the clock reminded the old man that time was running out.*

Heighten The Intensity

Tie your descriptions to emotion. Certain scents such as the aroma of baking bread or cookies comfort us.

Other scents, such as sea spray free us, while musky fragrances intoxicate us. The same is true of tastes, of touch, of sounds, of sights.

When you describe a scene from your senses, you seduce your readers into your own vivid Passion as a writer. And they love it! Sensual, emotional scenes will be part of your re-writes.

As you re-write a scene; take the initial emotion of the reader one more step. Then take it another step. If the emotion you have developed is curiosity, intensify it into an insatiable appetite, and then perhaps into obsession – if it is appropriate for your character.

Clichés

An occasional cliché can be both expedient and succinct for your reader; but more than a few in your book reflects your writing as trite and unimaginative. The talent of your writing is your ability to 'translate' an idea into *original* parallel comparisons, which we just discussed in the use of metaphor, simile, et cetera.

I cannot list all the clichés in our language; but I will list a few to make you aware of clichés. Your inner ear will then become more attuned to clichés and to avoiding them.

Pretty as a picture	Happy as a lark	Straight as an arrow
White as snow	Brown as a berry	Red as a rose
Good as gold	Hungry as a bear	Honest as the day is long
Pearly white teeth	Green with envy	Hard as a rock
Busy as a bee	Sharp as a tack	Last but not least

When is there 'too much' description?

When more description is given than the Situation or Character or Setting requires, there is too much description.

For example, if the Situation is a divorce, decide if your chapter is going to reveal the moment your Character decides to get a divorce – and describe the Setting your Character is in at that moment.

Or you may decide to have your chapter be the moments after the divorce is granted and your Character leaves court, your description of the Setting would flow naturally out of that moment.

Or you may decide to have a chapter containing some of the actual divorce proceedings and your description of the Setting would include the courtroom. My point is, you describe what brings the Situation to life and build it into the Action of the chapter – only what is needed that makes the Setting 'pop' (like the difference between viewing black and white television versus color) but nothing more than that.

Descriptions of the Character, too, should flow naturally out of the 'Situation.' Descriptions are only as important as they apply to the scene and bring it to life.

If you are reading your scene and your mind wanders, there may be too much description or not enough Action.

Chapter

27

Mood, Pace, Variety
The Glue Of Good Writing

Keep your readers with you through skillful use of Mood, Pace, and Variety. – Ginie Sayles

All great writing that I have read contained more than striking Characters, a good Plot idea, and clear descriptions. They also contain the skillful use of Mood, Pace, and Variety. I consider these three to be literary glue that holds your writing together with power. These are easy to learn and critical for fine writing.

The Power Of Mood

Often ignored in writing classes, Mood is as much an element of fiction as Setting. Mood is vital for moving your reader from one feeling to another and not getting bored.

Mood reflects the emotional state of a scene, a Situation, a Character. Give great attention to creating Mood when you describe a Setting.

Ask yourself "Does my Setting/Action/dialogue convey a comfortable, homey Mood?"

"Does it convey a tense, anxiety-ridden Mood?"

"Does it convey a Mood of imminent threat, suspense?"

"Does it convey a convivial social occasion?"

"Does it convey a sensuous invitation?"

Know the Mood of each scene – each chapter – as well as you know your Main Character.

The Power Of Pace

Pace is another, often ignored, element in teaching Fiction; and like Mood, Pace keeps your Reader *'with you.'* Pace is Action-Related; but Pace and Action are not the same thing. A kiss is Action; but the Pace of the Action of kissing can range from slow and tender to fiercely fervent.

There are times when the Pace of Action in your book should be momentarily relaxed: your Character may be lazily stretched out in a canvas hammock that swings slowly back and forth, generating a leisurely, easy Pace.

Suddenly, your Character is confronted by an angry maniacal neighbor who waves a hatchet and threatens to kill your Character for some ongoing infraction. Instantly, the Pace picks up. Your Character struggles out of the swinging hammock just as the hatchet slices the canvas hammock in half. Now a chase ensues, changing the Pace into fast, suspenseful Action.

Pace and Mood can work hand-in-hand to change not only the Pace of the Action, but also the *feeling* of a Mood.

The Power Of Variety

Typically, variety is not listed as an element in Fiction writing; but I consider it an element of its own – and vital! Variety combines all the other elements into one overall element of making your writing compelling.

Have you ever put down a book because it seemed to be going nowhere; or flipped through it to skip over the 'slow' parts to find more interesting (active) parts of the book? If not, I will bet you have done that with a television movie – which gives us the term of 'surfing the airwaves with a remote control.'

Action, Pace, Mood, Setting, and Characters will all die on too many pages of sameness. Rarely should any Action, Pace, Mood, or Setting remain the same very long. Variety is needed.

Begin almost EVERY CHAPTER or at least EVERY OTHER CHAPTER with:
- A change of Setting
- A change of Mood
- A change of Pace
- A change of Action

Yes, there are times when the Mood and Action of one chapter runs for a couple of chapters; but longer than that can bore. Changing these four provides Variety and stimulates the Situation – which prompts your reader to ask the all important question... "What happens next?"

Chapter 28

Page-Turning
Anticipation

When your reader looks forward to 'what happens next'
in your book, you have a page-turner. – Ginie Sayles

There are specific techniques to keep your reader asking "What happens next?"

Opening and Closing a chapter can help keep the momentum. There is no exact 'right' way or 'wrong' way to open or close a chapter.

But in order to 'work,' Chapter Closings and Openings should be:

- Relevant – a continuation of the natural flow of the story.
- Move the story forward.

Opening A Chapter: The first sentence of a chapter can invite "what happens next..."

1. Begin a chapter with your Character in the **middle of a serious problem**:
   - *"Take your hands off my wife!"*
   - *(from **Her Secret Life** – by Ginie Sayles)*

2. Begin a chapter with **anticipation**:

A crash of thunder woke her. Kytra glanced out the window and, in a flash of lightning, saw Ransom standing on the edge of the cliff in a violent rainstorm. He stood naked, his muscular legs apart and arms outstretched, his head thrown back, receiving the rain fully onto his face and over his body.

His hair clung in a slick, yellow streak down his back. His wet body glistened outlines of his muscles in brief light flashes as a swirling black firmament roared around him.

*(from **Her Secret Life** – by Ginie Sayles)*

3. Begin a chapter with **foreshadowing**:

It was harder to rewind the string that day. The kite tugged, resisting. It longed, instead, to catch a fresh blazing current from the sun that promised to sweep it higher than it had gone before.

Kytra felt it, too, from where she stood. A warm blast of air breathed around her neck, her face, her ears, rippling loose strands of her black hair in waves over her eyes and back again. The sun's hot breeze teased her hairline in kisses that took her breath away. ...And then she saw him.

*– (from **Her Secret Life** – by Ginie Sayles)*

Closing A Chapter: Closing a chapter should fulfill the energy of the chapter. At the same time, vary the ending of each chapter to keep a satisfying flow of "What happens next?"

1. End a chapter with **mild suggestion and curiosity**:

But then, all her promises to her husband were meant to be broken.

*(from **Her Secret Life** – by Ginie Sayles)*

240

2. End a chapter with **suspense**:

> *They were interrupted by a loud male voice in the*
> *backyard, gruffly shouting a command, "Come out with*
> *your hands up! You can't escape! The house is complete-*
> *ly surrounded!"*

*(from **Her Secret Life** – by Ginie Sayles)*

3. End a chapter with a **satisfying close of a scene**:

> *The ketch dipped into the water and then rose, then*
> *dipped, then rose in the smooth rhythm of the sea.*
> *Kytra stood on deck, welcoming the cold salt spray in*
> *her face, welcoming dim warmth from the frozen ball of*
> *winter sun.*

*(from **Her Secret Life** – by Ginie Sayles)*

Your goal is to **vary** not only the **chapters,** but **also VARY** the **openings and closings of each chapter** to keep your reader turning the pages to find out what happens next.

Writing Dialogue
Clear Attributions

He said, she said, or who said? Be sure your reader knows. – Ginie Sayles

I once had a professor who insisted we always write 'said' or an equivalent word – i.e. asked, replied, et cetera – to indicate which Character is speaking. He often emphasized that we must never follow a dialogue with 'smiled,' such as "What are you doing?" He smiled. My professor insisted that it is impossible for a Character to 'smile' the dialogue.

Whereas that may be literally true; it is just as true that a person can say something and then smile and you still know the person made the comment.

However, as a student who wanted to pass the course, I wrote the way he said to write while I was in his fiction writing class.

But bestselling fiction writers today have realized they do not have to pepper every dialogue with 'said' to identify who is speaking. It is mentally tiresome for both the writer and the reader.

Let's give credit to readers for intelligence and for being able to deduce who is speaking if the dialogue is written in a context that indicates the speaker. If so, you do not have to use 'said' ad nauseum.

For Example:

"This is my favorite time of day," she **said** (use it once to set the conversation in motion)

"Mine, too." His brown eyes scanned the sunset.

"Do you live here?" It was easy to talk to him, as if he were an old friend.

"I have a house here" He shrugged slightly, "but I am only here about once a month. What about you?"

"This is my first visit."

"And...will you be here tomorrow?"

"Yes."

"I am having coffee and croissants at the sidewalk café across the street at ten o'clock tomorrow morning. Is it all right if I ask you to join me?"

"Coffee and croissants seem pretty harmless." She flashed a smile and then looked at her watch. "I have to go now. See you in the morning."

"At ten?"

"At ten."

As you read through this snippet of dialogue, you did not need 'he said,' and 'she said' after every comment each Character made to know who was talking.

Do be sure you describe an action from time to time, after a Character speaks, that will identify who is talking and also keeps the dialogue and action flowing together smoothly.

Let's read the example again with 'said' or its equivalent attribution:

"This is my favorite time of day," she **said**.

*"Mine, too." He **said**. His brown eyes scanned the sunset.*

*"Do you live here?" she **asked**. It was easy to talk to him, as if he were an old friend.*

*"I have a house here." He **said** and shrugged slightly, "but I am only here about once a month. What about you?"*

*"This is my first visit." She **said**.*

*"Will you be here tomorrow?" He **asked**.*

*"Yes," she **said**.*

*"I am having coffee and croissants at the sidewalk café across the street at ten tomorrow morning. Is it all right if I ask you to join me?" He **asked**.*

*"Coffee and croissants seem pretty harmless." She **said** and flashed a smile. Then she looked at her watch and **said**, "I have to go now. See you in the morning."*

*"At ten?" He **asked**.*

*"At ten." She **said**.*

As you can see, it works just fine both ways; and you can write with specific attribution if you like. However, it works just as well and sometimes better to use a small Action or expression as an attribution, instead of said. Too, if there are only two people talking, it is pretty clear that the next response is from the other person.

However, if you have a third person – or even more than that; you will want clear attribution either by behavior of the person speaking; or by using 'said' or its equivalent.

Example:

At that moment, Julie waved at them. "I see you have made a new friend. Invite him to my party tonight."

- Or –

*At that moment, Julie waved at them and **called**, "I see you have made a new friend. Invite him to my party tonight."*

Either method of attribution is fine. As long as it is clear who is talking, you can write dialogue either way.

Punctuation also Indicates Who Is Speaking

Rule 1: Enclose all dialogue by each Character in quotes
(" ").
*"is the mark to **Open a Quote**.*
*" is the mark to **Close a Quote**.*

Rule 2: If you change paragraphs while a Character is talking, *do NOT close any sentence or paragraph with quotes until
the dialogue spoken by that particular Character is complete.*

For example:

Julie said, **"I** *(*open quote with first word*) was going to the
store to buy groceries and paper goods. (*no end quote because
she is not finished talking; however, she is changing topic*)*
"Did (open quote with first word of new paragraph) *I tell
you that Joey called me?* "(close quote because she is now finished speaking.)

It reads like this:

Julie said, **"I** *was going to the store to buy groceries and
paper goods.*
"Did *I tell you that Joey called me?"*

Further explanation: Notice that her first sentence begins
with a quote mark ("I) but there is no quote mark at the end of
that sentence. Why? Because she is not finished talking.
The next sentence she is still talking but because it is another paragraph, it also begins with an open quote (*"Did*). When she
finishes talking, her dialogue is closed with an end quote (*shop-
ping."*).

Rule 3: If a Character's dialogue is interrupted with an attribution or a description, then separate the first part with both open and closed quotes and commas.

"I am going to the store," Julie said as she unlocked the door, "to buy groceries and several paper goods."

Rule 4: EVERY TIME YOU **CHANGE WHO IS TALK-ING**, MAKE A SEPARATE PARAGRAPH WITH QUOTES TO ENCLOSE THE DIALOGUE OF THE NEXT SPEAKER.

"This is my favorite time of day," she said.
"Mine, too." His brown eyes scanned the sunset.

NEVER, ever combine the conversation of one Character with the other in the same paragraph. It is confusing. Each Character gets a new paragraph each time he/she speaks.

Chapter

30

Author's Voice

*How do **you** tell a story? – Ginie Sayles*

Students often ask how they can develop a 'Voice' in writing. I suggest that you not develop your Author's Voice, but that you *discover* your Author's Voice in your writing. When you write one complete manuscript you still may not yet 'hear' your Author's Voice. You know how your story goes, but you may have no inkling of 'your Author's Voice,' yet.

However, if you start writing a second manuscript – about half-way through it, you will begin to hear your distinctive flow of writing – your Author's Voice – your writing style.

What is Author's Voice? ***Author's Voice is a person's manner of telling a story***. Your Author's Voice is the way *you* tell a story in writing, the way your writing 'sounds' to the reader's inner ear. Because you are also a reader of your work, you will eventually be able to 'hear' your unique voice, too.

When I worked in Public Relations for Houston Grand Opera, I also worked closely with the prestigious advertising firm, Ogilvy & Mather, who designed ads for the Opera.

Through Mike Turner, President of the Houston Ogilvy & Mather office and also President of the Opera Board, I met a very talented and hard-working songwriter named Ken Sutherland, who wrote songs for some of Ogilvy & Mather's ad campaigns.

As a favor to me, Mike put us in touch with each other because I had written 16 songs at the time and I did not know if I wanted to seriously pursue songwriting and what it would entail. Ken and I got together to see if we might want to collaborate. Both our lives were in flux – job changes, moving to different cities – so it never got off the ground; but we had mutual respect for our musical interests during that brief interaction.

About three years later, I visited a new community being developed called The Woodlands, Texas, which is north of Houston. Watching their promotional film, I became aware of the film's background music – and even though I had never heard this particular music before, there was an identifiable resonance to it – a fingerprint, a style – in the sound.

When the film ended, I went to the film projection booth.

"Excuse me," I said to the man working inside the projection booth, "Can you tell me if the music in the film was composed by Ken Sutherland?"

The projectionist was surprised. "Why, yes it was. How did you know?"

"I recognized his style," I said, "It sounds like something Ken would compose."

It turned out the projectionist was a musician, himself, and he knew Ken Sutherland and about the making of the film.

My point is, I could recognize an underlying unique style in the music that identified it as having been written by Ken Sutherland – who, incidentally, went on to write movie scores, as well as music for top recording artists – plus Ken also won many music awards.

An Author's Voice is the same way. When you tell a *story the way you see it in your head, the way you feel the story*, your writing reveals your unique attitude, your specific tone.

Each author has his/her own way of "talking in writing" that is the author's literary 'fingerprint' or 'Author's Voice.'

I urge you to flow with your feelings as you write and to see what you discover about yourself as a writer.

The Gift Of You

You are a special talent, overflowing with uniqueness. You bring a magnificent originality to your work. You are a gift to Life, to people, and to your own writing. Keep it that way. Through your writing, discover and reveal the gift of you.

As a new writer, if you take a writing class or workshop, be alert as to whether or not a particular style of writing is considered 'the right way to write.'

If a workshop concentrates on telling you what you do 'wrong,' the instructors may be working from what they consider wrong according to how they, themselves, write – or according to the school of thought they embrace. But the end result can be confusion and loss of confidence …maybe giving up. If so, the workshop is wrong, not you.

There are many writing workshops that end up producing writers who all write alike, which diminishes the value of the writers that such schools produce.

If a writing workshop embraces a particular school of thought about writing – let's say Earnest Hemingway's writing – it may teach a Hemingway style with limited description and end up producing 'Hemingway Knock-Offs' who have no more literary value than Gucci Knock-Offs do in high fashion. Hemingway was primarily of value as a writer for his originality.

Certainly, there are many good workshops and I include mine in that category. Good workshops strive to find and encourage the sacred spark of originality in a writer. A workshop is good if the workshop does not teach you a *specific* way to write. Above all, do not let one school of thought change your natural inclination.

Most people who sign up for writing workshops are adults who know how to put sentences and paragraphs together. They just lack confidence; or they do not know what their strengths are.

It is more important for **each writer to understand what he/she is doing that '*works*' – that '*connects' with a reader* and**

what is effectively *'unique'* about the writing – which allows a writer to emerge with his/her originality and voice intact. Writers develop faster from learning what they do *'right.'*

BE ORIGINAL WITHOUT 'TRYING' TO BE – and the only way you can truthfully be original – is to be you in words. You may not know exactly what that means, yet; but just keep writing and you will.

Yes, there are authors who have 'contrived' a unique sounding voice and it can work up to a certain extent; but even then, there are echoes throughout the writing of the writer's original creativity. If a writer surrenders to his/her own writing, it will flow in a true Author's Voice and with motivated Passion.

Some beginning writers complain that if they read a particular author, they end up writing in the style of that author.

Do not worry about that. If you find yourself writing in the style of a writer you just read, I assure you, that as you get deeper and deeper into your writing, and your mind is focused on the storyline inside your head, that you will instinctively begin switching into your true originality, without thinking about it. Then as you re-read the early parts that you wrote in another author's style, you will begin editing it to the way you now feel and see your story – suddenly being true to your emerging voice.

Your Author's Voice also includes your writing STYLE – perhaps florid or sparse. If there is change in your voice or style, let it EVOLVE naturally. Sometimes a particular period in writing is like an artist's particular period in painting or sculpting: it evolves but it does not copy; and beneath the new emerging expression lies the identifying undertones of the writer's unique self. The gift of you in this world.

Treasure it.

Chapter 31

IF
You Get Stuck
– Troubleshooting Fiction

*Use the elements of fiction and a few tricks to get
'unstuck.' – Ginie Sayles*

Some people claim they have writer's block when the truth is, the writer is simply stuck – meaning he or she does not know what to do next in their story.

Getting stuck can be narrowed down to something as simple as having written too long on one idea, or of finding yourself bored and not knowing what to do about it. Remember, if your writing bores you, it will bore your readers.

Using all the elements (tools) we discussed in the previous chapter, you can learn how to get unstuck. A reader craves variety of experience and feeling. The cliché that variety is the spice of life can well read "variety is the spice of writing." The next time you feel stuck, try one of the following tools and elements and use them as a lever to get you going again:

- Interrupt Whatever Is Going On
- Introduce A New Problem
- Change Mood

- Change Pace
- Resolve A Problem
- Create 'Time Constraints' For Your Character
- Work On A Different Part Of The Book Altogether/ Come Back Later And Connect This Part You Are Leaving For Awhile - Or Eliminate It Altogether Later
- Use Your Timer To Find Out What The Problem Is
- Just Write
- Yes, But…

Interrupt Whatever Is Going On

"Suddenly, there was a loud crash in the next room" is an example of shifting out of a 'dead moment' in your chapter. "And what happened next?" is the question in your reader's mind – and that is exactly what you want your reader to ask.

The loud crash immediately perks up the reader's interest and now your job is to take your reader into another Action with your Characters – move them out of the dead spot and into vitality again.

Introduce A New Problem

Your Character is in the middle of one problem that has dragged on a bit – so you must heighten the suspense by adding a new problem to the existing one.

For example, your hero has spent the last several pages feeling his way through a dark room. The reader will get bored with much more; so now, something else needs to go wrong. He hears someone coming and slips inside a closet – and as he eases it shut, the lock clicks and he is trapped inside. You can even make it more intense if he discovers a dead body, or blood, or a snake – or someone else hiding inside. Your reader is asking "What happened next?"

And you may be asking yourself the same question because you are in the process of figuring it out – which keeps you interested in what you will create to 'happen next.'

Rework Or Change Mood

One of the easiest and most masterful ways to get unstuck is simply to change the Mood of your story. One way to do that is to note the Mood of the chapter that is stuck.

Is the Mood the same as the previous chapter?

And is the Mood the same as the one previous to that?

If so, change the Mood of this chapter` altogether. Switch to a different Setting or have another Character change the draggy Mood.

For example, your two main Characters have been bogged down in trying to resolve a personal conflict between them with ongoing angst. The door opens and in runs their giggling five-year-old daughter, eager to show them a baby kitten she found among the first bloom of spring daisies. The Mood switches to the happiness of their daughter, cuddliness of a baby kitten, refreshing spring flowers.

Go with that for a few paragraphs…let there be a meaning that the quarreling couple draws from it – perhaps the pettiness of their fighting.

Then, in the very next chapter – COMPLETELY CHANGE FROM THE CURRENT MOOD INTO A MOOD NOT USED BEFORE OR NOT RECENTLY USED IN YOUR BOOK.

Mood is such a wonderful tool to keep your reader interested, that I suggest you change Mood at least every other chapter, preferably every chapter, and even at times within a chapter – although you do not want your chapter to lose cohesiveness by jumping from Mood to Mood – so it should only be occasionally within a chapter, if needed to get unstuck.

Rework Or Change Pace

Related to Mood change is the change of Pace to get you unstuck or to prevent getting stuck. As discussed in the previous chapter, Pace is Action-related. The dragginess of a chapter can liven up very quickly if the Action changes – an unexpected kiss, a fistfight, a chase, a near drowning, a slap, a woman tossing her glass of wine in a man's face.

Conversely, if there has been a lot of rapid-fire Action, change the Pace with an absolute slow-down. *He fell exhausted onto wet moss near the creek bed. Hours passed in a drowsy haze, filled with nothing more than cool breezes that slowly dried the perspiration on his shirt and body. He drifted in and out of sleep to a soft lullaby of cooing doves overhead.* Now, you are ready to change Pace again – either easing out of this tranquil state or suddenly having to leave.

When you feel stuck, it is likely you have stayed too long on one idea, Mood, or Pace. You need Variety of Action and Mood.

Resolve A Subplot Problem

Maybe you are stuck because one of the Subplot problems confronting your hero has dragged on too long. You can either introduce a new complication to the problem, as previously mentioned; or you can resolve a current Subplot problem, only to have your Character discover yet another problem in the resolution. Or it may be time to resolve this issue satisfactorily and move into a new level of the story.

For example, amid bigger issues of your Character's life, he at least learns the name of his father or that his true love has returned…one of the smaller but important issues (subplot) in his life that has a strong measure of satisfaction and perhaps inspires him as he moves on to resolve the big issue or Main Problem (Plot) of the book.

Time Is Running Out – Create 'Time Constraints' For Your Character

In Cinderella, the final stroke of midnight is the moment she loses her magic. In Action movies, a ticking time bomb may explode if the main Character does not figure out how to diffuse it. Fear of getting caught, time running out, racing against time add juice to your story.

Time Constraint – a deadline, a ticking bomb or the stroke of midnight, or a moment when it will be too late to create anticipation and suspense. Time Constraints are a marvelous trick of writing that keeps readers turning your pages.

Work On A Completely Different Part Of Your Book

Sometimes, you have done all you can do FOR THE MOMENT on a part of the book. Your Creative Mind wants to invoke new ideas in other scenes and come back to this later. That's okay. Do that.

A Ginie Sayles Rule is to always, always, *always work on whatever interests you most at the moment and you will never run out of motivation.*

One day as I dutifully started the next logical chapter in *Her Secret Life*, I kept having flashes of a scene that were completely unrelated to the chapter before me. It was a love scene on a cliff in the middle of a violent thunderstorm.

After a few false starts with my current chapter, I simply skipped down a few pages and started writing the scene that was on my mind at the moment. There were no false starts at all. It flowed like lava from start to finish with only a few pauses. It is one of the best scenes in the book and my agent loved it.

Come Back Later And Connect It – Or Eliminate It

Once I had the particular scene above out of my system, I found it had unplugged the other chapter – and I could see how this chapter could set in motion the dissatisfaction of my heroine's life. The love scene ended up being many chapters later, but now I was able to weave together all the ones before it into the events that led up to it.

Sometimes, when I skip ahead in my writing and come back to a chapter, I end up eliminating the chapter I was working on because it did not work, at all – and I had to get a new vision of it by working on another chapter in order to see that it would not work.

At other times, I come back and see what I need to do clearer than ever.

Skipping around is a perfectly legitimate way to write – and then all you have to do is to connect the various chapters together with transitional chapters – occasionally eliminating or elaborating on those you wrote. This is simply the writing process – liberate yourself to 'go where you want to go that day with your novel.'

Set Your Timer And Find Out What Your Problem Is

Your Timer can be a best friend for getting you unstuck. If you feel stuck, get a sheet of paper, and title it "Possible Solutions." Set your Timer for 10 minutes. As your Timer ticks down, list as many possible solutions to the problem as you can. If your Timer goes off and you have ideas bubbling out of you, just keep writing.

Write any problem at the top of a page, set your Timer for 5 or 10 minutes, and then list as many solutions as possible, without analyzing or thinking about it before your Timer goes off.

You can even take one of the items from your list, use it as a title at the top of another sheet of blank paper, set your Timer, and list everything that comes to your mind about that item.

If you are writing fiction and having trouble with a particular Character; you can write the name of a different Character in your story at the top of a blank page, set your Timer for 10 minutes and ask the Character what he/she thinks about your problem Character. Start your Timer and write down what you think that Character would say is the problem.

For example, in *Goldilocks And The Three Bears*, I might ask the butterfly that led Goldilocks into the forest to tell me what made Goldilocks such a sucker to follow the butterfly and get lost. Then, writing as fast as I can, the butterfly might tell me she was unhappy in school and looking for an excuse to leave – or that she was hoping her parents cared enough about her to come find her. Putting yourself into the mind of one of your Characters is often the answer.

You can do this with several other Characters, too.

Just Write

Some writers find that if they just write something…anything…it helps them get unstuck. I agree that just writing something helps – but I think if you write on some part of your project – maybe even just an analysis of your feelings about it – you are less likely to become distracted. You can set your Timer for 20 minutes and write until your Timer goes off. Re-set it another 20 minutes – and then another. Bite-sized pieces get it done.

Yes, But…

If you think you have tried these techniques but you still are not getting anywhere, and you find yourself saying or thinking, "None of it helps" or "Well, yes, but…"and then launch into a new problem; then you need to ask yourself if you really have Passion for your project.

Psychology tells us that when a person thinks or says "yes, but…" to every solution offered; that person does not want a solution. The person only wants a problem, something to complain about, an excuse not to finish.

Be sure you have Passion for your work; and if so, the troubleshooting techniques will work. If not, then you do not really want a solution because you do not really want to write the project at all.

New solution? Find a project you truly love and all the elements will be solutions and you will finish with no excuses.

Review This Important Process: *Write In Layers*

Remember, the first question to ask yourself as you open a chapter is "What is the **Situation**?" Then choose a Setting – time and place – in which the Situation will unravel. *The Situation should be related to the Plot* (which is the Main Problem the Main Character must solve by the end of the book) – and you will use *all* the previously defined elements (tools) to write the chapter.

Your main goal is to get the story down with all the major parts in place. Once you start your book, write – without edits – until you are finished, even if you do not write in order. However, if you find yourself re-reading what you have written before finishing; at least limit your edits in a chapter to no more than twice as you work through your First Draft. Then add more **layers that bring your book to life!** Writing in layers works! And it works like this:

1. **Layer 1 – Your First Draft Layer** – your first draft is your basic story.
2. **Layer 2 – Your Mental Paintbrush Laye**r– Read your first draft and paint a layer of description into your Character, Setting, Situation and so on, in each chapter. This is part of Creative editing.
3. **Layer 3 – Your Sensory Layer** – be sure you have added all 5 senses in each chapter. This is part of Creative editing.

4. **Layer 4 – Your Final Editing Layer** – add to – and then take away whatever is not needed. *Do this several times.*

When you write in layers, your writing becomes better and better.

Chapter 32

Children's
And Teenage Fiction

Make It Fun! Do Not Overly Moralize. – Ginie Sayles

Children's books can be liberating for both you – as the author – and the child who will either read the story or listen to it being read. Everything depends on the "Appropriateness" of several factors in the development of a child for a child to enjoy your book.

A child MUST identify with the storybook. Consider the following guidelines:

- Vocabulary understanding for a child's age
- Age-appropriate topics
- Length that fits the interest-span for the child's age
- Colorful, exaggerated pictures
- Interactive projects for a child
- Help a child...
  - o Understand a current situation in his/her life
  - o Express his/her feelings or ideas
  - o Feel pride in his/her culture or heritage
  - o Discover his/her uniqueness – Like himself/herself – Raise self-esteem
  - o Enjoy life

- Empower a child to make choices
- More entertainment than morality

Age-Appropriate Vocabulary

I am also certified in reading, which includes the development of reading skills. A child will pay more attention to words the child understands. And, children – like the rest of us – learn by building new information onto what they already know.

Most University bookstores have textbooks for college students who are majoring in elementary education or receiving certification to be a reading teacher. These books can identify vocabulary levels of an average child at a certain age.

You will know to include those words often in your children's book, while *adding only a few new words* that can be made clear by the context of the word, perhaps a picture of what it represents, an explanation of it, and the use of it several times in context. This builds a child's vocabulary but does not overwhelm the child with so many new vocabulary words that the child loses interest or confidence.

Most three year olds have a spoken vocabulary of about three hundred to five hundred words; and a clear understanding of five hundred words that are spoken to them. This increases several hundred-fold each year.

A sample of a child's early reading vocabulary includes:

Early Nouns

Mother	Father	Sister	Brother
Dog	Cat	Bird	House
Floor	Door	Wall	Window
Chair	Table	Bed	Roof
Car	Hill	Water	Milk
Cup	Duck	Cow	Easter
Christmas	Hanukkah	Bunny	Cookie
Santa Claus	Doll	Dinner	Farmer
Game	Gift	Girl	Boy

| Family | Bread | Clown | Fairy |
| Chicken | Fish | Tree | Flower. |

Early Verbs

Go	Stop	Stay	Laugh
Cry	Run	Walk	Jump
Give	Take	See	Hit
Knock	Sit	Stand	Pick
Kiss	Hug	Sleep	Like

Early Adjectives:

Happy	Sad	Afraid	Glad
Good	Bad	Hungry	Sleepy
Pretty	Old	New	Red

As you can see, small children first learn their most intimate environment of home and family nouns, basic action verbs, and simple feelings and descriptions in adjectives.

You must think in a child's categories of thinking and of a child's environment as it changes. For instance, small children may – or may not – read the following words, yet; but they usually understand them quite well: cell phone, television/TV, story, CD, DVD, ipod, music, video game.

Age-Appropriate Topics

Children – like the rest of us – also favor topics that interest their peer-groups. Toys, games, and books are most effective if they appeal to the common interest of that age level.

For example, if you want to write about cars, a story about building hot-rods will not be as interesting to most six year olds as a story about a day at a theme park when a child gets to ride a bumper car.

And, of course, you already know that children have some variation in their development and that can even be the subject in a story.

Attention-Span Appropriate

The younger the child, the shorter the child's attention-span, so you want to grab the child's attention with action and a topic that you know fits the child's interest, and with vocabulary the child understands.

With all that working together for you, you can introduce a new word or two and repeat it several times – but have the outcome of the story to be very short if the child is very young, and slightly longer if the child is older or in early grade school.

Yes, children grow their attention spans, their vocabularies, and their understanding by hearing day-to-day language of their parents; but for pure enjoyment and better comprehension, a child will not tune-out if you keep your story short, simple, to-the-point and fun.

Respect the attention of the child, instead of constantly saying, "Are you paying attention to me?" The kid is not deliberately losing interest; the story is too long for his/her attention span. Respect it and children will love your books.

Colorful, Exaggerated Pictures

Remember that pictures are the first language a child learns to read by looking at it and figuring out what is going on. Colorful pictures bring a child's storybook to life and reinforce the story itself.

Before I could read, I looked at the pictures of Robert Lewis Stevenson's book, *A Child's Garden Of Verse* – and I could identify with it. I looked at the color picture of a swing and imagined myself in the swing as my mother read his poem that began:

"How do you like to go up in a swing,

Up in the air so blue?
Oh, I do think it the pleasantest thing
Ever a child can do!"

Because the poetry book had a picture of a swing and words I could fully understand as my mother read it aloud – even though I could not yet read the words – the poem was appropriate for my age in interest, understanding, and vocabulary.

As you can well imagine, I paid such sharp attention to it that even though I could not yet read, I memorized the words, looked at the picture that I could certainly recognize – and, yes, you are right – soon, as I soared high in a swing at the park, I was chanting the words as I went higher and higher, loving the wind on my face and in my hair. That was a children's book that spoke to me and that I love to this day. It began with seeing pictures and hearing words I could understand and enjoy.

If you are not only a good spinner of children's yarns but if you or your mate or a member of your family has a hint of artistic talent in sketches, water-color or other painting techniques – lucky, lucky you! As long as you can work together well, it is a fun project made in heaven. If it is just you doing both, it is still a project made in heaven. You can fully enjoy the double impact of words and pictures that appeal so to children and win them over to your books.

Otherwise, you may have to commission an artist. If you do that, be sure the artist is willing to assign the copyright to you before you undertake the work – and get it in writing! Have an attorney draw up a release that this is a work for hire and that all copyrights of the work are irrevocably assigned to you and the artist can never claim he/she did not understand. I am not a lawyer, which is the reason I am only giving suggestions that you consider with your attorney.

A Child's Interaction With Your Book

Interactive play within your book helps a child relate to your book. If you have a coloring section in your book, a child colors the easy Action in the story and then tells Mom or Dad or caretaker what is happening in the scene and in the story. The child's new language is reinforced in the child's memory.

There can also be a Mimic page – in which the child pretends to be the hero or Action figure of the story and acts out certain parts. Be sure it is a story that, if acted out, will not be dangerous to a child.

Any sort of interactive play based on your book makes it more fun and special – just keep it shorter than you think it needs to be.

Asking the child to tell the story – or even to elaborate on the story – what the child thinks happened next – can build the imaginative capability of the child.

Another wonderful point to this project is that it takes the control out of your hands as the author and puts it into a child's hands – giving the child more control over the story – as a little co-author which makes the story more meaningful to the child and makes you more fun as a writer of children's books.

Help A Child...

Children's books are a marvelous way to help meet some needs of children and in a way they can comprehend on their own level of immediate concern or interest.

For example, your children's book can help a child:

- **Enjoy life**. Perhaps at the top of the list for the benefit of any book, including children's books, is pure, simple enjoyment. Books can make life more enjoyable for any reader and certainly we want that for a child.

- **Understand a current Situation in his/her life.** When my daughter was three years old, I almost died from a new birth control method called an intrauterine device. I was in the hospital recovering from it for most of the summer. My husband at that time was a physician who had been drafted into the Army and he was overseas; so my daughter and I lived alone in San Antonio, Texas.

I will forever love my dear friends, Susie McGee, Sarah Dennis, Voncil Barnhill, and Diane Henneke for their steadfast support and help in getting me to the hospital, contacting my parents, and taking care of my little daughter until my parents could arrive from West Texas.

After a few weeks in Intensive Care, I was finally allowed to have a nurse take me downstairs in a wheelchair to visit my daughter and parents. When I saw my little girl, I saw worried concern in her face and noted her anxiety when visiting time was over. I had another month to stay in the hospital and I did not know how to explain it to her.

Perhaps it was Divine inspiration, but I came up with a children's story on the spot – short, simple, and to-the-point. "Once upon a time (not too original – but at least she knew it was a story), there was a little girl named Kae whose mother had to go to the hospital. "Where is my mommy going?" little Kae wondered. "Why can't I go, too?" and "When will my mommy be back?"

My daughter instantly related to the story. She looked up and said, "Mommy, you had to go to the hospital, too." And as the story of little Kae answered each of the questions, she looked up at me with comprehension and nodded. Sometimes she would elaborate, "And did Kae's granddaddy come get her?"

When I ended the story with Kae's mother returning home , she asked, "When will you come home, Mommy?"

I took sheets of paper and drew a series of smiley faces. Each sheet of paper had a big number on it. The last one had two great big smiley faces.

I put the paper in order and told my daughter that when she got out of bed each morning she could throw away the paper for the day before and look at the next one. And that when she got to the last one with two smiley faces, I would be coming home that day.

With Mother's help, my daughter did exactly that and when she got to the last one, Mother had her carry it with her when they came to the hospital to pick me up.

I have always felt – and so did my parents – that the story and the interactive slips of paper helped my daughter to partly understand and to deal with the scary situation of Mommy going away to the hospital.

- **Express his/her feelings or ideas.** Children have feelings they may not understand. As infants, the only language they have is a cry when they are wet, hungry, bored, have a headache that we will never know they have; but because they are crying we know something is wrong – we just don't know what. They also laugh or smile or reach for something of interest. That is pretty limited language – but it is all they have.

  As they grow from infants to children, they learn to understand some words and to communicate a little bit – often by acting out. Again, to use my own situation, when I was in college and my daughter was about one and a half – toddling – she did not like my attention being on my studies, so she toddled to the coffee table where my books were stacked and shoved them all onto the floor.

  Acting out her displeasure was her language at that time – and it taught me to create more quality time with her before studying and to have new games for her to play alone while I studied. It also taught me to stack my books on the kitchen table where they were out of her reach!

  As children get older and relate to stories they are told, the stories can often be used to elicit feelings which they may not understand. The story I told my daughter when I was in the hospital is an example of not only helping her understand the situation she and

I both experienced; but it also allowed her to express her feelings and ask questions through "Kae" the main character.

Sometimes, such stories can help children express ideas about how a problem can be solved. Reading a children's book is not just a story, in those cases. Such books are a launching point for asking the child what the hero in the story should do.

It stimulates their problem-solving thinking – and gives both the adult and child a chance to interact about various choices and finding the best one.

- **Discover his/her uniqueness/Like Himself**. I am fond of children's books that have a "who am I?" theme. Posing questions to a child about his/her likes and dislikes, interests and activities that reinforce the right of a child to have choices different from others and to feel pride in individuality of choices, of likes and dislikes and feeling pride and happiness in his/her uniqueness. Such a children's book can give a child new confidence and strength of self, and a feeling that he/she is good, okay, and completely likable.

- **Empower A Child To Make Choices**. Children's stories that develop situations in which the child makes choices or sees how the story's hero makes choices can help strengthen discernment and realize the power of making appropriate choices for the child.

If possible, a good writer of children's books with this motif will not coerce the child in a particular choice as good or bad or right or wrong but enable the child to reason the probable consequences for him/her.

Of course, a very small child needs small choices that are part of his/her everyday life, such as choosing a red ball or a blue ball.

More Enchantment Than Moralist

Having said all of the above on the "mission" of children's books; the most valuable key for the child's enjoyment of books is *fun*.

When my grandson, Grant Scott, was small, I told a story to him. When I finished, he said, "And so the moral of the story is...??"

Realizing he had probably been hearing stories that were "overly moralistic or overly preachy," I had the great pleasure of saying, "Well, Grant, there is a point to the story; but there is no *moral* to this story except fun."

His face lit up and he said, "Tell it to me again!"

Morals to a story are fine, of course; but my grandson was happy that he did not have to be burdened with heavy-duty meaning and could just enjoy the fun of the story.

The fabulously successful *Harry Potter* books should teach us all that children love unfettered imagination. Yes, the storyline included triumph over a foe. And it was fun, too.

Harry Potter is a child's Science Fiction book. It is no different from Superman or Santa Claus or the Easter Bunny or Tom and Jerry cartoons where the cat and mouse blow up each other with dynamite and no one protests that it is teaching immorality!

Yes, children should be told that books such as *Harry Potter* are fantasy, just as the imaginative ploys of cartoons and other make-believe heroes are not true life, just fun fantasy.

Entertainment, itself, is its own reward. *Entertainment is enchantment in the unlimited fun of a finely-told story.*

Teenage Fiction

Teenagers today are far more sophisticated in many ways than earlier generations of teenage readers. They like to read about teenagers dealing with issues that they are dealing with in their teenage worlds, too.

As an author, though, you may want to be selective about the issues you choose in order to tread on safe ground. Alcohol, tobacco, and drugs are definitely prominent issues in the lives of teenagers; but teen readers will tune-out anything that borders on lecturing.

So what are the so-called 'safe' issues that will be compelling to teenager readers? Every teenager can relate to issues concerning:

- Self-esteem
- Popularity – fitting in
- Best friends – a true blue or a betrayal
- Self-consciousness – shy
- Teachers – a favorite, a least favorite
- Grades – easiest classes, ones struggling through
- Parents – not evil; but not always understanding
- Getting grounded – maybe for a real reason, maybe for something not warranted
- Siblings – maybe close or a rivalry
- First love – maybe a fantasy out-of-reach person; or a next-door neighbor or classmate– who may end up being the right person; or may be the wrong person who seems right long enough to cause problems.
- First love rival – may end up being best friends; or if not, the hero triumphs.
- First kiss – sweet, awkward, tender
- First date – nervous or casual friends
- Embarrassing moment
- Wanting to impress someone
- Sports – a jock or not a jock
- Weight issues – too skinny, overweight (or thinks so) and how it is handled
- Physical development issues – small breasted, late bloomer
- Extra-curricular activities – clubs, school float, car wash fund-raiser

- Dressing like the other kids – and any issues related to that
- Jobs, allowance, making extra money, handling money
- The social standing of their families
- Shame about anything
- Pets – the comfort of a special animal friend

Go to the Chapter 23 on Character and go through the in-depth Character questionnaire for your teenage Character.

Be sure to add current fads of iPods, text messaging, cell phones, and earpieces for phones and music. You can venture into the deeper issues of body piercings, tattoos, teenage sex, temptations of tobacco, alcohol and drugs if you want to, but you may face opposition.

I do not tell authors not to do something. I think if you have a strong feeling about it, it is in your hands. If you can find ways for a positive outcome, it may be a stronger book; but, again, the message you want to give is your own.

Chapter 33

Ethnic
Fiction

Add a sparkle of magic to your writing with ethnic fiction. – Ginie Sayles

When I learned that my great-great grandmother, Phana Luan Ratten, was Native American, I looked at her picture that showed her dark haired, dark-eyed beauty dressed, not in tribal attire, but in the clothing of a pioneer woman.

In the 1800s, she married a man of English descent, who was born in North Carolina. He painted houses and signs and fences for a living. They moved around, from Missouri to Kentucky to Tennessee to Oklahoma and finally to Texas, where she died of tuberculosis when she was in her forties.

So often, I have wondered how difficult it must have been for her to live in a time when Native Americans were viewed as terrorists by settlers. No wonder she tried to dress and act and to look as much like the other wives of American settlers as possible. Conquered races of people often feel shame and in Luan's case, her children were taught to deny their heritage.

Today, people jump at the chance to claim they have a Native American heritage in their bloodline. Times change, viewpoints evolve, and increasingly, it is the uniqueness and joy of an ethnic culture that people crave now when reading books.

Most readers have tired of the beaten-down, victimized stereotype of an ethnic character in books and movies. We want ethnic heroes – whose heroic qualities are tied to their great ethnic heritage and not flooded with hate and anger. We want to expand our understanding of the magical effects of an ethnic superstition or religion.

Academy Award winning *Slum Dog Millionaire* that makes heroes out of an Indian (India) ethnic hero; and Amy Tan's *The Joy Luck Club* that lets us experience a fascinating Asian ethnic story.

Perhaps one of the reasons *Fiddler On The Roof* was so popular was because it concentrated on the joy of life and the respect for Jewish traditions in the family of Jews in Russia around the turn of the Twentieth Century; and made the prejudice and persecution an underlying story of their migration not a pronounced theme.

Formality and class consciousness is often associated with the English culture; although Charles Dickens shows us a seamier side of English life and human nature. Some groups – such as Muslim and Jewish – are more faith-based than race-based ethnicities.

Today, ethnic writing– especially if it is authentically yours – can make your writing glitter with originality in an otherwise typical or ho-hum story.

Consider the following ethnic groups to interweave into your writing, as well:

- Indian (India)
- Jewish
- Muslim
- African American
- Caribbean American
- Asian
- Hispanic
- Irish
- Scottish
- English
- Native American
- Alaskan Eskimo

- Native Hawaiians

The cultural practices of each group bring unique beliefs, practices, and values that enrich a writer's palette of color. Perhaps someday I will write a story based on the thin facts I have of my Native American great-great-grandmother's life; just as you may want to write ethnic stories from your heritage – or research an ethnic group and plait it into your own story.

If you do want to write ethnic books, be sure you follow these general guidelines:

- Introduce a fresh perspective.
- Show an evolving image.
- It is okay to include the magical qualities, the handed-down stories, religious strengths.
- If political views are part of the ethnic reality, such as those my great-great-grandmother faced; then make the point clearly, with sympathy, and without apology.
- Be careful dressing your ethnic character in stereotypical garb, unless it is an important part of the character's life and personality.
- Do not pigeonhole your characters with expected typecasts or stripped-down stereotypes.
- The same is true with settings – avoid an overly predictable backdrop.
- Give a clear emotional insight into what it is like to live "in-between" two cultures that may not understand each other or may be vastly different from each other.
- Avoid colloquial speech patterns associated with that ethnic group.
- If ethnicity is part of the Main Problem (Plot), resolve it satisfactorily – do not leave it hanging.
- Show common human threads that are cross-cultural, cross-ethnicity, such as love. And, yes, interracial love/cross-cultural love – sometimes between two unexpected cultures – is an acceptable theme.

Part 3

SPEED SKILLS

Non-Fiction

Chapter

34

Why
Write Non-Fiction?

*Establishing yourself as an expert in your field with a
non-fiction book can lead to more money.*
– Ginie Sayles

Pretend you have just entered a new career with dreams of success. Without knowing it, you already stand at a crossroad. You can either work diligently for twenty years and become recognized as an expert in your field; or you can write a small non-fiction book and be an instant expert in your field!

A number of years ago, a young Houston, Texas stockbroker saw me on a national television show. During the course of the interview, it was mentioned that I am a former stockbroker.

The young man telephoned me later in Dallas, Texas where my husband and I were living at the time. He explained to me that he gave local investment seminars, which is a typical way stockbrokers drum up business and develop their clientele.

"Do you think I could turn my investment seminar into an investment book?" he asked me.

"Yes, I certainly do," I replied, "and I hope you will do it."

As it turned out, I was not the only person who encouraged him to write his book. He later told me that Tony Robbins, a famous author and speaker, also encouraged him to do so.

A few years later, my husband and I were in a Borders Bookstore in downtown White Plains, New York and I saw the workers unpacking brand new hard cover books and stacking them in the front part of the store.

Immediately, I recognized the title of the book as being the title of the seminar the young man had told me he taught in Houston. His picture was on the cover and he was a cute young man who looked as if he might be in his twenties.

"Look, Sweetheart," I called to my husband, "The kid did it (he was not a kid but because he was such a young broker to be writing a book, that is what I called him)!"

Indeed, he had turned his seminar into a hard cover book (which is the highest royalty writers receive). It was a beautiful book and he was quite a young man to be giving such astute investment advice.

Several years passed and I was a guest on a national daytime talk show on the subject of money. And guess what? This young man was also a guest, in a separate segment of the show. Backstage in the Green Room (that is what rooms are called where guests wait before their appearance), he and I caught up with each other's lives.

Let me tell you how his life had changed – just from writing his non-fiction book. He was no longer a stockbroker in Houston, Texas. He owned his own investment firm in another major city. He and his wife had a second home in another state.

The Crossroad – And A Shortcut To Success

As we talked, catching up on each other, I marveled again at how young he was for the success he had attained.

I thought back to my days as a stockbroker and the admiration I had for a much older gentleman who was very successful and highly esteemed as a stockbroker.

Then I compared him with the young stockbroker who was even more successful.

What made the difference?

- Each man – the older gentleman and the young man – stood at the same crossroad to success on the day they became stockbrokers. They began with the same knowledge of investing.

- The older gentleman chose the usual way of climbing the ladder of success – diligently working hard, day after day *for twenty years* and he was, indeed, successful and recognized as an expert in his field by a small circle of investors.

- But the younger man short-circuited the long route to success by writing a book – and that made him an *'instant expert'* in his field. He was recognized as an expert by a nation-wide circle of investors.

Now, did the young man get rich from his book?

Well, I do not believe he made a fortune in book royalties, even though it sold well.

But yes – as a **'by-product'** of the book, he probably made a lot of money.

This is what I think happened: First, ask yourself, who reads books about investing? Rich people and others in the investment industry are the ones who most read books about investing.

Poor people seldom read books about investing because they have no money to invest in the first place and have no understanding of how to build money through investments.

Middle-income people are gaining an increased level of financial savvy in today's world; but most of them depend on money advice from their bankers, their insurance agents, and maybe advice from a good friend or relative, occasionally.

But rich people have to do something with their money – and they had better read books and learn about investments in order to know enough about what to do or they may end up getting bamboozled by an investment counselor who takes advantage of managing the funds for the rich person. An example of this is Bernard Madoff who perpetrated a "Ponzi" scheme of fraud that lost 50 billion dollars of money his rich clients invested through him.

Many celebrities have found themselves broke after years of hard work because they turned all their money over to someone else to invest for them and never bothered to learn what the investments were all about. This is a heartbreaking truth.

So, the rich individuals who understand how to protect their money and how to build it at the same time stay abreast of investment information by reading books.

Back to our young man. Suddenly, rich people all around the country were reading his book – and what do you think they wanted? They wanted 'him' to be one of their stockbrokers. Why? Because he's an expert! Oh really, what makes him an expert? He is an expert *because he wrote the book!*

His hard cover book sold for about $25 – which means he received the highest royalty, which is 10% - or $2.50 per book. His agent received 15% of the $2.50 per book. That means for every person – rich or not – who bought his book, he received only about $2.12.

But when the rich people who read his book called him and said, "I like your investment strategy. I will send about $300,000 as an initial investment and see how it does. If it does as well as I think it will, I will invest more. Now, he was making a lot of good money on commissions as their investment advisor – all as a *by-product of his book.* So writing the book paid off in more ways than royalties.

Writing a book can be a simple and direct short cut to financial success as an expert in your field.

What Is *Your* Expertise At This Moment?

Whatever vocation – or avocation – you have (or have had in the past) – you can leverage your credentials into a book that makes you an instant expert in that field.

And you don't have to write a book on the 'whole subject' of your profession. You can take just a segment of your profession and write a book about that.

Plus it does not have to be a big book – a small book will work just as well as a big one. For example, let's pretend you are a teacher writing a small book about the way you deal successfully with problem students. Keep in mind, you will not write a book about education in general – that would be quite an undertaking. And you are not writing a book about the actual subject you teach in school. Instead, you only focus on this one specific topic.

Naturally, if there are shootings in schools or other problem situations, you can make yourself available as an expert for the media to give input on dealing with problem students. Why? Because you have written a book about problem students and that qualifies you as an expert on that subject.

If you are a janitor, you can write a small book about the best cleaning equipment for industrial cleaning or businesses or for homes – or about timesaving methods of cleaning. You are then an expert and an author.

There are many perks for establishing yourself as an expert in your field with a book:

- You usually make more money in your company.
- You are the one sought for information on the subject if there are media inquiries.
- You are often invited to be a guest speaker for organizations and your fame grows.

Whenever you write a non-fiction book, it requires a certain amount of personal experience, opinion, minor research, thought, and logical sequence of information that supports your topic.

Whether you are writing a non-fiction textbook or informative data about a topic or if you are explaining a how-to for anything from carpentry to job skills, the detailed and comprehensive work you put into the book turns you into an expert on the subject.

Non-Fiction
Book Outline
In Just 30 Minutes To 1 Hour

Completely Outline Your Book In About
30 Minutes To 1 Hour. – Ginie Sayles

In my seminars and on my DVDs, I demonstrate the steps in this chapter. Be sure you follow each step exactly. You can use this technique to write a book and also a thesis. A psychology professor wrote a letter to me and stated that several students told her that my *Write A Book In 3 Weeks – Or Less* seminar helped them write their thesis.

As with her students, there are a lot of applications for you, also, to use with this information. But first, let's see about writing a non-fiction book.

Let's pretend a publisher tells you that if you can write a book about washing a car, it will be sold through driver's education classes around the country. They need your manuscript in three weeks – or less.

And let's pretend you have wisely accepted the opportunity to write the book for publication. This is an opportunity you have dreamed about; only now, you find yourself stymied. You cannot seem to get started. Don't worry, with my simple five-step method, you can completely outline your how-to book in about thirty minutes!

For this basic, 30-minute step, you will need:
A. Several sheets of blank paper
B. A pencil or pen
C. A Timer (I use Radio Shack timers because they don't give distracting 5 minute warning signals the way cooking timers often do.)

Now, get comfortable on your sofa, with a cup of coffee or tea, if you wish. Being comfortable accelerates the process.

Perform each of the following steps – and study the examples.

Step One: Make A Quick Master List For Your (Working) Book Title

Sample title: How To Wash A Car
1. Set your Timer for 10 minutes.
2. From memory, and as fast as you can:
   1) Make a list of everything you think is important to tell a teenager about washing a car. (*No, you cannot write down 'Take it to the car wash...'*)
   2) Use as much of the page, front and back, as you wish.
3. Do not write sentences – only a list of single words or phrases
4. Do not worry about the order – just write.

You may be surprised that it will probably take you less than 5 minutes. But, if it takes the whole 10 minutes, that's fine, too. Then, number your list in order.

When I first wrote this course, I enlisted my husband, Reed, to be my guinea pig. He has a degree in Business with a major in economics and a minor in math – so I figured that was as polar opposite from literary experience as I could hope for. Frankly, I was very impressed with Reed's list. This is what he wrote in 3 minutes.

Step One Example: How To Wash A Car

(Reed's list)

Location
Water source
Types of equipment and products to use
Washing and drying procedures
Detailing
Cleaning interior
Preparation checklist
How often to wash your car
Car windows and side mirrors

Congratulations!
If you did this step, then…

You just CREATED A WORKING TABLE OF CONTENTS in mere minutes!

Each topic you listed is a chapter title. Do you remember when I made a list of topics for pageant brochures? Well, that list turned out to be my Table Of Contents for my *How To WIN Pageants* book.

Step Two: Organize Your New Chapter Titles For Table Of Contents

Next, number your new chapter titles in the order you think best for your working Table Of Contents.

Step Two Example: Reed numbered his list as follows:

Chapter #   Chapter Title
4. Location
5. Water source
3. Types of equipment and products to use
6. Washing and drying procedures
9. Detailing
7. Cleaning interior
2. Preparation checklist
1. How often to wash your car
8. Car windows and side mirrors

Step Three: Write Each Chapter Title On A Separate Sheet Of Blank Paper

Count and set aside the same number of blank sheets of paper as you have topics on your list. At the top of each blank sheet of paper, write one of the topics from your list as a title.

Step Three Example: Reed counted out nine sheets of blank paper because he had nine topics (or chapter titles) on his list.
He titled the first blank sheet of paper, "Location."
He titled the next sheet of blank paper "Water Source"
He titled the third blank sheet of paper "Types of Equipment and Products to Use"

… and so on until he had a stack of nine papers, each with nothing but a title on it, taken from his list of chapter titles.

Then, Reed restacked the papers in the order he wanted them for his Table Of Contents.

Step Four: Outline Each Chapter In Minutes

Pick up one of your papers with a title on it and set your Timer for ten minutes. Once again, make a list – in any order and as fast as you can – of everything you think your Reader will need to know about 'that 'specific topic. In the following example, Reed listed everything he thinks you need to know about the 'location' for washing a car.

Step Four Example: **From Reed's list, he chose : LOCATION.**
After Setting his Timer for 10 minutes, he listed the following that he thought a person needed to know about choosing a *'Location'* for washing a car:

Each topic Reed listed above will now be a Subject Heading *within* his Chapter on Location for washing a car.

Now, you do it.
1. **Choose a blank sheet of paper with your chapter title**
2. **Set your timer**
3. **List everything you consider relevant to tell someone *about that specific topic.***
4. **Stop, note your time.**

Chapter 4 Location

Concrete or hard surface
Location that drains well
Shady or covered area for washing
Open sunny area for drying
Easy area to clean up
    time: 2 mins. 6 secs.

You have just OUTLINED YOUR CHAPTER – in about 2 minutes or so!

1. Go back through and number your list in order
2. Repeat this exercise with every sheet of titled paper you have made.

When you finish making a list for every chapter title, you not only have your Working Table Of Contents; but YOU HAVE COMPLETELY OUTLINED YOUR BOOK!!

Often, it takes only 30 minutes. But, if it takes an hour or so, you still have completely outlined your book in a remarkably short period of time within one day, rather than several days or weeks.

Step Five: Write Each Chapter – It Is Just *'Fill In The Blanks'*!

Once you have put all this information into your computer (see Day-By-Day Calendar for instructions), then you simply write an **introduction paragraph** which can be one sentence or several sentences. Next, you start with the **first Subject Heading** and **explain it in paragraphs** – however many paragraphs it takes to explain it well. It may take just one or it may take several.

Go to the **next Subject Heading in that Chapter** and **repeat** the same writing procedure.

Basically, this is a process that I refer to as just 'fill in the blanks' When you finish this process with every chapter, **you have written your book**. Write a conclusion and you're finished. In some cases, this entire project can be completed in 12 days!

Step Five Example:	(Reed's chapter)
I. Chapter Title	**CHAPTER 4** **LOCATION**

Step Five Example: / **I. Chapter Title**

II. Introductory para-graph

III. Heading from outline
Explain topic with as many paragraphs as needed.

IV. Heading from outline

Explain topic with as many paragraphs as needed.

(Reed's chapter)

CHAPTER 4
LOCATION

When you wash your car, it is important to pick a location that protects you and your car as you do your wash job.

Location That Drains Well

If you choose a slightly sloping surface for washing your car, it will allow water to run off to a lower area, away from your car.

Number one, you don't want to walk around your car, standing in mud or water puddles. Furthermore, when the washing procedure is done, you want to be able to drive your car away without picking up mud or other substances that might cling to your newly completed wash job.

Hard Surface
For Washing Your Car

A hard surface location will not become muddy when you use an abundance of water around and under the car.

So, the most logical places to wash your car will be the concrete driveway or the paved street in front of your house.

If you choose the street, please park your car near the curb, and always be careful of traffic that will continue to pass while you are out there, working away.

Repeat the same processes for each heading and your chapter will be written in no time. Do this procedure for each chapter.

Editing Notes – The first sentence in a paragraph is a 'topic sentence' that tells what the paragraph will explain. After you finish each paragraph, re-read each sentence and eliminate those sentences that do not help explain the topic sentence and the 'heading' and the chapter.

Writing Non-Fiction – Write The Way You Talk

Do write the way you talk. A book is much more readable if people feel as if they are 'hearing you' and understanding clearly what you are saying.

If you think writing non-fiction is different from talking, think again. Some people will pompously say it is; but it is not. I am a very effective communicator with a degree in English and Speech; and I can assure you that people who write non-fiction the way they talk are the best communicators.

The very worst thing you can do is to sound 'bookish' or too clinical or so academic with words that you sound more as if you are showing off than trying to communicate. You alienate readers rather than embrace them into your understanding.

For that reason – even though I have been an English teacher – I find the use of words that are too objective, such as "one must do what one must" are not reader-friendly. It may be accurate, yes; but it is a starched accuracy that calls attention to itself, rather than to the idea being communicated.

If propriety calls attention to itself, it fails in its purpose of communicating. And *communication is the whole point of writing that is shared with others.*

Instead of writing "one must do what one must," it is less self-conscious and therefore more effective to write "you must do what you must" – using 'you' in the impersonal sense that feels more relaxed, comfortable and communicative.

The same is true about beginning sentences with 'and.' It is true that you do not want to run sentences together with 'and' used repeatedly. Of course not. But it is perfectly okay to begin a sentence from time to time with 'and' if it has a natural flow.

The same is true of having an occasional 'incomplete' sentence such as the one I used above 'of course not' because it completes the flow of an idea in a conversational tone, even though technically it is an incomplete sentence.

It is also true of ending sentences with a preposition – of, about, with – so that your writing does not become tortuous in an effort to avoid it.

My greatest strength as an English major was grammar. Even as a girl, I would read books and mentally diagram the sentences as I went. And yet, this grammar-loving English teacher can tell you in good conscience that slavishly following rules of grammar to the letter can take the heart and soul out of your communication with others.

I repeat – the whole point of language is to communicate and, yes, having a standard of grammar is good, too – as a strong guideline; but not as a whip-lashing technician that takes the breath of life out of your words.

You will have less editing if you write the way you talk. Words embody ideas. Writing an idea the way you would say it, is more powerful than propriety. Cleaning up minor points comes later. When you do edit, all you have to do is to make sure you have mostly complete sentences (complete ideas) and that your ideas are grouped together.

Write In Layers

Good writing requires that you read and re-read your writing – and each time you read it through, you take certain steps to enhance the quality of your nonfiction book, by writing in layers.

Non-Fiction Layers Of Writing

1. **Layer 1 – Your First Draft Layer** – your first draft is your basic book (Creative Mud).

2. **Layer 2 – Your Mental Paintbrush Layer**– as you read your first draft, paint a layer of Examples and Analogies and Human Interest cases-in-point to flesh out your logic or step-by-step explanations. This is part of Creative editing.

3. **Layer 3 – Your Clarity Layer** – read each chapter with one question in your mind – is this clear? Is it sharp? Does each chapter stay 'on track' with the chapter topic? This is part of Creative editing.

4. **Layer 4 – Your Final Editing Layer** – add to – and then take away whatever is not needed. Do this several times. The human body sloughs off or eliminates what is not needed – that is what you do with your manuscript in the final stages of editing.

The MONTHLY CALENDAR and DAY-BY-DAY CALENDAR THAT FOLLOW will itemize how to use these steps in a daily manner for 3 weeks. Of course, you should adapt these steps to your own life and use them as a strong guideline.

Chapter

36

Day-By-Day
Non-Fiction Calendar

Success begins in your mind and is fulfilled by a deadline on your calendar. - Ginie Sayles

I have given you the Process for Writing A NON-FICTION Book In 3 Weeks – Or Less in the previous chapter. Now, I will set it out in a daily calendar you may want to follow for about 3 weeks or so.

Preliminary Steps: Create 'Readiness'

✓ Copyright Forms – Order TX forms online or by calling 1-202-707-3000.
✓ Timer – be sure it is a Digital Timer.
✓ Build Faith in your Creative Spirit.
   You can say a brief prayer, if you like.
   Affirm, aloud your positive Faith Statements (which I consider to be positive prayers) – set your Timer for 1 minute and say:
   I, your name, am a writer. I am an author. I am creative.

I, your name, now attract to me all things necessary for fulfilling my writing goal.

✓ Surround Yourself with uplifting, encouraging posters/ pictures.

✓ Post a note on top of your computer with this question written on it: *"What is the single most important thing I can accomplish today?"*

Day 1: Outline Your Entire Book And Chapters In About 30 Minutes to 1 Hour

➢ Carry a PDA or pocket-sized spiral notepad at all times: use only for ideas for your book.

➢ Transcribe ideas each day before continuing to write your book.

➢ Set Timer for 1-minute – Faith Statements.

➢ *What is the single most important thing I can accomplish today?*

✓ One sheet of paper:
  • Choose a Working Title for your new book (a title makes it 'real').
  • Write the Purpose for your book in 1 sentence.
  • Write who needs this book (Target Audience).

✓ List why a reader should learn to do this – 8 to 12 reasons.

✓ Write a Summary of what your book will be about and why. This can be the introduction to your book.

✓ Set Timer for 10 minutes.

✓ Take one sheet of paper and – as quickly as you can – list everything a person needs to know about the subject. No sentences, just single words or phrases – and in any order.

✓ Stop Timer. Count items on your list. This is your Table of Contents. These will be your initial number of chapters.

✓ Get the same number of blank sheets of paper as the number of chapters on your new Table of Contents.

✓ Title each sheet of paper with one Chapter title from your new Table of Contents list.

✓ Set Timer for 10 minutes.

✓ Take one of your titled sheets of paper and – as quickly as you can – list everything a person needs to know about that particular topic. No sentences; just single words or phrases – and in any order.

✓ When finished, stop the Timer and note how quickly you did this.
  • Number the items in the order you think they should go.
  • You have just outlined your chapter!

✓ Repeat this process with each titled sheet of paper.

✓ Open a file in your computer for your book – such as how to wash car.doc.
  • Type Working Title for your new book in a large font that looks like a book title.

✓ Input your new Table Of Contents into your computer.
  • Make it look nice, the way a Table Of Contents should look.

✓ Input each chapter page into your computer.
  • Type in your outline for each chapter – upper-lower case bold.
  • Double space.
  • Indent paragraphs.

Day 2: Create

- ➢ Transcribe ideas each day before continuing to write your book.
- ➢ Set Timer for 1-minute – Say Faith Statements aloud. Hear your voice saying each one – DO NOT JUDGE what you think about it. Just say and hear it.
- ➢ *What is the single most important thing I can accomplish today?*

- ✓ Select any of your Chapters that interest you most at this time.
  - • Write an introductory paragraph for that chapter. It can be just one sentence if you like.
  - • Fill in each sub-topic of your outline by explaining it with complete sentences.
  - • Write at least one to ten paragraphs per sub-topic.

- ✓ Write as if you are talking to your Target Audience. Use simple, clear, direct language. *Do not sound 'bookish.'*

Day 3 – Day 13: Create

- ➢ Transcribe ideas each day before continuing to write your book.
- ➢ Set Timer for 1-minute – Faith Statements.
- ➢ *What is the single most important thing I can accomplish today?*

- ✓ Continue filling in your chapters. Explain each sub-topic, thoroughly.

- ✓ Put a question mark (?) next to any sub-topic you are not sure you want to include.

✓ Put an asterisk (*) next to any sub-topic you need to better research on Research Day. Do not stop to research it, yet. Keep writing as much as you know.

✓ Follow this procedure with each chapter, one at a time, until you have completed each sub-topic in each chapter.

✓ Give specific, step-by-step instructions for subjects that apply.

✓ Use bullets, numbers – break down your information in clear, easy-to-follow instructions.

Day 14: Research

➤ Transcribe ideas each day before continuing to write your book.
➤ Set Timer for 1-minute – Faith Statements.
➤ *What is the single most important thing I can accomplish today?*

✓ Global your asterisks throughout your new book – Control F (find) (On Mac: Apple F)
✓ As each asterisk comes up on your screen, jot down on a notepad what you need to find out.
✓ Go online and look for each item you noted.
✓ If you are not able to find what you want online; visit your library and search for it.
✓ Incorporate new information at each asterisk, then remove the asterisk.
✓ Do not violate copyrights of others, do not paraphrase. Understand the information and then explain it in your own way.
✓ Credit your sources.

Day 15: Edit

> ➤ Transcribe ideas each day before continuing to write your book
> ➤ Set Timer for 1-minute – Faith Statements
> ➤ ***What is the single most important thing I can accomplish today?***

✓ Organize Chapters. Get out your old handwritten Table of Contents. Decide what order they logically or most effectively belong. Change them in your computer.

✓ Be sure the topic headings in each chapter relate to that chapter.

✓ Be sure the paragraphs under each topic heading fully explain the topic heading.

✓ Eliminate any sentences that do not directly relate to the topic heading.

✓ Write a summary of what you have told your reader and why. Be sure to point out how all of this has helped your reader. This summary will be the conclusion of your book.

✓ Print out your book – preferably using pink paper for your 1st draft.

✓ Look at each sub-topic with a ? next to it and decide whether to keep the topic or to eliminate it. If you keep it, be sure to delete the ? from your manuscript.

Note: Using different colors of paper on your drafts keep you from going crazy if you get them mixed up. You know instantly by paper color which draft is which.

Be sure to number your pages.

Day 16: Edit

➢ Transcribe ideas each day before continuing to write your book.

➢ Set Timer for 1-minute – Faith Statements.

➢ *What is the single most important thing I can accomplish today?*

✓ Read your print-out.

✓ Make corrections as you go.

✓ Make notes in the margins for new ideas you may get or changes.

✓ After each chapter ask:
  • What was the purpose of this chapter?
  • Have I fulfilled that purpose?
  • Have I explained the topic or this chapter thoroughly?
  • Clearly?
  • Simply?
  • Would my reader understand it?

✓ Re-read parts that bother you and work on them – but do not judge the worthiness of your writing – just particular parts that can be made clearer.

✓ Re-read parts that interest you and preen.

Day 17-20: Edit

> ➢ Transcribe ideas each day before continuing to write your book.
> ➢ Set Timer for 1-minute – Faith Statements.
> ➢ ***What is the single most important thing I can accomplish today?***

✓ Clean it up! Make revisions. Can you say something more clearly?

✓ Add anything that comes to you that you consider relevant.

✓ Read your overall book purpose statement. Does your work fulfill the purpose?

✓ Have you answered the 8 – 12 reasons why the reader should read your book?

✓ Insert your introduction. This is the summary you first wrote of what you were going to tell your reader and why. Put it at the beginning of your book. You can rewrite it, if necessary.

✓ Insert your conclusion. This is the summary from day 15.

✓ Run your spell-check.

Day 21: Edit

➢ Set Timer for 1-minute – Faith Statements.
➢ *What is the single most important thing I can accomplish today?*

✓ Print out your manuscript.

■ Use light yellow paper.

■ Read it.

■ Is it clear?

✓ Make revisions.

✓ Finalize.

HOORAY!

YOU HAVE FINISHED YOUR BASIC (FIRST DRAFT) MANUSCRIPT

CONGRATULATIONS!

YOU ARE NOW AN AUTHOR!

Day 22-Day 24: Release it

➢ Leave your notebook at home.

For 3 days – or 3 weeks if you wish do the following:

✓ Release your book mentally!

✓ Put your manuscript away – and do NOT look at it – no matter what. Do not sneak a peek. Do not add a great new idea to it. If you have an idea, write it in your notebook when you get home, but do not touch your manuscript.

✓ Have a good time. Enjoy restful, fun activities.

✓ Go out with friends – but do NOT tell them about your new book.

✓ Let everything steep on the back-burner of your Creative Spirit in your subconscious by forgetting about it, dismissing it from your conscious mind.

Day 25: Final Decisions

➢ Set Timer for 1-minute – Faith Statements.
➢ *What is the single most important thing I can accomplish today?*

✓ Print out your manuscript on light blue paper.

✓ Read it again.

✓ Make final revisions.

✓ Use spell-check.

- ✓ Use word-count.

- ✓ Re-think the name of your book from a working title to a marketing title. The title sells the book. Try several titles. Choose one.

- ✓ Coordinate the page numbers of each chapter with your Table Of Contents page.

- ✓ Print out final draft on white paper.

- ✓ Fill out your copyright form *immediately;* and either:

  - *Mail it to the Library of Congress Copyright Office by Certified Mail with your copyright form, payment and required copies of manuscript.*

  - Or go online and fill out your form and upload it with your payment and your manuscript.

- ✓ Decide if you want to make additional revisions. If so, give yourself another three weeks and then repeat each step on this page.

Monthly Calendar

Non-Fiction

Sun	Mon	Tue	Wed	Thu	Fri	Sat
LEGEND H = hours of writing CS= Creative Spirit FD = Final Decisions The first 4 days are structural & creative Carry small spiral notebook.	**Positive Faith Statements:** "I (your name) am a writer. I am an author. I am creative." "I, (your name), now have a writing awareness. I now attract to me all things necessary for fulfilling my writing goal." Enjoy this special time – Your very own Creative Adventure!	**POINTS TO REMEMBER** As you write, put a Star * next to anything you think you need more research on or information about. But keep writing. Limit Editing to twice for each chapter until finished. Start each work period with what interests you most at the time.	**1** 3¾-H 1. Temporary Title for book 2. Set Timer. 3. List every thing important about your topic 4. Count items on list. 5. Get that many sheets of paper. 6. Repeat #2 for each item. 7Input computer	**2** 3¾-H 1. Target readers 2. Summarize your book idea as the Introduction to your book. 4. List 8-12 reasons reader should learn this - put in summary 5. Begin with topic that interests you 6. Write intro, fill in each topic	**3** 3¾-H 1. Always work first on topic that interests you most. 2. Write intro, fill in each topic and each sub-topic	**4** 12 H Continue explaining in paragraphs the importance of each topic and sub-topic you have listed.
5 12 H1. Repeat Process	**6** 3¾-H Repeat Process	**7** 3¾-H Repeat Process	**8** 3¾-H Repeat Process	**9** 3¾-H Repeat Process	**10** 3¾H Repeat Process	**11** 12 H Repeat Process
12 12 H Repeat Process	**13** 3¾H Repeat Process	**14** 4 H Library-Research Make Corrections from research	**15** 3H Organize chapters Edit	**16** 3¾H Clean up	**17** 3¾H Work for Clarity	**18** 12 H Free-form writing
19 12 H Free-form writing	**20** 3¾H 1. Read 2. Revise 3. Final writing	**21** 3¾H 1. Spell-check 2. Print-out End of 3 Weeks ♥	**22** CS Have fun – rest & relax	**23** CS Put your copy away Have fun unrelated activity	**24** CS No peeking! Keep it on your mental backburner	**25** FD Send 1ˢᵗ draft to Copyright office by certified mail
26 CS Have fun -	**27** Read Manuscript	**28** CS Make Decisions	**29**	**30**	**31**	**1 Month**

Chapter
37

Elements Of
How-To, Informational,
or Textbooks

Heart is everything! – Ginie Sayles

Non-fiction books range from instructional – how-to self-help, textbooks, directories, handbooks, guidebooks, manuals, workbooks – to informational books about antiques, theses, history, and the like.

Let's look at what they have in common and then examine the major components of each. The one factor they have in common is vocabulary you use when writing for the average reader.

Don't Write Over Anyone's Head: *Age 13 is the Target Vocabulary*

When I was in junior high and high school, I was on the school newspaper every year.

In junior high, I was assigned a gossip column, which I named "Now Hear This" and it was a lot of fun to write.

In high school, I was assigned an advice column, which I titled "Dear Ginie" and I turned it into a satire of the syndicated Ann Landers and Dear Abby advice columns.

I made up letters from our teachers asking Dear Ginie for advice– such as a letter from the speech teacher, confessing stage fright and from the science teacher as being squeamish about dissecting frogs.

The kids loved it and the column was a great success. Everyone knew it was just for fun and I really loved writing it.

It was a great lesson in writing, too. *My journalism teachers told us that newspapers write to a general readership with an average vocabulary level of a thirteen year old.* That way, news media publishers know that just about anyone can read and understand the news. That information has been one the most significant contributions to me as a writer. I still use 'can a 13 year old understand?' as my yardstick.

Don't write 'over the head' of anyone. Talk directly to your readers in a simple, clear vocabulary they will definitely understand. If a lofty sounding word comes to your mind, it is good that you understand it; but when you write, choose a simpler word that means the same thing.

You write a 'How-to' book to help people learn something that can make their lives more effective–more satisfying. You are not writing to impress someone with your vocabulary.

How-To Books

Non-fiction how-to books are best written when it has the feel that you are 'sharing' information over a hot cup of coffee with a good friend you want to help. Or that you and a friend are in your workshop and you are explaining how to build something.

And that is pretty much the style of writing I employ in my How-tos. Very simple. Very me. And very specific. And very effective.

To Be A Super How-To Author - *Ya Gotta Have Heart!*

The bigger your heart, the better your book.

When writing a how-to book, give that extra little push that gets someone up and over the top of their dreams and beyond their expectations. True, it does not mean you will achieve that goal, every time; but I think it has to be part and parcel of your book.

Your heart is the beginning and the end. It is the urge in your heart to help people that will keep you going when you get a little tired. And it is your heart that makes sure you write so that readers can understand. For a super how-to, *heart is everything*.

In order to be successful in the marketplace, how-to books should follow this recipe:

1. **Create A New Niche**. This was the door for my first book, *How To WIN Pageants*. At that time, the how-to market had not significantly tapped the lucrative pageant industry, which was an ever-growing market then.

2. **Build A Better Mousetrap – Or At Least A Different Version**. If your how-to book is on a topic that is already flooded with competition, you have to build a better mousetrap of information. Your angle must be new, different, exciting – or why would anyone buy it?

   If your book just regurgitates information from other books, you are liable for lawsuits – and readers are disappointed that they learned nothing new.

   Most successful how-to books are different from the avalanche of books on the same subject.

   The second question a publisher will ask you is "How is your book *different* from the ones that are already published in that genre?" You had better be able to answer that question.

   And finally, whatever you write must make sense with the basic concept of your book.

3. **Give Step-by-Step Information**. A how-to book should be laid out in a logical development – i.e. "first you do this and second, you do that..." easy-to-follow sequence of behavior that provides a good result if the reader follows the order of behavior you set forth.

4. **Very Specific Information**. No generalities are allowed in a how-to book. You must provide specific procedures and reinforce it through the use of examples.

   Also highlight important points with numbers, bullets, charts, outlines or diagrams.

5. **Credibility**. You should have some relationship with the subject that accounts for your writing the book. Your credentials let readers know they can trust your information.

   If you are writing a book on how to climb Mount Everest but your only climbing experience is a rock climbing wall at your local YMCA, then you need to interview actual mountain climbers who have attempted or succeeded in climbing Mount Everest – to up your credentials as author of a book on the subject.

   Be sure you include your credentials in your Author's Bio.

Informational Books

History books or books about antiques or other factual information work best if they include the following:

1. **Logical Organization Of Material**. This can mean giving a timeline or providing the information in a chronological sequence.

   For instance, you may want to write a book about Antiques. If you want to take on the whole world of antiques, you will definitely need to create a world timeline and culture timeline and break the book – a volume or more, really – into time periods that you then break down into cultural pieces within each time period and eventually how each culture influenced the other, as they learned of each other.

On the other hand, you can write a book *on just one time period and one particular culture* –concentrating only on the antiques produced by that particular culture during that particular time period.

For example, you may be knowledgeable about American furniture during the time of the American Revolutionary War. Or you might narrow your scope of antiques even more by zeroing in on 'drinking vessels' used by Americans during the American Revolution.

Do you see how you can narrow your timeline and your subject matter? Yet, even then, you must show a timeline of the evolution of styles and quality of drinking vessels within the overall timeline of the American Revolution and limit it to those used during the war itself.

2. **Anecdotes Or Cartoons That Mix Emotion Into The Facts**. To write a winning informational book, be sure to insert a human interest story into a sidebar on every third or fourth page that gives a glimpse of the human connection to your facts.

    For example, if you are writing a book about antiques of the Revolutionary War, and you are explaining the workmanship of a highboy chest of that period; you could insert a sidebar recounting a brief tale of someone's ancestor who hid an important map between the drawers of her highboy (like the one depicted on that page of your book) and the British Redcoats were unable to find it. Such stories make your facts come to life with human interest and human emotion.

Clever cartoons that provide momentary relief from the seriousness of facts can make it easier for a reader to remember.

Textbooks

Textbooks combine the requirements of the How-To plus the Informational Books. Often, they have a chronology or time-line with educational background of events or developments; and they may also provide step-by-step procedures for a student to follow in order to work a math problem or to diagram a sentence in English class or to build a motor for shop class or to cook a meal in Home Economics class.

Emotion Hooks Readers

We live our lives through our emotions. Yes, we use our minds to analyze our lives and to try to keep ourselves on course; but we human beings are emotional. We judge whether or not we are on the right track by our emotional response to it. We judge the fairness of others by our emotional response to what they do.

Thought is still the basis of our emotion because – *emotion is a response to thought*.

What does this mean for you as a writer? It means that if you, as a writer, are able to express thoughts in such a way that people *feel* the power of your facts and thoughts, you will be a popular author and one whom publishers will want..

Fear, love, hate, tenderness jealousy, forgiveness, revenge, reconciliation, anger, justice, desire, humor – these are just the tip of the iceberg of emotions that hook a reader if you are able to show how stodgy facts in an informational book can affect the everyday life of that reader. And you do that by generating emotion in the way you write it, perhaps with stirring examples.

Cogent thought is the bedrock for good informational writing; and emotion gets the thought across! Be sure to inject emotion into your facts to help your readers get your message.

Solutions Hook Non-fiction Readers

I have said this before, but I want to emphasize again that most people buy a non-fiction book because they are looking for solutions to something in their lives. Solutions to washing a car, building a house, finding love, getting on with life after divorce, budgeting for retirement – the list is as endless as the needs of life itself. Always give solid solutions.

Chapter

38

Elements of
Poetry Books

Trust your own vision in your poetry. Do not second-guess its value. – Ginie Sayles

Poetry is extremely personal. It is a metered flow of emotion or thought that may or may not rhyme. It can be graceful or abrupt, tender or harsh, symbolic or to the point – and perhaps more than any other form of writing, has a distinct Author's Voice – or Poet's Voice – that is typically unlike most others.

Because of its intimate self-expression, there is no 'right' or 'wrong' way to write poetry unless you choose existing styles of writing that are clearly defined. These are Classic styles, typically with Iambic Pentameter, typical of the Elizabethan period and Shakespeare; or other traditional patterns.

While not musical per se, Poetry is musical in nature with core rhythms of language. Sometimes it comes all at once, and sometimes a piece of it comes to you and when you begin writing it, you sense what comes next or simply decide what comes next within the flow of the beat your poem has.

Trust your own vision in your poetry. Do not second guess the value of it. Does it flow to the beat of your poetic heart at the moment? Does it communicate your feeling, your thought? Does it feel right? Do you like it? If so, it is good, period.

For quick review of the major classic beats in poetry, I have listed the better known rhythmic patterns. Rhythm is measured in the number of sounds in a syllable. For example if a girl is named Sue, her name has one sound, which means one syllable, no meter.

Meter is determined by the accented syllable/sound. If a girl's name is Susan, it has two sounds/syllables— and since the accent is on the first sound/syllable, it is SU-san.

When the accent is on the first sound/syllable, it is called a **Trochee.** When the accent is on the second/syllable – such as Marie – ma-RIE – it is called an **Iamb.**

In poetry, two sounds/syllables = 1 foot of meter. The two names above are respectively measured as a one foot Trochee (SU-san) and a one foot Iamb (ma-RIE).

You can have two, three, four, five, six, seven, eight, etcetera meters.

Iambic Pentameter

Iambic pentameter – meaning a line of five feet – is the most common of the rhythms and sounds like this:

ta-DA/ta-DA/ta-DA/ta-DA/ta-DA

Accent on a syllable/sound is the key to identifying metric feet in conventional forms of poetry.

Iamb	=	unaccented -ACCENTED
Trochee	=	ACCENTED-unaccented
Anapest	=	unaccented-unaccented-ACCENTED
Dactyl	=	ACCENTED-unaccented-unaccented

In addition to meter, there are also names of poetic lines.

Verse	=	a single line of poetry.
Stanza	=	a series of lines.
Occidental	=	a number of syllables to each line, both uniform and regular.

2-line Stanza	=	A Couplet- 2 lines that rhyme.
Quatrain	=	4 lines – only the 2nd and 3rd lines rhyme; or 1st & 2nd rhyme and 3rd & 4th rhyme, like a double-couplet.

Stanzas may exceed four lines, but the ones listed above are most common.

Lyric	=	stanzas in musical or almost musical meter/tempo. A song.
Sonnet	=	lyric of 14 iambic pentameters with a definite rhyme pattern.
Ballade	=	3 stanzas, each 8 lines, followed by a quatrain; or 10 line stanzas, 10 syllables each in iambic pattern.
Ode	=	lyric poem in varied or irregular meter in tribute to a subject.
Chant	=	evenly metered repetitive speech within one or two note range, rhymed or unrhymed, à capella.
Rap	=	evenly metered repetitive monotone chant, rhymed or unrhymed, with or without music.
Free Verse	=	rhymed or unrhymed verse without a typical metric pattern.
Blank Verse	=	unrhymed, unmetered writing of any line pattern.
Narrative	=	poetry that tells a story.
Epic poem	=	very long narrative poem that exalts heroic legends.
Limerick	=	light, humorous, or bawdy verse of 3 long lines and 2 short lines

Consider discovering your natural 'inner meter' and follow its flow, rather than striving to achieve a particular rhythm – unless it interests you to try it. Familiarity with the older forms of poetry can deepen your personal respect for the art; but keep the 'truth' of your style.

Example of *Rhymed Free Verse*: Cradle Clocks
by Ginie Sayles Written 6/27/1989

I hug my daughter and say good-bye
and feel blood flow from my heart and into her distance
But do not cry
with tears that dry
but lingering wistfulness
that time cannot be reached back into
and pulled upon my lap in the sweet form of a child
my life lived for;
and feel the impatient fidget of her life,
of her age
so like a cage
to us both at that time, but precious now if retrieved
and reconceived
with Retrospect to sire fatherhood...*It would be good*
It would be good
It would be good.

I would not risk her kidnap this time
by reason or rhyme
of an hour's chime.
from the sinister plots
of clocks that ticked above her cradle
traded for a bed
when toys were shed.
Her toys now old and stacked in silent witness...
as phantoms they deceive
and tempt me to believe
her tiny fingers will pick them up again for play
someday.
Yet I know that child has passed away
In the death of cradle clocks.

Was I the child
and she the daughter-toy
to whom I clung
and rocked and sung
in the play-like of my life?
Husband-less wife
whose unmated heart had just cause to be alone
a heart that had no room for any
thing or one
but its own
belief in the make-believe of motherhood.

With shadow memories lived in joy,
this mother-toy
is of no more use than other toys
that remain
but tries to learn new games
to play with this child-turned-woman
half my age but now my size.
She, too, cries
for me
and the comfort that I was in yesterday;
For the ticking knives of cradle clocks
severed the cord for both of us
and I became a woman again
and loved a man
and married a man
whose heart my own can rest in
and grow in
like an eternal embryo
so like the one of her in my own heart's womb

Does that fetus of her yet abide
inside
a woman I see
looking back at me

and who looks like me?
Perhaps the cord
still ties
and lies
unseen in placental love,
that all-enduring food.

From cradled womb, to cradled arms, to clasping hands,
I carried her – And now I stand
and wave good-bye
feeling blood drain from my heart into her distance
but do not cry
with tears that dry.
I feign a smile
to ignore all aching aftershocks of cradle clocks
with tick and tock
in words that mock...*It would be good*
It would be good
It would be good.

Example of *Conventional Rhyme, Irregular Meter*: Serious Subject

During my last year of high school, I felt that everywhere
I turned, adults inquired about my future, what I wanted to do or
be and giving unsolicited advice at every turn.

At Seventeen
Ginie Sayles
Written on my 17th birthday.

"Follow the star"
    Comes the command
"Follow and search
    in every land.
Sow the seed
    and harvest by hand.
Follow the star!"

"Look for the pot of gold
in the west
You'll see it shine
when you do your best
For the gold is your life
given its test.
Look for the pot of gold.

"But where is the west?"
Despairs my cry,
For I know not
where directions lie.
Must I live only to die?
or is there a 'pot of gold'?

I know there's a star
somewhere in the night
But how can I follow
if it sheds no light?
For I'm like a bird
Who is lost in flight
but 'you' say,
'Follow the star.'

Example of *Conventional Meter*: Whimsical Subject

'Lines' on being Thirty
by Ginie Sayles on 30th birthday

Twinkle, twinkle, little Wrinkle.
Laugh and frown lines – equal crinkle
To tattletale days I've been bad,
And glad, and sad, and mad – and had!
So if you ask me what I thinkle,
I'll say, "You're a dirty, rotten
stinkle finkle, wrinkle!"

317

A Rhyming Dictionary

For a serious poet who wants to utilize rhyme, whether regularly or occasionally, a wonderful tool is a Rhyming Dictionary.

In some poetic circles the use of a word that rhymes more than once is considered bad form and limited. But more importantly, there are moments in writing poetry when you are working with a meter you like and you do not want to use an ordinary rhyme. Typically, your rhyming dictionary can produce exactly the word you need.

Chapter
39

Elements of
Cook Books

Cook Books tell the story of a society at a given time through food. – Ginie Sayles

Like good non-fiction, cookbooks are best written with human interest stories inserted every so often, plus very specific step-by-step information. Most people enjoy knowing why you took the time to put together a certain type or style of cooking; so share why you are writing the book. You readers will especially like a brief history of the recipe or your personal history with a few of the recipes.

Be a hero to your readers by emphasizing cleanliness procedures – especially hand washing; and also safety procedures – such as not cooking with skillet handles or pot handles extending over the stovetop that a child might bump into, overturning it and causing injuries. You can look up additional ones.

Be sure you also provide:
- Exact measurements. If you use 'a pinch,' as a measurement; it may be fairly well self-defining; but 'a dash' can vary from cook to cook; so give your definition.
- How long it will take (typically) to prepare each recipe.

- How many people it should serve. This helps the cook to decide when to start cooking and whether or not to double the recipe so it will serve everyone or to cut it in half for a smaller group; or to cook it as is.
- Time it takes to bake, noting that ovens vary.
- Degrees of heat for your oven.
- Refrigeration times/temperatures.
- Thermometer reading when it is done.
- Any particular cooking method – conventional oven, convection oven, grill, stovetop.
- Any nutritional advantages of the recipe – if you know it. Otherwise, this is optional.
- Suggested menu to include this recipe and category of the recipe: entre, dessert, et cetera.
- The best pairing of wines or alternate beverages to serve with a particular recipe.
- Beautiful pictures of the final result of a recipe.
- Make your book unique by adding entertainment suggestions, such as music that goes especially well with it.
- If you can dig up/or write a few poems about this type of food, include them.
- Cookbooks with a spiral binding are especially flexible for a cook to keep open while preparing a recipe.

I am including my own super nutritious recipe.

Life Is Wonderful Muffins
Copyright © 2009 Ginie Sayles

Before using this recipe, be sure to check with your physician to be sure you or those you serve have no allergies to any of the ingredients and that it works toward your best health goals.

A. Set the following on your kitchen counter top before you start:
   - 2 Quart Glass Measuring Cup with pour spout– to use as your mixing bowl for dry ingredients

- 2 Cup Glass Measuring Cup with pour spout – to use as your mixing bowl for liquid ingredients
- 1 Cup Measuring Scoop
- ½ Cup Measuring Scoop
- 1 Teaspoon Measuring spoon
- Muffin tin for 12 muffins
- Digital Cooking Timer
- Cooking Gloves for oven safety
- Two clean, dry hand towels
- Roll of paper towels
- Liquid soap dispenser next to your kitchen sink

➢ Preheat your oven to 400° for 7 minutes.
➢ Spray your muffin tin with Pam
➢ Wash your hands with soap and water. Dry them on one of your clean, dry hand towels

B. As you measure your ingredients; if you put each container back where you keep it – as soon as you finish measuring it – you will keep your counter top clean and uncluttered. Measure the following dry ingredients into your large 2 Qt glass measuring cup that has a pour spout:
- 1 Cup All-purpose flour
- 1 Cup Wheat Bran
- ½ Cup Natural Organic Cane Sugar
- 2 Teaspoons Non-Aluminum Baking Powder
- 1 Teaspoon Powdered Cinnamon or Nutmeg
- ¼ Cup Oatmeal (uncooked)
- ¼ Cup Sunflower Seeds (unsalted)
- ¼ Cup Pumpkin Seeds (unsalted).
- ¼ Cup Chopped Walnuts.
- ¼ Cup golden and brown flaxseeds mixed together.

Stir all the above dry ingredients together with a fork.

C. Measure the following liquid ingredients into your 2 Cup glass measuring cup that has a pour spout:

- Pour skim milk to the 1 cup line in your 2 cup glass measuring cup.

- Pour corn oil on top of the milk until you see the liquid rise ¼ above the 1 cup line of the milk

- Pour ¼ cup of Aunt Jemima Lite Syrup (or honey if you don't mind the calories) on top of the milk & oil combination in the same 2 cup measuring cup – until the bottom ¼ line is met. Your measuring cup is now registering 1 ½ cups of liquid.

- Add egg white of 1 organic brown egg (from non-caged chicken farm) into the milk, oil, syrup (or honey) combination in the 2 cup glass measuring cup.

Wash your hands and dry them.
Stir the liquid combination with a fork thoroughly. Pour liquid into the pre-stirred dry ingredients in the large 2 quart glass measuring bowl.

D. Pour or spoon your muffin mixture from the pour spout of the 2 Qt glass measuring cup you used as a mixing bowl into your pre-sprayed muffin tin.

- Put your filled muffin tin in the preheated 400° oven.

- Set your Timer for 13 - 17 minutes (oven times vary. Check after 13 minutes.

- Rinse all equipment you have been using and put them in your dishwasher. This keeps your kitchen clean as you work.

- Make hot tea or coffee or whatever you like to drink with muffins.

- Set your table.

E. When your Timer goes off:
  - Put on your Cooking Oven Gloves.
  - Open the oven door.
  - Remove the muffin tin.
  - Close the oven door
  - Test doneness by inserting a sharp knife and if nothing clings to the muffins, they are done.
  - Turn off the oven.
  - Quickly rinse and dry your hands.
  - Run a thin knife around the edge of each muffin and using a clean dry cloth to protect your fingers, immediately lift and remove each muffin onto a large plate.
                Enjoy your muffins!

The Story Behind My Life Is Wonderful Muffins

I was told that Wheat Bran is a food that requires more calories to digest than calories it supplies, making it a zero calorie food. Let me emphasize that I do not know if this information is true and I have not been able to find it on the Internet. However, at the time I learned this tidbit of information or misinformation, I knew for a fact that wheat bran keeps the intestinal tract clean and functioning well.

I also liked that muffins made with wheat bran were filling and I did not feel hungry shortly after eating. At that time, I jogged every morning, and after a shower, would enjoy a cup of tea with a bran muffin.

Deciding to make my own muffins and to make them as nutritious as possible, I devised the recipe I have shared here. My husband, Reed, loved my Life Is Wonderful Muffins. I would make a dozen each morning, and we would eat what we wanted

– sometimes topped with vanilla yogurt and sprinkled with fresh blueberries – and have a pot of hot tea. Then throughout the day, anytime either of us felt hungry, we would munch another muffin. For dinner, we had steamed vegetables – usually carrots, green beans, and squash – drizzled with a capful of extra virgin olive oil, salt, pepper, a sprinkle of turmeric and a tall glass of water.

During the evening, any left-over muffins with non-fat de-caf lattes were very satisfying.

We never felt hungry – ever – because we could always have a muffin anytime we wanted it. We both became trim and felt great.

I did not measure my weight by pounds but by how I felt and how my favorite clothes fit. Most important of all, I felt great – and my mantra was "Life is Wonderful!" – my muffins were part of that.

This sample recipe and story are merely that – examples of how to put together a cookbook recipe and procedures. If this were an actual cook book, a color picture would complete the project.

Chapter 40

Elements of
Photojournals

Photojournals tell a visual story. – Ginie Sayles

Photojournals are self-defined as a journal of photographs. It is a pictured diary or chronicle of a specific event or theme.

I fell in love with a photojournal I saw in a store in downtown Goliad, Texas. The photojournal contained 'winter in south Texas' pictures that brought "oohs" and "aahs" from me with the turn of each page that gave another unique look at a south Texas setting in snow.

Such a book – with a clear-cut theme – makes a perfect gift for Christmas, or for Texas lovers, and especially for south Texas lovers. And it was a beautiful coffee table book for anyone.

In New Orleans, I saw a photojournal that covered the funeral of musician Louis Armstrong. After going through the pages, I felt as if I had attended it.

Your photographs will have your Author's Voice in images – pictures with your unique thought process as you chose a subject to photograph.

Make your images distinctively yours.

Consider the following:

- Perhaps you use your camera to create character studies – a variety of people whose faces tell a story.
- Whether candid or carefully staged, your work should have the variety of Mood and Pace as people turn the pages of your work.
- Your individual stamp of light and shadows or color or black and white or enhanced or monochromatic or some tell-tale uniqueness comes through.

I once purchased a black and white photograph of a man's hands. The minute you looked at the picture, you knew the man's life, just by his hands. Clearly, he was a hard working laborer, broken nails, dirty knuckles, and a hand-rolled cigarette butt between two fingers that had stains from the many cigarettes held before. I regret that I no longer have the photograph and do not know the name of the photographer; but I wish I did. It was a strong story in a single photograph.

Before you photograph the faces of people, hire a good lawyer to obtain an airtight written release that you can ask each person to sign, granting you permission to publish and to sell the person's picture.

As I understand it, a photographer owns the copyright to a photograph; but a human being whose face is the subject of the photograph is another matter. Check with a good lawyer.

When I was Public Relations for Houston Grand Opera and Editor of the in-house Opera magazine, I had the idea of having a photographer take pictures of our audience milling around in the lobby during Opening Night of a performance – a mini-photo-journal – for a segment in our in-house magazine.

I went to Rice University and found a talented photography professor, named Geoff Winningham, who agreed to do it for us.

Geoff's pictures were wonderful. He captured the glamour and the lively interactions of people as they sipped champagne or conversed about the opera. Everyone enjoyed the magazine when these pictures appeared in the next issue.

Anyone could flip through the pages and instantly feel as if they had attended the event. That is what a photojournal is all about – drawing the viewer into the moment, letting them 'meet' the people, see the action. On his website, geoffwinningham.com I saw that Geoff has continued his art to "create seven books, three films, and numerous exhibits" which you can enjoy.

One Thanksgiving Day, our daughter and son-in-law invited us to Rock Port, Texas, a gulf coast community. Our grandson, Grant Scott, was eleven years old, and that morning, I woke him and handed him a Kodak digital camera. Then I took him outside just after daybreak, which is supposed to be one of the most perfect times to take pictures because there are no shadows. The 'light' is virtually ideal at that time (and also late day is supposed to have good light).

Showing Grant how to use the camera, I then turned him loose and he walked around, taking as many pictures as he wanted. When my husband and I returned home and downloaded the pictures into our computer, we were both amazed at how beautiful they were.

We framed them and presented them to Grant for Christmas. He was surprised and thrilled. He had created a framed photojournal of his experience that Thanksgiving Day.

Photojournals can include breathtaking landscapes; slice-of-life pictures like the one I mentioned of a man's hands that tell you his life; a panoramic span of an event; a formal headshot, a political demonstration, and on and on.

Photojournals can be in black and white or full color or even monochromatic or sepia or a combination. Photojournals share with us or tell us something about ourselves or reveal a new world of visual experience.

The brilliant marketing cliché, *"One picture is worth a thousand words"* has been attributed to F. R. Barnard in 1921 (Wikipedia); although the concept has been summed up in similar ways by others.

No where should the words be more true than in the art of creating a photojournal.

Chapter

41

Common Elements
Poetry Books, Cook Books,
Photojournals

These books have specific missions for their genres. –
Ginie Sayles

Genres in books define themselves. Many genres were popular
at different times in history and certain others, such as children's
books, are ever-present. All of them evolve in some way or another, so keep your eyes on the market while always remaining
true to yourself and who you are as a writer.

Poetry Books, Cookbooks, Photojournals

Poetry books may be non-fiction or fiction; however, they
are listed here because they have common threads for marketing
with cookbooks and photojournals, even though they are vastly
different from each other in content.

Poetry books, cookbooks, and photojournals appear to be
most marketable if they are *developed around a 'theme.'*

True, some poets have created a name for themselves and can produce a book of poetry with poems on many different topics and the book will sell because of the poet's name.

But the average reader who picks up a book of **poetry** wants it to address a certain event or situation in their lives – and this is especially true if the person plans to give it as a gift.

Likewise, **cookbooks** that target a particular type of cooking will set it apart from the many generic cookbooks that tell you how to boil water to cooking everything under the sun. Zero in on a particular type of cooking and there can be more excitement to your work. Add an inviting cover picture to command a bigger price.

Photojournals with a theme gives readers a reason to pick it up and to look at it. Otherwise, a photojournal with no theme is no different from looking at random pictures. You want your specific style as a photographer to come through – which it will with a theme – plus it will communicate more effectively.

Marketable Themes

A clear-cut theme gives you a reading market for selling your book! Here is a list of themes that work great for Poetry Books, Cookbooks, and Photojournals (and also for novels or how-to books).

1. A Holiday - or a Collection of Holiday Verse, Recipes, Photojournal:
   - Christmas
   - Kwanzaa
   - New Year
   - Hanukkah
   - Easter
   - Passover
   - Valentine
   - St. Patrick's Day
   - Memorial Day
   - Independence Day/4th of July

- Birthdays (life cycle)
- Labor Day
- Columbus Day
- Halloween
- Thanksgiving
2. Ethnic Interests
3. Special Needs
4. Current Concerns In The World
5. Motherhood
6. Fatherhood
7. Parenthood
8. Grandparents
9. Ancestors
10. Love
11. Marriage
12. Divorce
13. Spiritual Awareness
14. A Certain Event – homecoming, family reunion
15. Seasons

The list above can help you organize your work into a sensible book, help you sell your book, and help you market your book.

For instance, a poetry book, cook book or photo journal developed around the 4th of July USA Independence Day will be timely every single year on that holiday. Bookstores and businesses can put your book in the window as part of their holiday scheme.

Elements Of
Biographies, Autobiographies, Memoirs

*Do you really want to tell a compelling story; or do you
just want to 'nail' somebody? – Ginie Sayles*

Students invariably ask me if they can write about a true event in
their lives.

My answer is, "Ask yourself if the true event would be a
good story, even if you fictionalize it into a novel and do not use
the real places or real people?"

If your answer is "yes, the story would be just as good,"
then fictionalize it and save yourself legal problems. Most publishers will not touch a book that even remotely sets them up for
liability.

"Gotcha!" is not a game to play as an author. It can backfire
on you.

Are you secretly airing a grievance? If so, you should fictionalize it. If not, fictionalize it.

Do you want to 'even the score' with someone? If so, fictionalize it. If not, fictionalize it.

As you can see, I am urging you to fictionalize a true story about people you know, no matter what your motive, in order to protect yourself.

Listen, we have all had our share of being done in by 'bastards' and 'bitches' (b&bs) – absolutely. And these b&bs probably deserve a top notch lambasting – true, true, true. But even the b&bs have legal rights – and so, if you write about them, they will get to rake you over the coals one more time by suing you for defamation– giving them the last laugh as well as your money! Don't let them win again.

Look at it this way – we have all been b&bs ourselves, even if we didn't mean to be and we would not exactly like finding our worst selves in print – so naturally, we would lawyer up and go after anyone who wrote about it. That's a fact.

SO! Work out your fury at the b&bs in a way they cannot come after you – write about it in a way they can never prove and probably would not realize it is about them – fictionalize it and make money from it.

If the true story is about someone who is dead and who was a public figure, you may have greater latitude as long as you can support your facts. *Check with a lawyer on this.*

However, whether a person is dead or alive, if you want to tell a true story about them, most publishers suspect that you may have an ulterior motive for writing it.

Rule-Of-Thumb Changes

How can you successfully fictionalize a true story and avoid being liable? One of my editors at Penguin-Putnam Berkley Books told me there is no sure and fast guarantee; but she said there is a basic writer's Rule-Of-Thumb to follow.

The Rule-of-Thumb she told me is to change *at least* 5 things (preferably more) to make each real person unidentifiable. Some of the 5+ changes could include:

- Gender
- Ethnicity

- Age Range
- Geography
- Career
- Situation for the events that happened

The Rule-Of-Thumb is basic – but try to change up to 7 or more for greater safety.

Yes, I know that fictionalizing the b&bs takes some of the satisfaction out of it; but your success as an author is the greatest revenge, whether they realize it is about them or not.

And even with the Rule-Of-Thumb in place, do *check with a lawyer anytime you write about true stories or real people.*

Autobiography or Memoir

I was impressed when a young woman who was kidnapped by a terrorist organization was later rescued and asked to write her autobiography. She declined, stating something to the effect that she thought it was presumptuous to write an autobiography while only in her twenties.

Although the modesty and good taste of her reasoning impressed me, she nevertheless had a significant story to share with the rest of us who had kept up with her saga on television news.

Bottom line: I do not think age has as much to do with writing an autobiographical account for publication as does the significance of the story to the general public. Of course, all lives are significant and it is true that everyone has at least one story to tell – an autobiography. But, certainly, if you have had an experience that was thrust into the limelight, you can limit your autobiography to the story of interest, with highlights from your life leading up to the event.

There are many justified reasons to write an autobiography, including:

- Genealogy Preservation – for research by future generations of your descendents. Be a stickler for accurately documenting your claims and crediting your source of information.

- Self-examination to evaluate where you have been in life and where you are now... possibly what you hope for your future.
- Lessons you have learned, lessons yet to learn.
- And maybe the best reason of all is that you just plain want to write it. No quarrel from me on that one. Passion is its own justification.

Begin with the following steps:
1. List 20 moments or events that were key to your life.
2. Put them in chronological order.
3. Now, narrow them down to the 10 most important and why they were important.

Another way to approach your autobiography is to divide it in the following ways:
1. Early Years – 5 important memories.
2. Teenage Years – 5 to 8 important memories.
3. Adult Years – education, careers, love, marriage, affairs, children.
4. Senior Years – 3 important or special events/people in your life now.

Still another way to write your autobiography is to narrow your scope to one major focus:
1. Zero in on one particular event in your life.
2. Summarize or briefly flash-back to your life before this event.
3. How this event changed or impacted your life.
4. Your path since the event.

Memoirs should give the feeling of 'reliving warm moments, and describing the emotions and sensations of it. Finish by telling how it has continued to impact your life or how you released yourself from an undesirable situation.

A Christmas Heritage For My Daughter

When my daughter was about five years old, I went through Mother's shoebox of old family photographs and arranged them neatly in a series of photo albums, asking Mother to tell me who they were.

Looking into the faces of my bloodline ancestors – faces I had never known – I wondered so much about their lives and I made up my mind that I did not want my grandchildren to grow up with just pictures of my parents as strangers whose faces have no story of their lives.

So, at Christmas that year, I recorded each of my parents telling their favorite Christmas as a child and then their favorite Christmas as an adult. Then I told mine and my five year old daughter told her favorite Christmas.

I transcribed the stories and titled it "A Christmas Heritage For My Daughter" and gave copies as a gift to my family the next Christmas. It is a wonderful collection of true Christmas stories.

Two years ago, at Christmas, I gave a CD copy of "A Christmas Heritage For My Daughter" to each of our grandsons. The boys loved hearing their mother's voice at age five telling her favorite Christmas; and of me, their grandmother as a young woman, telling mine; and of their great-grandparents who are no longer living, telling their favorite Christmases when they were children in the early 1900s.

You can make a DVD of your family members telling their favorite Christmas, Easter, Fourth of July, Valentine, Anniversary, birth of a child – and/or any other stories of their lives that you care to record.

If you also make a written book just for family, it can be a great hit.

Other Perfect 'True Stories' For Your Family

One year, while I was constantly traveling to give seminars throughout the USA and Canada, I found myself ending my seminars by talking about my Aunt Mertie Jane Barker Moncrief, a woman whose love and kindness was dear to me as I grew up. I had never talked about her before in my seminars; but for some reason, she was on my mind and I used her as an example of someone with a generous spirit, a woman who shared whatever she had, even though she had so little of material value at times in her life.

I said to my husband, "I wish I knew Aunt Mertie's telephone number. I want to call her and talk to her." This strong pull that I felt about her continued for about three or four months. I had not seen her or talked to her in several years and I suddenly wanted so much to talk to her; but she had moved into a nursing home and I did not know which one. With constant travel, it was all I could do to get from one city to the next on time.

And then she died. Her death was very, very hard for me. We were kindred spirits in many ways and I loved her with all my heart. She had a limited education, and yet she wrote poetry and gospel songs – some that are sung to this day in fundamental churches – and she played piano by ear and sang with such conviction, it could make me cry.

Of course, I have always regretted not having called my dear Aunt Mertie, when it seems obvious to me that our souls were calling out to each other…that some spiritual connection knew she did not have long to live.

The same month Aunt Mertie died, an old friend of mine also died. And almost exactly a year later, my father died – and six months after Dad, my older brother, Lefty, died. Over the next few years, I lost Mother and another close aunt, and two close cousins.

I decided to work through my grief in a positive way, which was family research in genealogy. It turned out to be a wonderful and healthy method for dealing with my loss.

I found a cousin, John W. Odam, Jr. who is a lawyer, like my brother, Lefty. They knew each other, practiced the same kind of law in Austin, Texas at one time. Both Lefty and John had served as Assistant State Attorney General, both had run for office and both liked to play guitar and sing. John had even talked to my brother when he was in the hospital, dying of lung cancer. – and neither of them knew they were blood-related.

My brother died without knowing John was his cousin. John did not know it either until I found him through my genealogy research. Our great-grandfathers were brothers who fought in the Civil War.

Perhaps the genetics John and I share may be writing; because John was writing a novel before we met. His novel, *The Conspiracy Candidate* utilizes his understanding of political parties in spell-binding fictional intrigue; and he wrote a non-fiction book about his run for office. John's wife, Peggy Kurtz Odam – my very dear cousin-in-law – has co-compiled two spiritual books. Two more Morris cousins – Betsy Griffin Shuble and her sister, Diana Griffin Franklin – are also talented writers!

Another cousin I found went to TCU with my brother and they were both left handed and volunteered together in the same political party. So through genealogy, I found a little bit of my brother to love in a common bloodline of family.

It was natural for me to want to put together a family book; but then it dawned on me how much better a book it would be if all the new cousins I found would write *their* memories of their family members and contribute pictures of them.

This was a huge success – and the resulting family tree book that I collected compiled, and arranged of all our writing is available in various genealogy libraries.

IF
You Get Stuck –Troubleshooting Non-Fiction

Use the elements of non-fiction and a few tricks to get 'unstuck.' – Ginie Sayles

If you get stuck while writing non-fiction, go back through the elements listed for the type of non-fiction you are writing. Frequently, you will see what you need to do to get back on track.

If need be, go back to your original outline of your book or outline of your chapters and review them.

- What is your purpose for writing this book?
- Who is your audience?
- Is your writing 'tone' appropriate for your purpose? For your reader?

Paragraphs

Non-fiction relies on strong paragraphs. Looking at each chapter, ask yourself what is the goal for this chapter? Ask yourself if you clearly had something to say in the chapter – not just rambling.

Then, look at each paragraph within that chapter. For each chapter ask yourself:

- Is there one central idea for the paragraph? Can you identify it?
- Are the supporting ideas in good order, giving coherence and a logical flow of information?
- Eliminate ideas that are unrelated to the central idea (topic sentence) of the paragraph.
- Do you need to develop the paragraph by use of examples?
- Are instructions you give clearly stated and easy to understand?
- Have you written with an 'assumption' that the reader knows what you are talking about? Explain everything that seems built on an assumption.
- Give direct explanations of a process or even of a word that can make it clearer to your reader.

Remember that non-fiction thrives on facts and examples, arguments or reasons, comparison and contrast and clear definitions.

- Use comparisons to explain a process or an idea. Compare an everyday event that is readily understandable to your reader with new information you are introducing to your reader.
- Use diagrams or graphs, pictures or cartoons (if it does not add much to the expense of publishing) in order to better explain your ideas.

And, finally, be sure your writing sounds like *you* talking – even if it means breaking a few of the rules I have just given. It is more important that you sound conversational and real than it is to have starched perfection. Do your best to execute the rules of writing, while writing the way you talk.

The only exception to writing the way you talk is that if you talk in a professorial, bookish manner, you will be boring, both as a speaker and as a writer. So keep in the front of your mind that the most forceful language is simple and direct. Eliminate long, pretentious words.

Also, review the following, important steps of writing and editing in layers, which I have already included elsewhere in this book.

Non-Fiction Layers Of Writing

1. **Layer 1 – Your First Draft Layer** – your first draft is your basic book (Creative Mud). Write from start to finish without editing until you get your first draft finished

2. **Layer 2 – Your Mental Paintbrush Layer**– as you read your first draft, paint a layer of Examples and Analogies and Human Interest cases-in-point to flesh out your logic or step-by-step explanations. This is part of Creative editing.

3. **Layer 3 – Your Clarity Layer** – read each chapter with one question in your mind – is this clear? Is it sharp? Does each chapter stay 'on track' with the chapter topic? This is part of Creative editing.

4. **Layer 4 – Your Final Editing Layer** – add to – and then take away whatever is not needed. Do this several times. The human body sloughs off or eliminates what it not needed – that is what you do with your manuscript in the final stages of editing.

Part 4

WRITING BEYOND 3 WEEKS

Taking Your Time – Finding Your Pace –

Chapter 44

Write A Book In
6 Months – 1 Year
– Less Than 2 Years

You can write as a hobby; or find your own pace with at least 10 minutes a day. – Ginie Sayles

A man in La Jolla, California attended my *How To write A Book In 3 Weeks – Or Less* seminar because, as he said, "My CPA told me that if I don't get my book finished and submitted for publication, my research expenses cannot be counted as a write-off. My CPA said I will have to change writing from a profession to a hobby and foot the bill myself."

Humor aside, there is truth to what the man said. Some people find they diddle and dawdle, hoping to finish their books but years pass by and they have nothing to show for it.

However, it is just as true that many people who have demanding careers in some other field; enjoy writing as a hobby or avocation. They do not know if their writing is good enough for publication – or even if they think their writing *is* good enough for publication – they simply find a casual, lassez-faire attitude toward their writing to be restful, relaxing, completely enjoyable.

There is nothing wrong with that – whether it is consciously writing as a hobby or just taking your time as you write for relaxation – both are viable reasons to write.

Yes, markets may change and the book idea you initially had may pass out of style – but so what, as long as this gentle tempo of writing feeds your soul. There is always the pendulum swing of time that brings some types of writing back into vogue.

If you are a bit market-driven, then kick up your writing speed in ways laid out earlier in this book; or, once you have finished your book, you can check current markets and modify a few chapters or situations to put your book in the current flow.

A friend of mine said he enjoyed writing from time to time and the idea of writing a book often entered his thoughts; but that he really did not know if he could write a book or not and wanted to dabble for awhile…just to get his feet wet, first. He wondered if writing as a hobby is a feasible way to write a book – and I assured him, it is.

A woman in Austin, Texas said to me, "I feel that my life flashes by in a blur of schedules – of watching the clock and keeping appointments and rushing to be on time and checking my calendar. Daily life is stress for me."

Then her facial expression softened when she added, "but when I sit down and start writing – sometimes a few minutes, sometimes until midnight – all the stress melts away and I enjoy writing on my own timetable. I don't have any deadlines for getting finished."

"Then writing is your salvation," I said, "And you should write the way you have been writing – as a hobby. A hobby is any activity people do in their free time as a leisurely pastime of enjoyment."

"But I want it to be good," she protested, "and maybe even be published…someday."

"And it can be good and it can be published, one way or another," I answered, "Many times the pleasure of a hobby can lead to wonderful success. It is not either/or; it is either/and for you, meaning you can do it for real and yet as a relaxing expression of yourself."

As always, when someone says 'someday' I suspect Fear is the thief of their time; but if writing slowly is the only way a person *thinks* he or she can write, I encourage them to go ahead because it is a starting point and it keeps them writing.

I replied to the woman, "If your story begins to take shape and you feel excited about it, the word 'someday' will change. You will want to finalize it and maybe to do something with it."

What do I do in the meantime?" she asked.

It is a question you may be asking yourself, too.

Here is the answer:

How To Write A Book In 10 Minutes A Day

Writing is like any other skill: the more you write, the better your writing becomes. The less you write the more skills you lose without realizing it.

But if the idea of writing 3 hours a day is mind-boggling, then find a length of time that is comfortable and do-able for you. Make it a length of time that may seem ridiculous to other people but they don't count – because this is *your* time and not theirs. Besides, you are not going to tell them, anyway!

Keeping your writing pleasurable is most important for those of you who view it as a hobby – perhaps as a hobby with potential.

For relaxing days of writing, you may surprise yourself by writing almost an hour or almost all day (wow) and that is great.

But rather than a complete hit and miss twice a year writing spree or writing every so often and not really getting anywhere, consider *keeping your writing times relaxing – and daily* – even if it is *just 10 minutes every single day – and finish it in about 1 year and 9 months.*

Your 10 minutes is your 10 minutes. So, if you sit down and think for 10 minutes and all you write is one sentence, it is one sentence you did not have before! Hooray for you and your sentence. I am very serious about that. Each addition – no matter how small – is significant.

But, *in 10 minutes of actual writing, you will typically write 1/3rd of a page – roughly 94 words.*

Make your 10 minute writing period a very relaxing time for you, as well. Maybe when you first come home from work and feel a little frazzled, change into comfy clothes, brew a cup of tea or coffee and sip it as you settle into your writing chair and switch on your computer.

Or maybe just before you go to bed, turn off the television, take a hot bath or shower, and wearing your robe or pajamas, write for at least 10 minutes before going to bed.

Or 10 minutes in the morning before you go to work, or 10 minutes at noon before you meet your buddies for lunch or 10 minutes after work before you go to happy hour.

The super-neat magic of 10 minutes is that your writing gets better and better – and you also find yourself getting deeper and deeper into your story. There will be numerous times you find you don't even think of stopping after 10 minutes and suddenly you look up and 30 minutes or an hour or several hours have passed.

This will happen increasingly and one day, you really are a very serious writer.

At that point you may decide you want to bump up your speed – so turn to the 3 Weeks – Or Less sections of this book and take it from there.

But if you want to continue to write at a leisurely pace, just stick with at least 10 minutes a day or more and find your own pace.

Let's look at how you can leisurely write your 200 page book and finish in 6 months, 1 year, or even less than 2 years!

Leisurely Writing A Book In – 6 Months – 1 Year – 2 years

200-220 Page Book @ roughly 275 - 300 words per page

10 Minutes a day   =   732 days   =   2 Years, 2 days

20 Minutes a day   =   366 days   =   1 Year, 1 day

40 Minutes a day   =   183 days   =   6 Months, 3 days

In Chapter 2 Why Write A Book In 3 Weeks- Or Less?, I told the true story of a **woman who leisurely wrote a book in ten years and by then her husband was too ill for her to leave him in order to promote her book.** Even so, I still contend that a leisurely pace is as viable as a fast pace if it is your only entry point of confidence into writing – OR – if it is the only way you enjoy writing – OR – if writing is a hobby for the time being.

In any case, 10 minutes is your super best friend! It WILL get you there, if you are faithful to at least 10 minutes a day. Choose the time period given above for your goals that will allow you to savor a leisurely pace of writing enjoyment – and still get it done.

Now, that is do-able – and livable for those of you who just do not want to be rushed.

10 Minute Magic In Revisions

If you are revising your First Draft – spend at least 10 to 15 minutes a day (or longer) brushing up the following:

Week 1 Revisions: **just 10 to 15 minutes a day** perfecting Situations and your Characters in each Situation.

Week 2 Revisions: **just 10 to 15 minutes a day** perfecting your Settings – include all senses – and try for a metaphor or simile in at least every third chapter (or more frequently).

Week 3 Revisions: **just 10 to 15 minutes a day** checking the changes in Mood and Pace.

Create "Extra Time" With Your Digital Timer

A Timer lets you discover how to measure time, how to save time, and how to make time your friend. With a Timer, you become increasingly effective, less judgmental on yourself, and accomplished. You do so much more than you ever imagined. A Timer teaches you to 'trust' your flow of instant thought.

If you can cram an extra 10 minutes in before you have to go somewhere, set your Timer for 10 minutes and you will achieve more in that 10 minutes than you imagined.

If you have a spare 10 minutes before you expect someone to arrive, set your Timer for 10 minutes, and work on your manuscript.

Or, if you know you should write a long time; but you are not sure how inspired you feel, set your Timer for 30 minutes or for 1 hour and start typing.

I use this method frequently to create extra writing time. And I am amazed at how much I get done in a short period of time. If we are going somewhere and I only have a few minutes, I will set my Timer for 5, 10, or 15 minutes and start writing. When my Timer starts beeping, I am always surprised to find I am in full flow and ready to write more.

But since I have to go somewhere, I stop, pick up my Sacred Idea Book – small spiral notepad – and take it with me so that I can make notes in the ladies room when ideas start coming to me.

The minute you sit down to write, set your Timer for at least 10 minutes – or if you have more time, set it for 30 minutes or for 1 or 2 hours – and then lose yourself in your writing. You will be surprised when your Timer goes off.

A digital Timer is your very special friend – your magic genie of Creativity. A Timer lets you discover how much faster you are than you think.

Set Your Timer And Just Start

Sometimes, you may feel that you do not know what to write or where to start. Using your digital Timer keeps you going.

On most days, I set my Timer for 1 hour or sometimes for 2 hours and start writing. On slow idea days, I set it for 1 hour. At the end of that time, if I have done reasonably well but I still do not feel red hot inspiration, I make tea, coffee or cocoa, re-set the

Timer for 1 hour and go at it again. I find that this method 'gets things done' no matter what.

Just starting – and having a time frame you can live with – 10 minutes, 15 minutes, 30 minutes or an hour – brings a greater reward than doing nothing.

Listen, 10 minutes of writing is better than no minutes of writing! You discover you get more involved in it than you thought you would.

Time Can Translate Into Setting A Quota Of Pages Per Day

Rather than hours per day; some authors set a rigorous task for themselves of writing a specific number of pages per day. I offer you both – pages per day and hours per day. As long as you have written at least 200 pages at the end of your book, it does not matter how you accomplished it.

Numerous writers have patterned themselves after the two prolific writers below:

- **George Sand** – A notorious 19th century French author and feminist (without knowing that was the word for it); Amandine Aurore Lucile Dupin, Baroness Dudevant was a married aristocrat who wrote under the pen name of George Sand. Despite flaunting customs for women's dress by wearing trousers and smoking tobacco in public, and despite her numerous love affairs with many famous men of the time (including the famous composer, Frederic Chopin); George Sand steadfastly kept to her quota of writing 20 pages a day. No matter what time she started, she did not go to bed until she finished writing 20 pages – often writing from midnight until dawn.

- **Janet Dailey** –An Internet source states "during her most prolific years, Dailey set a goal of writing 15 pages per day. Her day began at 4 a.m. On good days, she would meet her quota in 8 to 10 hours; other days would require 12 to 14 hours of work." The minute she met her goal, Janet stopped writing even if it meant leaving a sentence unfinished. This 'unfinished sentence method' appears to have jump-started her writing the next day. It seems this 'unfinished sentence' method to jump-start writing was also a method used by Ernest Hemingway.

Goals For A 200 Page Book Can Translate Into Chapters Per Book

You can also set a goal of writing a certain number of Chapters per book.

For example:

1. A 10 Chapter book of 20 Pages per Chapter = a 200 page book.
2. A 20 Chapter book of 10 Pages per Chapter = a 200 page book.

The late Barbara Cartland wrote exactly a Chapter per Day; and other authors like the feel of such precision. You may want to write a Chapter per Week; or a Chapter per Month, to keep a leisurely pace and still have a goal for a 200 page book. The reason I use 200 pages is because that has evolved into the minimal standard for a book in the traditional publishing definitions. Even so, standards do change over time.

Writing For You

If you do not plan to 'make a living' as a writer; but you enjoy writing, then write for you. If you toy with the idea of writing a book in a leisurely way, it is just as valid to write a book over time as it is in 3 weeks or less.

There are drawbacks to writing slowly and those drawbacks have already been covered in this book; but it is far more important to write, period, whatever the timetable you establish.

Chapter 45

Writing
As Self-Therapy

If an author's writing is consistently 'dark,' it is time to examine personal issues that may be leaching into the work. – Ginie Sayles

I have noticed in my Fiction-Writing Workshops that new writers often write sad pieces or unhappy sketches. Even with talent and fine skills, these writers express a hopeless or depressed or bitter scene, sometimes with futile endings.

Most of the time, the writers, themselves, define their own writing as 'dark.' Some of them think their work is 'realistic.' But it is their own view of 'realistic.'

The truth is that writing in a dark mode often indicates the writer's own unresolved personal issues leaching into the work, even though it is not an autobiographical story. In most cases, there are painful issues with parents or spouses or love relationships in general that have colored the lens of 'dark' writers. And, as well-written as a piece may be; 'dark' or negative writing is amateurish in its one-dimensional nature.

Yes, I know there are authors who made a name for themselves writing dark pieces. Sylvia Plath and Virginia Woolf had tremendous talent but the leeching of their unresolved neuroses into their work became self-reinforcing to the point of developing an illness to the point of suicide. Both great writers were self-indulgent in their darkness and nursed their depression through their writings to fatal harm.

Had these brilliant writers developed their range of writing by 'exploring new mental and emotional experiences they wished for, the brilliance of their writing could well have given a breadth to their writing that would have been even greater than they or we could imagine.

From Amateurish Writing To Maturity – Darkness To Light

Any writing – no matter how skilled – with self-indulgent and limited scope remains undeveloped and therefore immature. Writers who stretch themselves into new emotions and explore a wider inner universe, are truly 'creative' in the full meaning of the word. This form of self-expression limits the writer's scope. Limitations are not creative. Remaining in a limited emotional view of life stagnates your writing.

There are two specific ways – using two specific writing modes – to develop your writing into mature creativity with a wide range of perceptions and creative discoveries.

Self-Therapy Writing

If you have unresolved personal issues; writing about them can be a form of self-therapy but only to an extent. Yes, it can provide an outlet for your feelings, which can be good. On the other hand, it can stir up volatile feelings that can make matters worse if you then act on them.

The greatest danger, though, is that your perspective of the events may become self-indulgent in a deepening one-sided view – prejudicial to the point of discoloring the issues. This complicates your issues into nursing your grievances, rather than dealing with them.

Another down-side to writing about your unresolved issues is that you may find yourself so upset or so depressed that you stop writing at all.

If this happens or if you find yourself more upset than ever, then consider working with a licensed therapist who does *not* prescribe drugs for depression (that only masks the issues and keeps you dependent and undeveloped) and a therapist who works the old fashioned 'talk it through' method and offers a new perspective of the situation plus helpful choices.

Self-therapy writing can alleviate the stress of unresolved issues and help you analyze how they continue to play out in your day to day life. If there seems to be no way to resolve the issue to your own satisfaction; you can pose possible 'solutions' rather than 'resolutions' for managing your pain or anger.

But the most positive form of Writing As Self-Therapy is when you mature in the following, very healthy ***method of developing as a writer and healing yourself.***

Creative Writing

Many people have heard me say that Creativity is our ultimate survival tool. We adapt and we solve problems through our wonderful Creativity.

In a TCM profile of actor/producer/director Ron Howard, I was taken by something he said about the comment made by John Forbes Nash, the subject of Howard's biographical movie, *A Beautiful Mind.* Nash, a Nobel Laureate, who once suffered from mental illness, said that if his mind had made him sick, then his mind could make him well, and he worked at making mental choices (thought processes) for healing, which worked for him.

You most likely do not have such extreme complications; but the answer is still the same: forging a mental state that makes your life most effective – both as an individual and as a writer.

Writers have a distinct advantage over many people for accomplishing this.

Ask yourself, "What do I wish had happened in my life?" And then write the story you wish you had lived.

One of my male students, whom I will call Samuel, was adopted as a newborn by a couple who had tried for years to conceive and finally gave up and settled for adoption. No sooner had ink dried on the adoption papers than the wife discovered she was pregnant and gave birth to a boy, whom I will call Dave.

His parents were determined to love them the same; but their good intentions failed almost on a daily basis. If both babies wanted the same toy, it went to their natural born son, Dave. If Samuel exhibited more natural ability in a sport or music than Dave, then Samuel was taken out of the sport or music and Dave was allowed to develop and excel. In every instance, Dave was the Golden-Haired Boy.

Daily, it was clear that Samuel did not have permission to equal or to excel Dave. Any problems that Dave had were always blamed on Samuel. Of course, the parents always claimed they were fair and equal with both boys, but that Samuel was just a problem and Dave was not. In reality, they told themselves this lie until they believed it. But they had programmed their adopted son, Samuel, to be a loser and their natural born son, Dave, to be a winner – and it was playing out exactly as they programmed it.

Without a doubt, this was an explosive situation – like the Cain and Abel story from the Bible – and it enrages all of us. Samuel's hurt was fully justified – unless it destroyed his life. If so, the misguided parents would have won because he would have lived up their programming which would have made them feel justified. But most devastating of all, he would have let them define him.

Fortunately, through writing, that did not happen.

When I saw that Samuel's writing was dark, I asked him to write a story with a Character like Samuel who, instead of reacting to the situation by languishing in his sadness, becomes a proactive winner who secretly achieves and in the end 'shows 'em' with a positive triumph and frees himself emotionally from their grasp.

The assignment had a magical result. Suddenly, Samuel was 'trying on' a variety of experiences and emotions and a winner mentality he had never considered before. He became increasingly passionate in his writing and looked forward to it.

It took him just over two years to write his novel – two years of writing and rewriting, learning how to make his Character into a winner. By the time he finished his book, Samuel no longer had the 'loser' identification that had been pasted on his self-esteem by his adoptive family. Through his writing, he had experienced a new mental state of achievement and set forth how his Character – or alter ego – became a happy person and an achiever. Samuel had learned how to deal with and to overcome the situation by reframing his Character's (his) triumph over it.

…and, yes, by the time, he finished writing his book, that is exactly what he had become…a happy, more confident person and an achiever. He wrote a novel, a good novel – which is something Dave never did. And even if Dave ever does write a novel, Samuel's success stands alone…as his and Samuel did it first.

Through his writing, Samuel healed himself. Through his writing he defined himself as he wanted to be and he learned not to let anyone else define him. He reclaimed his ego and in the end, that is what we all must do, whether we are writers or not.

*A happy state of mind can be created from the **outside-in**.* How? Several ways. I once read that just as feeling happy on the inside releases endorphins (happy feelings) causing us to smile on the outside; that conversely, if we simply choose to smile, that behavior can also cause the release of endorphins, causing us to feel happier. So, yes, happiness can work from the inside-out; but also from the outside-in.

I have also found that speaking affirmations has much the same result – as does hypnosis if you have a very good, non-controlling but supportive, encouraging hypnotherapist – and even positive CD messages that enhance self-esteem.

What all of this means is that we have a choice. And that includes the choice of experiencing a state of exalted success or simple happiness through our Characters when we write.

To use Creativity as self-therapy, put a 'character' in your place and enjoy rewriting your life in a new and vibrant novel, the way you would like to experience it or wish it had been.

Do not ask the people who have hurt you to read it and do not seek their approval or praise for your achievement. They will not give it. Accept the fact that giving them the power to hurt you by seeking their approval is hurting yourself. Keep your power. Keep your writing sacred. This belongs to you and to you alone. And then, you really are successful. You will have a success they cannot take away from you.

Creative Writing means exploring many different ranges of emotion from your own unresolved issues.

- Write the same scenes from a variety of vantage points.
  a. How would a Character behave in this scene if newly and happily in love?
  b. How would a Character behave in this scene if having fun?
  c. How would the Character behave if feeling confident?
  d. How would the Character behave if figuring out success?
- Write scenes you have not experienced but as you imagine it in a proactive success.

Can your dark feelings or unhappy experiences help your writing? In small doses, yes, when you have a chapter in which a Character feels the loss of a loved one or a disappointment – but this should only be an *occasional* – very occasional – scene in your book. Most of your book should deal with the proactive forces of your main Character, not the self-pitying ache of a reactive loser.

If you want to write as self-therapy even in a creative mode; you do not have to try to write fast. Just write new facets of experience and thought, however long it takes.

Be sure you study **Chapter 13 Key Factor - The Fire Of Your Creative Spirit.** The processes of Creativity and of writing in layers will be totally important to you as you take your time in writing.

No matter how long it takes you to write your book, the process is the same and being aware of writing in the layers set forth in that chapter will greatly improve the quality of your work.

Part 5

IMPORTANT EXTRAS

Chapter

46

Layering
Write In Layers – Edit In Layers

When you write and edit in layers, your book-writing experience is easier. – Ginie Sayles

Think of writing the same way you think of a human body – first is the skeleton, then muscles and organs are layered on top of it.

That is how you write, too. As you write your First Draft – the skeleton story of your book – your main goal is to get the story down as quickly as possible, with all the major parts in place. During that time, it is best not to edit until you are finished; but if you feel you must, then limit edits on a chapter to no more than twice as you work through your First Draft. Then add more **layers that bring your book to life!** Writing in layers works!

I also use the analogy of a potter, to provide the following layers of writing. I have listed them them several times in this book, as they applied:

Non-Fiction Layers Of Writing

Layer 1 – Your First Draft Layer – your first draft is your basic book.

Layer 2 – Your Mental Paintbrush Layer– as you read through your non-fiction first draft, paint a layer of Examples and Analogies and Human Interest cases-in-point to flesh out your logic or step-by-step explanations. This is part of Creative Editing.

Layer 3 – Your Clarity Layer – read each chapter with these questions in your mind – is this clear? Is it sharp? Does each chapter stay 'on track' with the chapter topic? This is part of Creative Editing.

Layer 4 – Your Final Editing Layer – add to – and then take away whatever is not needed. Do this several times with your manuscript until you release it for a time and then come back for the final stage of editing. At that point, add finishing touches.

Fiction Layers Of Writing

Layer 1 – Your First Draft Layer – your first draft is your basic story.

Layer 2 – Your Mental Paintbrush Layer– as you read your first draft, paint a layer of description into your Characters, Settings, Situations and so on, in each chapter. This is part of Creative Editing.

Layer 3 – Your Sensory Layer – Re-read again and be sure you describe all 5 senses in each chapter. Be sure there is Variety in Mood and Pace. This is part of Creative Editing.

Layer 4 – Your Final Editing Layer – add to – and then take away whatever is not needed. Do this several times with your manuscript until you release it for a time and then come back for the final stage of editing. Then add finishing touches.

When you write in layers, your writing becomes better and better. And that is the process of 'polishing' the prose.

Edit In Layers

Back to my initial analogy of thinking of writing the same way you think of a human body. Well, a human body also 'sloughs off' what it does not need and this keeps us healthier. Our bodies eliminate what is not needed and we would die if we could not eliminate them.

So, in the same way, we make our writing cleaner and more vigorous by editing in layers, sloughing off and eliminating what is not needed.

Even with a little bit of 'fat' in minor digressions – keep writing in layers to build the body of your book – and editing in layers to trim excess from the body of your book – just as nature does with a human body. It works the same way.

How To Organize Your Mind For Editing

Sometimes you may feel overwhelmed and stare at your work, feeling that you do not know how to organize it. If you work hard at it for an hour and cannot seem to get anywhere; you need to get away from your manuscript and just get your mind into an orderly focus.

Organizing requires skills of sorting, putting things together that belong together and throwing away what is not needed. So, you can prepare your mind for organizing your manuscript by organizing something you already know how to organize. Familiar skills in small jobs, such as cleaning a room or cooking an easy recipe will do it.

Just the orderliness of putting things into place or carefully measuring ingredients and following a recipe focuses your mind into an orderly process.

Do not get into a major clean-up job of finally attacking the garage or cooking a complicated dish or you will find that you are using it as an excuse not to work. The clean-up or recipe should be simple and not take more than half an hour.

During that time, the Creative Spirit in the back of your mind will follow suit automatically and begin sorting and organizing your material when you return to your manuscript. Your mind can be focused with greater clarity.

A few methods that work are:

1. Light house cleaning that takes no more than 20 – 40 minutes – or some part of it, such as the bathroom or the kitchen – or straightening it up. Remember, I said 'light' house cleaning.
2. Organize a single drawer, one shelf on a closet, or a single book shelf.
3. Cook something simple – i.e. cookies or muffins – and cleaning up as you go. Measure everything precisely. No pinch of this or pinch of that. You can cook that way later – just as you write that way, intuitively. Right now, organize ingredients rather than intuit them.
4. Vacuum your car and throw away trash.

Choose one of the above or something similar that requires precise thinking, and do it quickly to get your mind organized, and then come back to your work.

Editing And Your Workspace

Take 5 – 10 minutes to clean up your sacred writing space. Sometimes a messy workspace can subliminally drain your mental energy. A chaotic environment can make you feel psychologically scattered...and you will not even realize that is what the problem is.

You may say to yourself, "but I think it is part of my creative nature and I know where everything is this way. If it is cleaned up, I will be lost." I used to feel that way, but I learned that this concept is not true.

It is an excuse to postpone cleaning it up. No, it does not have to be perfect – and do not stop to read *any*thing. Just stack neat piles and straighten. Even just taking a second to stack papers neatly can do wonders for setting your mind in an orderly mode before you edit.

Editing And Your Over-all Environment

For a really out of control environment, filled with papers you are afraid to throw away because you may "need them... someday;" buy plastic garbage bags at the supermarket and stuff armsful of 'papers-you-may-need-someday' into the bags. Do not bother to examine them. You will be able to find them, if you really do need them...someday.

Tie up the bags and stuff them out of sight...under a bed or in a closet. If you have too many of them, rent a tiny storage space for a small amount of money and put them out of sight.

Get control of your work environment and watch yourself gain a new control over your work, itself. Chaos breeds chaos, and order breeds order.

The very universe operates on order – the sun rising in the east each day and setting in the west, et cetera – and we count on it; otherwise, we could not survive.

Once your workspace is orderly, your mind has room to think without subliminal distractions of clutter. And your mind is in an orderly mode. You have everything it takes to organize your ideas. Rely on familiar skills and transpose them into editing skills.

And remember – all books are written one word at a time. And all books are corrected one word at a time.

Editing Tips

Because editing is the process of making revisions to your writing, try the following:
1. Re-read your manuscript – This is something you will do automatically. Anytime you have written a manuscript, you will be so proud of having completed it that you will re-read it as much as fifty times!

2. As you read through it, DO NOT JUDGE THE WORTH OF IT, just check for typing errors, omissions, and misspelled words.
3. Delete anything that seems unnecessary (or 'cut and paste' it in a separate file – you can call it scrap.doc file – if you are not sure that you want to delete it. You can retrieve it later if you think you need it; but eliminate it for the time being from your working draft.
4. Revise any sentences or paragraphs that you think can be better. Again, you can use your separate scrap.doc file to copy and paste the original sentence or paragraph before editing it in the main file – so that you can come back and get it if you want to.
5. Insert any details or other ideas that come to you in various parts of your work.
6. After each chapter, ask yourself if the chapter is needed or if the book would make more sense without it.
7. After each chapter ask if it flows reasonably well, and if each paragraph invites the next paragraph. You may want to make a note of 'come back later to this' every once in awhile to a chapter that you are not sure you want to keep.
8. Check the way you opened each chapter:
   a) What did you want the main impression to be?
   b) Begin with a topic sentence stating this impression: *I had a good view of the party going on across the street.*
   c) Did you clearly describe your subject?
   d) Cross out items that do not add to the effect that you want to give.
   e) Arrange the remaining items in an order that the reader can follow.
   f) Did you stick to one point of view?
   g) Does the end of your chapter put the question in the mind of the reader, "What is next?"

9. Preen over every single chapter, sentence, description, or paragraph that you feel really proud of. Preen, preen, preen. You deserve it!
10. Now, re-read it again – each paragraph one at a time – to see if you have one clear paragraph that best expresses an idea or scene and eliminates the need for some of the others before it.
11. Cut out the questionable paragraphs and put them into the scrap file, re-read the chapter with the tightened paragraph and ask yourself, "Does it make the meaning stronger?"
12. If yes, keep it, of course.
13. At the end of this editing session, preen some more. You can never preen too much.

Note: My separate Scrap.doc files – The great thing about not deleting questionable parts of my writing but putting it into a 'scrap' file is:

(1) My Scrap.doc file gives me the confidence to take out a sentence or paragraph I am afraid I might regret deleting. Most of the time I later realize I did not need the extra paragraphs or sentences that I cut and pasted into the scrap file.

(2) But sometimes I have found another place in a book for a paragraph or sentence I took out elsewhere; so I just go get it out of the scrap file and insert it where it does work well.

Writing and editing in layers is a simple way to improve your work; and your book-writing experience is easier.

Chapter 47

All-Important
Copyright

Spell It 'Right' – copy<u>right</u> not copywrite. It is a legal term
that means you own the **'right'** *of* **'copy'** *to your work –*
hence copyright, meaning others must have your written
permission or pay you a licensing fee in order to copy it.
– Ginie Sayles

A few years ago, I received letters from Readers around the country, telling me there was a book that plagiarized one of my books.

One Reader wrote, "Ginie, I can just see this author with your book propped up in front of the computer, copying you! It really makes me mad!"

At the time, I was incredibly busy, traveling around the USA and Canada, presenting seminars and I kept thinking, "No one would really do that. It must be a book on a similar topic."

Then, a Librarian wrote me and said, "If you have not seen this book, I strongly urge you to do so. This author has plagiarized your book."

I purchased a copy of the book in question and I was amazed at what I saw. But more than amazement, I was deeply disappointed in the author.

The author took my paragraphs, rearranged the sentences in the paragraphs, or paraphrased them or placed them in a different chapter.

The author even used my slogan I had coined as a trademark for my seminar and book. Plus, the author did not credit my work or me as a resource.

Paraphrase Is Plagiarism. Make no mistake. Paraphrase is plagiarism under the law. So, I mailed a side-by-side comparison of the paragraphs and pages of both books to my publisher's attorney who, in turn, contacted the other author's publisher and the matter was quickly settled in my favor. Printing on the other author's book instantly ceased.

Copyright is Key. My original copyright pre-dated the other author by eight years and my more recent copyright predated the author by three years. My copyright – secured by a number issued to me by the Library of Congress – protected me.

Legal Substitute For A Copyright?

Some people think if they simply mail a copy of their manuscript to themselves and keep it unopened, that the post mark is proof of their ownership?

Do not do that! Here's why…

In order to prove any author deliberately stole your work, the author would have to have access to your work in order to copy it.

How could an author who does not know you and has never visited you have copied your manuscript if you have only mailed it to yourself and put it in your closet on a shelf? The author must have access to your work.

If you file your work for copyright with the Library of Congress and they issue you a number, it is publicly available and with a provable date of when you filed it for copyright. If anyone publishes the same work at a later date; you can prove your work was viewable through the Library of Congress and that you have

369

a prior date. And later, if you publish your book, your ownership of the work is easy to prove by the **date of copyright, which is a legally recognized source.**

Copyright Forms Are Easy To Fill Out

You can fill out a copyright TX Form in about 10 minutes – and that 10 minutes can be the smartest move of your life. You can either do it online – paying the required amount and uploading your manuscript; or you can mail it in.

A copyright means you own the right of copy to your work and therefore people must obtain permission from you if they want to copy it. That is how money is made through copyright.

To order additional information about copyrighting your work, you can visit the websites, telephone or write:

The US Copyright Office:
Register of Copyrights
Library of Congress
Washington, DC 20559-6000
(202) 707-3000
http://www.loc.gov/copyright

The Canadian Copyright Office:
CIPO, Copyright Office
50 Victoria Street
Place du Portage, Tower One
Hall Quebec K1A 0C9
(819) 997-1936
http://cipo.gc.ca

These are the addresses and numbers at the time I first wrote this; so be sure to visit the websites and their 'contact us' page for any changes they may have made.

It usually takes quite awhile for the copyright office to process your copyright. If you mail your copyright form and your work and payment to the copyright office, be sure to send it certified mail with a return receipt which is a little green card sent back to you. I was told that when you receive the green return card, the day it is stamped as received by the copyright office is the date your copyright begins.

Be sure you check with the copyright office of your country to find out the following:

▪ How many copies of your manuscript to mail to them.

- How much money it currently costs.
- How to file your copyright for International Protection as well.

Only One Rule In Writing – And Copyright Helps Protect It

There is only one rule in my classes: YOUR WRITING IDEAS ARE SACRED. Do not share your ideas or your work with anyone. Even in my writing class I tell students to keep their ideas to themselves – and I do not allow students to share their private work with me.

How can you learn without sharing your work?

The way I do it in my Fiction Writing Workshop is by having everyone write about the same story – perhaps using Goldilocks and the Three Bears as an example – and each student reads his/her version aloud. It works out well because no one's private, original work is compromised – and yet we enjoy the variety of viewpoints told about the same story. Frankly, I have been amazed at the uniqueness and range of expression among my students.

They learn what they need to know from a generic assignment and then they can transpose those skills into their private work at home.

What about Agents And Publishers?

Only share work that you have filed for copyright. I mean that, seriously. And have your work marked with the copyright insignia.

A lot of people and books will tell you not to worry about filing for copyright before sending your work to agents and publishers and that it is a sign of an immature writer to copyright your work first.

Don't believe it! And who cares if they think you are an immature writer as long as your work is protected. Besides, why should they mind that you have been responsible to your own work – as you should be? If they like it, they will want it, copyright and all.

Even Agents and publishers who are honorable and honest MAY FORGET WHERE THEY READ AN IDEA and months later may innocently suggest it to their Star Author, not recalling they read it.

Agents and publishers do have their Star Authors and probably some in the genre you want to enter. You are an unknown and it would take money and time to build your name recognition – whereas if their Star Author is given a 'similar' idea the Star Author can peel out a book and instant name recognition makes it a quick bestseller.

I am not saying they do this; but you can better protect yourself from the possibility of it by having a copyright on anything you submit.

The Danger Of No Copyright On A Submitted Manuscript

Let me tell you **a true story.** An author wrote an entire manuscript and sent it to her Agent – a very successful Agent, too. The Agent called the author and said the manuscript was too risqué and turned it down.

Three years later, the author saw her exact story in a television movie that aired on a network for women. The author's exact story!!

What could the author do? Nothing, because she had not filed it for copyright before sending it to her trusted Agent. By this time, she had no proof and the Agent would likely claim not to remember it – and after all that time had passed, he probably would not remember exactly, considering all the manuscripts that flood his office each day.

Did the Agent betray her? I don't know; but I strongly suspect a leak in the Agent's office by a staff agent.

372

Questionable Staff Agents?

Like most big-time Agents, the author's Agent had several staff agents working for him. And there is often a rapid turn-over of staff in Agent offices (publishing offices, too).

Because top Agents are very busy, visiting publishers and negotiating financial terms of a sale, the Agent probably had one of his staff agents read the manuscript and give feedback before the Agent read it himself – if, indeed, he ever read it at all. Sometimes, a busy Agent will simply take the word of staff agents on a manuscript.

1. **Most staff agents have literary degrees and backgrounds as editors.** Most have worked in publishing houses before deciding to work for an Agent just to learn the ins and outs of agents so they can eventually write and sell their own books and know how to make it happen and how to get the best deal. Very smart.

2. **Staff agents are also 'agents' cultivating their own authors**– but they work under the umbrella of an established Agent/Agency because they cannot afford to go on their own, yet. They actively sign new authors of their own so that they can eventually go independent.

I think one of the staff agents, who was trusted by the Agent, probably nixed the manuscript to the Agent – and the Agent took the staff agent's word and never even looked at the manuscript.

Then the staff agent may have taken the book idea directly to a publisher who was friendly with the staff agent, and the staff agent either got a contract and copied the manuscript under another name; or the staff agent may have contacted an author who was already under contract with the staff agent and asked the innocent author to write it. The story was exactly the same. Exactly.

But, again, without a copyright, the original author had no claim.

If you have a copyright on your work before you submit it to an agent or to a publisher such a scenario is less likely to happen. Once again, I state that most agents and most publishers are not going to do this deliberately– but why take the risk? Just copyright your work and you have fewer worries.

Send only what you have filed for copyright to any agent; and mark the correct copyright insignia on your work. The correct way to mark a copyright on your work is:

Copyright © 2009 by <u>Your Name</u>
ALL RIGHTS RESERVED

What About Best Friends, Job Supervisors, Writing Clubs?

A little paranoia can be a healthy ally. Best friends, relatives (yes, relatives), and people in writing groups can be tempted to take a story idea if they see an opportunity.

"But I only tell my friends." you are likely to protest and with a shrug, add, "And my family."

I could fill a separate book with true stories of writers who have excitedly shared their book ideas with their very best friends or family members and were betrayed by the very people they loved and trusted most in this world.

This is especially true of employers or fellow employees.

A schoolteacher came to me in tears. The teacher had devised an effective system of helping special education students. So the teacher decided to write a book about it.

In the meantime, the Supervisor of Special Education for all the schools in that city came to visit one day and the teacher, eager to impress the supervisor and hoping it would help with possible job promotions, took the supervisor on a tour of her students and classes while explaining her new system she had developed.

Unknown to the teacher, the supervisor was working on a doctorate degree and yes, the supervisor went home, typed it up, and submitted it for the doctoral thesis – and then had it published as a book. There was nothing the teacher could do. Sharing without a copyright is foolishness.

Best friends, employers, and, yes, even family members can let you down.

What you do not share cannot be published by another person – and if you have it filed for copyright before sharing it, that person must have your permission to use your information and to attribute it to you or the person will be liable for infringement or violation.

This is why I say that the secret to success is the word 'secret' and it is why I insist that you copyright your work before revealing it to anyone.

You Want A Number Issued To You By The Library Of Congress

The Library of Congress will issue you a number for each copyright you file. This number is vital as your proof of the date you filed your manuscript for copyright.

Why is this important?

One of my publishers and I had a misunderstanding – something that occasionally happens between authors and publishers; and the publisher said he could take my manuscript from me and publish it under another name.

My husband, furious at this affront, took me to a literary attorney. When we explained the situation, the very first words out of the lawyer's mouth were, "Ginie, do you have a NUMBER issued to you from the Library of Congress that proves your work has a copyright?"

Before I could answer, he explained, "A lot of people just type the copyright symbol © on their work and think that protects them, but it doesn't. I need to know if you have an actual number issued to you from the Library of Congress. Do you?"

"Yes, I do," I said, and I did.

He gave a big smile. "In that case, there is absolutely no way the publisher can take your manuscript from you. The number issued to you by the Library of Congress is your proof of ownership."

The publisher and I eventually worked out our grievance on the matter and ended up with a stronger relationship. The book was published with no further problems because the smartest move I ever made was to have my work filed for copyright *before* the publisher ever saw it.

Chapter

48

Money
- Ways Authors Make It -

There is more saving than there is in making.
– Eva Addron Carroll

There are a number of ways authors can make money from writing books; and they include the following:

1. *A Book Advance* is a negotiated amount of money a publisher pays an author at the time of signing a publishing contract – sometimes before it is even written.
   An advance is often paid in two (or more) installments – half at the signing of the contract and the other half upon delivery and acceptance of the final manuscript.
   What you must realize is that you do not receive any royalty until the book earns the entire Advance back to the publisher. An Advance is much like a 'draw-against-commission.'
   The amount of the negotiated advance depends on many things:
   • If you or your work has had publicity, you may be able to receive more money from the Advance. For example, I was told that when *The Wall Street Jour-*

nal ran a story about the memoirs of a woman in her eighties, an agent snatched up a contract with the elderly woman and then negotiated a million dollar advance from a publisher – wow.

- If you have a widely known reputation on the topic of your book you may receive a higher Advance.
- If, for any reason, the publisher thinks the book will be very profitable and decides to get fully behind you, you may receive a higher Advance.
- If you have written a book before that has performed well, you may receive a higher Advance than a new unknown writer.

Some new writers sign a contract without receiving an Advance because that is the only way they can get published. If you get anything at all, it could be any amount from five thousand dollars – or less – to sixty-five thousand dollars or higher, depending on how the publisher views it – and if you have a good agent who can negotiate well in your behalf, or if you know how to negotiate well in your own behalf.

2. ***Book Royalty*** payments can vary among some publishers; however, they are typically paid twice a year – in the spring and in the fall. Your check usually arrives four months after the six-month cut-off date. For example, your royalty may be from July through December, but you may receive the check four months later, in April of the next year.

Your next royalty would be January through June, but you may receive the check four months later in October.

If you have an **Agent** your royalty is paid directly to your agent and your agent deducts his or her 15% commission from your royalty and then mails your check to you. Here is hoping you have an Agent who is prompt. An Agent who does not pay you within a few days after

378

receiving your check is not an agent you need. Find a new Agent.

3. *Foreign Rights* allow your book to be sold to foreign publishers. If you have an agent who insists you retain all rights, then it is your agent who will sell your book to foreign publishers, who, in turn, will translate it into another language. If you do not have an agent and if you do not retain foreign rights, your primary publisher will be able to sell your book to foreign publishers. Either way, you will get paid for it. And it is kind of exciting to see your book in foreign languages you cannot read, much less write!

4. *Subsidiary Rights* – Magazines buy 'subsidiary rights' to publish excerpts of your book as articles in their magazines. Typically negotiated between your publisher and the magazine, it can bring you extra money and extra recognition when the magazine credits you and your book with the article.

5. *Audio Books* are sometimes produced by certain publishers if they have a major author or bestselling book. Sometimes the author records the book; but just as often, the publisher hires a professional voice, such as that of Academy Award Winner, Lynne Redgrave. Also, the audio book will usually be released several months before the actual book is released. This is because an audio book normally commands a higher price than a book and after the book is released, people may not buy the audio as readily.

6. *Movie Rights* are fairly common purchases by movie producers scouting film ideas from new books. Be forewarned that you may never see a penny from the movie industry; but, if they make a movie of your book, you may end up making a tremendous amount of money

from people buying the book after seeing the movie. At any rate, if you make sure the movie producers credit your book by title and your name in exchange for the rights, you may find yourself becoming a famous author. And don't get upset if the movie bears little resemblance to your book. Just bank the difference and enjoy new fame as an author. It is worth noting that many times movie producers sign authors for movie rights to their books and nothing ever happens. They can't get the backing they thought they would have or some other happenstance. Don't worry about it. It's still nice to have the interest of movie producers.

7. *Money As A By-Product Of Your Book.* As mentioned elsewhere in this book, you can make money through a business that sprouts up as a by-product of your book. Speaking engagements, business consulting, new clients, endorsements, infomercials, product merchandising such as beauty products, clothing, or toys based on your book, spin-off plays, musicals, or comedy skits. Don't limit your thinking when it comes to the money-making by-products of writing a book. One thing can lead to another and another...especially if you coax it along.

Making A Living As A Writer

When a national magazine published a cover story article about one of my books and my work, the young woman who interviewed me for the story shared with me that her experience in the profession of writing entailed saving as much of her earnings as possible because, as she put it, there can be dry spells between assignments.

My grandmother, Eva Addron Carroll, used to say, "There is more in saving than there is in making." It can be a hard lesson to learn; but time has proven her right.

If you want to earn a living as a writer, try to save exactly half of every penny you earn. I saw a biography of a 1930s – 1950s Hollywood actor named Joel McCrea, who became one of the richest actors in Hollywood at one point. He claimed that his financial success was due in large part to the advice of his friend, Will Rogers. Will Rogers was a famous and influential 1930s personality and actor, and he told Joel to **save half of whatever he earned and to only live on the other half.** It certainly worked for both men.

These are wise words for writers, too.

Chapter

49

Odds N' Ends
Tidbits About
The World Of Writing...
Market Jargon, Pen Names

If you use a Pen Name, be sure to Register it for Trademark.

You may want to know a few odds and ends I find interesting about books and writing. Odds and ends that are not specifically related to each other; but they might mean something to you at some other time.

For example, the benefits and drawbacks of different sizes of books – and publishers' jargon that identifies reading markets.

Up-Market versus Down-Market

When publishers refer to readers, they use terms like 'up-market' and 'down-market.'

- *Up-market* – well-educated, affluent Readers who mostly buy Hardcover or Trade Paperback books (see below for description of Trade Paperback). Some Up-market buyers have personal libraries – small or large

– and they seldom buy a book in paperback unless it is a subject they want very much to read and it only comes in paperback.

- *Down-market* – refers to less educated and/or smaller income Readers who have less disposable income. Some of these individuals will not buy a book unless it is an inexpensive paperback or second-hand. When they finish reading a book, they may need the money and resell it. Down-market readers are not likely to have a private library.

Hardcover Books

Hardcover Books – are 'Up-Market' (see above) in publishing jargon. Hardcover books are the most expensively made and the most costly in bookstores.

If your book is published in hardcover, you may receive a royalty of as much as 10% on the sale of the first five thousand copies of your book, 12 ½ % on the second five thousand copies and 15% for all copies thereafter. (*note: percentages may be subject to change.*)

My book, *How To WIN Pageants* was published in hardcover and it is a beautiful book, although costly.

Trade Paperback Books

Trade Paperback Books – are also 'Up-Market' but readers are not as affluent as regular hardcover book buyers, even though they are typically well educated and do have some measure of disposable income. This reading market was once described as Yuppies (plural for **Y**oung **U**pwardly-mobile **P**erson).

Trade paperback books are not as expensively made as a hardcover book but they are better-than-average paperbacks. They are not as costly as a hardcover, but they are not cheap.

If your book is published in trade paperback, you may receive a royalty of about 7 ½ % on the sale of all copies of your book.

My books, *The Seduction Mystique* published by Avon Books (Hearst Publishing Co) and *How To Meet The Rich for Business, Friendship, or Romance* published by Berkley Books (Penguin-Putnam) are Trade Paperback books. I like the size very much.

Mass Market Paperback Books

Mass Market Paperback Books have all but disappeared in the publishing world. They were the cheapest made of all the books and therefore they sold for the cheapest price in bookstores. You will usually find the older copies for resale on the Internet or in used bookstores.

Mass Market Paperbacks are described as **'Down-Market'** for a readership with very little money to spend beyond their daily cost of living. They have little or no 'disposable' income; so hardcover and trade paperbacks are too costly for them. However, the cheap mass market paperback book gives them access to the same information as expensive books, but affordably.

Mass paperbacks are 4¼ X 6 ¾ which is a size that fits into any typical book rack in supermarkets, drug stores, truck stops, and so on. An editor once told me that a Mass Market Paperback was made so cheaply because the publisher expected it to have a shelf life of only 30 days; and yet, they think they can recoup their cost in 30 days – plus make a profit!

Well, I am proud of my little mass-market book, which was on bookstore shelves for over 10 years! When anyone saw me on television or heard me on a radio interview or read about me in their newspapers or magazines, they could affordably buy it at the corner convenience store, drugstore or bookstore.

Mass Market Paperbacks paid a royalty of 6% on the sale of the first one hundred-fifty thousand copies of a book, and about 8% thereafter.

The Real Skinny On Percentages

I use all the percentages in my examples as 'samples' based on my experiences. I don't know how much of the percentage situation is subject to change. If you have an agent, you have a go-between to negotiate all this for you. Consider all my examples as just that – examples – not absolutes of how the percentages run.

Up market? Down-market? What's Your Market?

Just as there are up-market readers who primarily buy hardbacks and almost never buy paperback; there are also down-market readers who would never buy anything else but easily disposable resale mass-market paperbacks. Either they cannot afford to or they just don't see the value in it.

Don't look down on the humble Mass Market Paperback. Don't be a snob about how your book is published. Remember Henry Ford and how he became immortal selling to the mass market. Other car manufacturers of that time who were snobbish about selling only to the up-market went out of business. And none of them ever reached the immortality of mass-market mogul, Henry Ford. The masses are wonderful people who are intelligent readers, too. I am proud to be a person of the masses.

Of course, you do receive a higher percentage of royalty with a hardcover, but, if it is priced out of the market, you only have a higher percent of nothing. A smaller percent of something makes more sense.

Never turn down a hardcover opportunity and at least try for a trade paperback, but the main idea is to get published. *Just get published.*

Using A Pen Name

I guess what surprised me most was when I learned that if you use a pen name; you should register it as a **trademark** in the trademark and patent office.

Why? It seems that if a publisher has spent money developing an author who uses a pen name and then the author leaves or goes to another publishing house; the original publisher may have the right to keep the pen name and simply assign it to another author! It doesn't sound right, does it? But, the old cliché is true that it's better to be safe than sorry. So, if you plan to pen another name to your work, register it with the trademark office to be on the safe side.

The idea of using a pen name has appeal. For one thing, you can be as wicked as you please under a pseudonym – that is, unless you get so popular that your identity is sought. And it is fun to think of wearing a new name that has always attracted you.

Certainly, some very prominent authors use one name to pen their mysteries and another name to pen their romances. There is a lot of sense in doing that, because some Readers do not like to see your name with one type of book only to find out it is another type. But, just as often, it is not that much of a problem. At this time, I use my legal name – Ginie Sayles – for both my non-fiction and my fiction books.

Chapter 50

E-Books
The Future Is Now

*Like each new century before this one; methods of
publishing and marketing are changing before your eyes
– and to your benefit. – Ginie Sayles*

Today, traditional publishers demand not only the printed rights
of your book; they also want your electronic rights (e-book
rights). THAT is how much the reading market change is due to
the ever-exploding electronic world (e-world) of the Internet –
and the media – television, radio, Internet magazines and such...

Major publishing houses know that distributing your book
as an e-book on the Internet can be much more profitable than
the traditional brick and mortar bookstore route. *E-books are
among the hottest profit-makers today for publishing houses!* And
writers of e-books are often discovered by agents and publishers
and brought into the current mainstream market (although mainstream market continues to be redefined.

Dan Brown, author of the mega bestseller, *The DaVinci
Code*, reportedly began his fiction-writing career on the Internet
by authoring e-books.

E-books are the future of publishing – and publishers know
this. If you sign with a publishing house, the publisher will get

the bulk of the money for your books even though you do all the work of writing it. It doesn't seem quite fair, does it?

In the past, if you wanted to write a book, you only had two choices for getting it to the public: either try to find a publishing house that will accept it; or self-publish your book and then find you have no way of selling it. That was the old-timey 20th century method of getting published – to find an agent or publisher or to publish it yourself.

Today, you live in the 21st Century – not the old 20th Century – and like each new century; methods of publishing and marketing are changing before your eyes – and to your benefit.

Why Write An E-Book?

1. You do not have to spend time – a year or even *several years* – trying to find an agent or a publishing house that will accept your manuscript.

2. You do not have to wait an additional year to two years to see your book in print – and possibly end up with your idea scooped by some other author.

3. You do not have to put your manuscript away and accept defeat because it has been rejected by agents or publishing houses.

4. You can be an author, NOW. If you wait to be published by a publisher, you are *hoping* to be an author. With an e-book, you *are* an author.

5. You can write your e-book the way you want to. You do not have to make changes you don't want to make – or watch publishing house editors whack some of the parts of your book that you think are important.

6. You may or may not make a lot of money as an author, whether it is with major publishing houses or with an e-

book; but whatever you make with an e-book, you have a higher percentage of return. Most major publishers pay an average of 7% to an author for every book sold (sometimes less, sometimes slightly more) – and if you have an agent, your agent gets 15% of your 7%.

Wouldn't it be nice to receive most of the money for your work? And you don't even have to write a big book to enjoy this success. You can write a small e-book or an e-document and have a better profit margin than you would with many publishers. However, if you hope to eventually go with a major publisher; they may consider an e-book as your first printing.

Additional BENEFITS Of An E-Book

1. **Length.** An e-book can be shorter. Whereas major publishers typically require 60,000 words – 200 + pages to qualify as a book; an e-book can be 49 pages.

2. **Technicalities.** With e-books, I do not think you need an ISBN number unless you market your e-book through certain markets.

3. **Topics.** If you want to write a book about growing petunias or some other pet hobby you have; publishers may not be interested. With e-books, you can pretty much write what you want without approval from a publisher or self-publishing house.

4. **Expense.** Writing and publishing e-books are as cheap as it gets.

5. **Time.** You do not have to wait for the printing process. Once written, it can be online in a matter of hours or a few days.

6. **Growing Market.** There are huge e-bookstores online now that are entirely selling e-books. And many major bookstores now have online venues with e-books, too.

Readership was revolutionized by the dot.com world of the Internet, where anyone can become an author with e-books, print-on-demand, blogs, video cam postings, and marketing online through websites, e-bookstores, paypal, clickbank, Amazon. com and Kindle and Sony Reader, small, portable devices for digital books, also mobile phones with digital reading capabilities and an exploding technology that keeps redefining the reading market.

Fiction or Non-Fiction

Which sells better as an e-book – fiction or non-fiction? I have heard conflicting information as to which sells more. Some say non-fiction sells better and there may be more non-fiction e-books on the market; but I am not convinced they sell better.

There are a growing number of fiction books being offered as e-books. They are instant-access and that is what more and more readers want – to read a book 'now.'

I have both. I have a non-fiction e-book and a fiction e-book. You can write either or both and turn them into e-books.

I believe that within 10-15 years, all publishing will be digital. Newspapers, magazines, and books – even school textbooks – will be paperless. I know of one small southern university that already has e-textbooks.

A bit farther into the future and in my imagination I see a pen sized device we can carry in our shirt or pant pockets – possibly even something much smaller – maybe a round penlight battery-sized device – that we touch and an almost transparent touch-screen emerges from it that can be sized up to a comfortable 12 inches. With it, we can read newspapers, magazines, books, and when finished, touch it again and – zip – it disappears back into the small device we put back into our pockets or wear on a chain.

Paper information will be a thing of the past. Libraries will be museums and books will be collectors' items and not used for reading. All library books from antiquity will be preserved and available to us in a digital format.

Even the wonderful books you write will be in a form that can endure. Right now, a paperback or hardcover book is something you should have – but do not limit yourself to paper. Have your new book digitized as an e-book that today's readers can download and carry with them and read wherever they go.

Do not be left behind with a 20th century mentality on publishing. Open yourself up to the hottest, most profitable new publishing market of the 21st century – the e-book. The future is now – why wait?

Chapter

51

Write
Your Way!

To thine own self be true. – William Shakespeare

I once read about an author who submitted manuscripts to agents and publishers, only to have the agents and publishers suggest specific and general changes in her manuscripts.

Like any writer who wants to be published, she rewrote her works, over and over, the way she was told. Each time, however, the manuscripts were returned with 'new' suggestions for her if she wanted to be published.

After many revisions and rewrites, she continued to receive additional advice of how she should write or how she could make her work better – and still she was not signed by a publisher.

In the midst of heartbreaking disappointment, she finally decided she was not going to make any more changes to her submissions – in fact, she defiantly decided she was going to write books the way she liked to read them!!

Don't you applaud her pluck? I do – but better than that, when she stuck to her guns on her writing, she was eventually published and became a bestselling author – wow! I love it!

Too many talented authors have 'given up' and stopped writing their books because of the opinions of agents, publishing house editors, writing groups, writing class professors – and so on.

Yes, agents and publishing house editors can sometimes help improve your work – but this should be after your book has been 'bought' by them and you are under contract for a book to be published.

At that point, it is mainly a matter of reorganizing parts of your book (which the editor normally does, anyway) or suggesting you add some material. That is no big deal because you typically have already been paid up-front money and it is just small polishing here and there.

But if you have not yet been signed by a publisher, take any suggestions with a grain of salt – because these are more often 'polite rejection excuses' not to sign you.

And even if you have been signed with an agent, take suggested changes with a grain of salt, as well. You can try one or two revisions of your work; but if your agent is unable to sell it with revisions the agent had you make, then it is probably the agent's inability to sell it or the publisher's polite rejection and preoccupation with other authors already in their stable.

All these rejections offered up as 'suggestions' keep you hopping about and making changes based on false hopes and not being published because they have no intention of doing so. *My rule is that I only make changes if I have a publishing contract first*; and it is a rule that has served me well. You will have to make up your own mind on this, of course; but I have found too many good writers with the heart beaten out of them by trying to please agents and publishers without even having a contract.

Do edit your work well, revising it to tighten your story or facts; but *do not let anyone kill your faith in yourself and in your talent and in your writing*.

Write for *you*, first!

Chapter 52

Three
Types Of Writing Success

Success is not 'static' – it is a learning curve. – Ginie Sayles

When you think of writing a book, your mind automatically wonders...

1. If you can write it.
2. And if you can write it, can you get it published?
3. And if you get it published, will it be a bestseller?

Talk about a mental deal killer – to think about all the things you don't know before you even begin (the voice of Fear)!

Success does not work that way. Success is incremental. Success works in stages. You cannot have the final stage worked out until you get the first stage of success worked out...and then you are ready to start working out the second stage of success, and so on.

The cliché is true that Success breeds Success: Success on one level automatically gears you up for achieving success in the next level.

But Success is not a 'static' thing – it is a learning curve – and learning by definition includes failure *as you learn what 'not' to do*. Failure in any category is not static either; failure is temporary, and part of the learning process that leads you to your Success.

However, unlike failure; Success is achieving something definite – a definable goal. When it comes to being an author there are three types of Success – and each Success is complete in and of itself. If you never go beyond each type of Success, you will always be Successful in that category.

Your Success As An Author

Completing your book is Success. Once you finish your manuscript, you are successful and no one in this world can take that definition away from you. You wrote a book. You are an author. Whether it is ever showcased in your neighborhood bookstore is not the point. You wrote a book. You are an author. You are successful.

But, Ginie, why would I write a book, if it will not get published and sold in bookstores? To satisfy your desire to write a book is the primary reason to write a book.

And it must be *your* desire – not your mother's desire for you to write a book – not your spouse's desire for you to write a book – not a feeling of obligation to write a book – but an honest, personal heart's desire to write a specific book.

If you look into the history of famous authors, you find they write books out of their own interest in a subject, their own ideas that have captured their imaginations and they become absorbed with ideas, sometimes to the point of feeling compelled to write it, no matter what.

On *Biography,* the television program that profiles the lives of celebrities, one author said that even though she was turned down by literary agents/publishers; that she knew that if she had to, she would run copies of her book, herself, and stand on street corners and sell them.

My paraphrase aside, she knew she had achieved success in the very writing of her book. Whatever the publishers or literary agents thought of her work, this author *knew* she was successful just to have written it.

Writing a book makes you an author – not getting published and not whether it sells. Those are separate successes altogether and you do not have to achieve either of the last two in order to be a success with the first one.

Don't worry about publishing. Don't worry about how it will sell. You cannot do either one without the first, anyway. When you have a book, you then know more about who should publish it or how you want it to be published. You also have new ideas about how to sell it.

Forget those things for now. First, just become an author.

Write for the joy of writing. Write for the love of writing. Write for the fulfillment of taking an idea and getting it from start to finish. Write for *you*. Writing your book is your ultimate success. The rest – publishing and selling – is gravy; and like gravy, it is a great addition to the main course of success, but not required.

Publishing Success

Getting published is another type of Success – but remember, it is dependent on your first success, which is writing a book. If you want to share your book – and some authors actually do not care to do that – then getting your book published is a second success all its own and it is a separate success apart from the success of writing it.

Bestselling Success

Wouldn't everyone like to be rich and famous and to live on book royalties? Yes, there are overnight success stories about authors who make a fortune from a one-book deal – and I want you to believe that your book will be one of those books. And it can be.

For some writers, there is another side to the reality of life as a writer. A number of years back, the television magazine *48*

Hours with Dan Rather, followed a woman who was writing a romance novel to submit to publishers. In the end, the woman's book was accepted for publication by a major romance novel publisher; but the amount of money she received caused *48 Hours* to close the show with the admonition that if you are writing books, "don't quit your day job."

Even a bestseller does not guarantee riches. Several years ago, a Dallas newspaper ran a story about a homeless man, Gary Shaw, who had once been the bestselling author of *Meat On The Hoof,* a book about the politics of football at the University of Texas. Let me repeat his book was a great 'bestseller.' Gary Shaw was interviewed by then famous Howard Cosell and other media greats of the time.

And yet, this bestselling author ended up homeless on the streets of Dallas, smoking cigarette butts he found on curbs and begging coffee and scraps from local diners. He slept outside, wore the same clothes, did not shower, and had to use the restroom outside if businesses would not let him use theirs. A far different world than he had known before.

Shaw's book is still cited by other authors and considered one of the most influential books of all time in its genre. But, bestselling author, Gary Shaw, died penniless. So, in the game of royalties, you are only as rich as your latest book.

Bread and Butter Authors

Most authors are what I call "bread-and butter-authors." They consistently write book after book, slowly developing a readership over a number of years until, finally, they 'arrive.'

By 'arrive,' I mean that the cumulative effect of prolific writing finally creates enough book royalties coming in simultaneously that the author can finally say he or she is making a living from writing books. One or two books are seldom enough. Sometimes, but not often.

Like any other business, it can take years for you to rise to the top of the publishing business; but the faster you learn to turn out books, the more prolific you become and the greater your chances of succeeding more quickly as an author.

This book is designed to help you become more prolific. And let me tell you something. There are many, many books that became bestsellers that were not nearly as good as some other books that did NOT become bestsellers. Why? Read on...

Bestselling Success Depends On Marketing Strategy

No one can deny that having your book become a bestseller is success. Like getting published, though; it is a separate type of success. And it is a success that depends almost entirely on shrewd marketing strategy.

Marketing strategy includes having the money to market a book. Some publishers will get behind a book and 'make sure' it succeeds. Selling a book has less to do with how good the book is and more to do with where it is placed and how well it is pro-moted.

I am told that some publishers may 'buy' the position the book will have in bookstores. They know that books placed in the front of the store where customers enter; and books that are well displayed inside the store will outsell a book that is lost on the bottom shelf in the back of the room – even if the latter is as good a book or better than the one they are pushing.

True, books are stacked alphabetically by the author's sur-name in bookstores; but if the publisher pays the bookstore for good display advantage; there will also be copies of the book dis-played in the front of the store as well as several on the shelves where the author's name alphabetically falls – and they make sure one of the copies is 'face out' on the shelf, not just the spines showing. They sometimes provide posters for the bookstore to display and book marks for the bookstore to stack at the check-out counter where customers can see them or take them free.

Marketing includes the publisher setting up book signings for the author at the bookstores. This usually coincides with set-ting up Internet, newspaper, radio, and television interviews for the author so that people know to attend the book signings.

Finally, when a publisher gets behind an author, they will pay the expense of a national or International book tour. This involves the author flying to major cities from coast to coast, being picked up and escorted by a hired service who takes the author to the bookstores for signings and to media outlets for interviews.

Depending on the investment of the publisher, the book tour can range from budget motel accommodations with a small allowance for food – to the rarer book tours that are truly first class in every way.

When the editor of Penguin-Putnam's Berkley Books asked me to write a sequel to *How To Marry The Rich,* I wrote *How To Meet The Rich For Business, Friendship, Or Romance* – which many people consider to be one of my best books.

The publisher liked it and got behind me. Berkley gave me a First Class Book Tour –booking my husband and me into the Ritz-Carlton and other five star hotels in major cities for television, radio and newspaper interviews on a tour around the country. We had an unlimited expense account, which allowed for hotel spa treatments, fine dining, and a paid chaperone to and from events. It was a beautiful book tour and one of the highlights of my career as an author.

But there are authors who have marketed their books themselves – which is what I did with *How To Marry The Rich* (a book the publisher also asked me to write) – and using the skills I had learned in Public Relations at Houston Grand Opera, I promoted my book entirely by myself and made it so successful I was able to assign my author's Royalty to create *The Ginie Sayles Scholarship For Single Parents.*

The most stunning success story of authors who self-promoted their work into bestseller status is that of two men were turned down by every publisher they approached.

However, according to the story, one small publisher told the two men that *if they could pre-sell 20,000 copies of the book, then the publisher would publish it.* Do you see that we are back to the old story of publishers being in the business of making money? The publisher was guaranteed no loss if the authors pre-sold 20,000 books!

Fortunately, both men were talented salesmen – and the story was that they went out and hustled 20,000 pre-book sales.

Since there was no risk of loss, the publisher then published the book and again the authors – masters of promotion – turned it into a multi-million dollar bestselling book with several spin-offs. The credit goes to the marketing strategies and promotion of the co-authors.

Writing A Book Remains A Success All Its Own

But here is the point. Whether or not a book is a bestseller; the success of the author as having written a book stands true. It can never be denied.

Profit is defined by money. *Success is defined by achieving a goal*, whether or not money is involved. In the world of writing, money may be a goal for you – but it is automatically not the primary goal because it cannot be achieved without the product of a book.

Writing a book is success in and of itself. It stands alone, inviolate as a personal success for you, forever.

Chapter

53

Winning!

Don't wait. The time will never be just right. – Napoleon Hill

The humble truth is that all authors feel fear. Be compassionate when you see and hear all the bravado we give ourselves. We are just as scared as you are – and we always have been.

Even with more than one book, we keep pinching ourselves to be sure we really wrote the books we were afraid we couldn't write.

But most published authors have one advantage – we have learned to recognize the many disguises of Fear, listed below. Sometimes, we still fall for one of the ploys, but, sooner or later, we recognize the ugly face of Fear and then we are okay, again.

Don't worry; you can defeat Fear, too. You will begin to recognize the sound of its voice in your head with a new lie – and by recognizing it, you will be able to defeat Fear – and to reclaim your power.

Postponement Is The Mask Of Fear

Fear is an insidious liar. It masquerades in many different disguises to fool you into postponing fulfillment of your dream.

Fear LIES to you with sensible sounding ploys that you need to do something else 'first' – before sitting down to write.

- *You will do it someday* – *Someday* is the calling card of Fear. When you find yourself thinking you will do it someday, know that Fear is visiting your soul.

- *You need to research first* – No, you don't. People ask, "But how will I know what to write, if I don't research it first?"

  Reverse that thinking. *How will you know what to research if you don't write what you know first?* Sometimes you don't know what you need until you start writing. **Research can become a great method to delay writing – which is an indication of fear and insecurity.** And you can get lost in research and feel overwhelmed by massive information.

  You know more than you think you do; so write your book first – putting an asterisk (*) next to anything you are not sure of. Then on your one research day, global your manuscript for every asterisk and jot down the topics you want to check out. Make Internet research your last effort to avoid getting sidetracked . Find what you need; and then go back through your manuscript and make your corrections. *Write first. Research last.*

- *You need to take a writing class first* – No, you don't. It is best to write as much as you can and then take a class or two to pick up extra tips for polishing techniques.

- *You need a co-author or a ghostwriter first* – No, no, no! No, you don't! More heartbreak, legal problems, and the end of great friendships – not to mention some rip-offs – are the results of co-authoring a book or hooking up with a ghostwriter. This is one of Fear's greatest tricks – to make you think you are inadequate and that you need someone else to do the work for you or with you – that you are not sufficient, not good enough. Be willing for your writing to be not good enough – that is called a first draft.

- **You need to host a bake sale for the Junior League or YMCA, or to volunteer for the hospital, et cetera first –** *Nobody needs you as much as you need you.* Memorize that. Your talent needs you – desperately – and you owe your first allegiance to your book. Call and make a plausible excuse that 'something has come up (you don't have to say what) and next month (that's after 3 weeks) you will check back, if you are able to help.

- **You need to go back to school first, maybe need a BA or MA or PhD –** Nope! Many hugely bestselling authors never went to college at all. Again, Fear is trying to make you feel inadequate.

- **You need to get pregnant first/wait until your baby is born first.** I read about a woman who was pregnant, had three children already, worked in a full-time day job and went to college at night. She had an opportunity to be published if she could write a book in 6 weeks. She did and even won an award for her work (I would cite the source but I read it years ago while I was standing in a bookstore in San Francisco, and I have since looked in vain for the book so I can credit it). My point is, this woman did not 'wait' for anything. And neither should you.

- **You need to get your kids through school first –** Not true. As you can tell from Chapter 1, many authors created time that insulated them from intrusion from their children and also gave them time with their children.

- **You need to accept invitations from friends for Happy Hour, dinner, the beach, a party, first –** Listen, this is just 3 weeks. For 3 itty bitty weeks – or for whatever writing time you allot yourself; your friends can wait – but your talent and your promise to yourself cannot wait. Your talent and your promise to yourself deserve first priority! Don't tell them what you are doing; just give a plausible excuse. You are your own best friend.

- ***You need to go to Europe first*** – If you get a chance to go to Europe, have fun – and take your laptop with you. It is my understanding that bestselling author, Nora Roberts writes even on vacation. You can do that, too.

- ***You need to make more money first*** – who doesn't? But you cannot wait for the proverbial ship of fortune to come in before you start writing. As far as you know, it is lost at sea for the time being. And who knows? It may come faster after you write your book.

- ***You need to wash the car first*** – Three weeks worth of dirt won't hurt your car permanently. If you are married, get your spouse to do it. If you are dating someone, get that person to do it as a favor (yes, really). The only way you wash your car is after you have fulfilled your weekend writing goals.

- ***You need to get rid of writer's block first*** – I saved this for last because it is one of Fear's most successful lies – and as you know by now, it does not exist. It is a catch-all phrase to cover all the excuses and lies that Fear uses to keep your dreams in suspense – and writer's block is the biggest lie of all. So you need to get rid of the LIE of writer's block.

Like a shrewd lawyer, Fear presents 'legitimate-sounding' lies to justify in your mind why it is more important to do *something else first*. These are ALL Fear talking – LYING to you! You will know Fear is talking to you if you think you should do anything else first. Fear is delay. Fear is postponement. Fear says 'wait.'

The ultimate trick is that Fear assures you that you *really will do it later.* There is no 'later.' There is only Now, Today, This Minute. You cannot live later. It is as impossible as living earlier. You cannot live earlier or later. You only live now.

Do not waste your time living in a dead past or in an imagined future – two great lies that keep your present life stalled out. REMEMBER to refer to Chapter 9 as often as necessary to keep building your Faith because Faith is the opposite from Fear.

If prayer helps you, you will enjoy the story of a 1920s stage actress who used to say, "God you know I can't, so you must," and then she would step on stage and go to work, doing better than she could have imagined. You can sit down at your computer and say the same words and then simply start writing, willing to do it poorly, if necessary, but just doing it.

And 'just doing it' even poorly – is action – and Action is Faith!

This is true for writing or for anything else we do. Hear yourself speak out loud whatever you need to hear because "Faith comes by hearing."

Show Faith over Fear in the following ways:

- When Fear says "Do it later," You say "No, *Now!*" out loud where *you* can hear you – and get started on it that very moment. Now is the cure for Fear's delay.

- When Fear says, "You can't write a book." You say "Get behind me doubt. I only need enough Faith to write what I am writing Now."

- When Fear says, "You will fail," you say, out loud, "Fear, I hear you. Yes, I may fail; but if I fail – I don't want to fail 'LITTLE' – I want to fail 'BIG!'"

Ah, that kind of moxie takes all the power out of Fear – because it cannot fight you when you are willing to fail.

And you know what? You won't fail...because just finishing your book is the success of an author – whether or not it is ever published and whether or not it is a bestseller. Remember that writing a book is a success that can never be taken away from you. You wrote a book and that's a fact.

You defied Fear and WON!

giniesayles.com would love to hear from you!

When you publish your book, please let Ginie know. State how Ginie's book helped you achieve your writing goals – and give us the name of your new book and permission to use your testimonial – so that we may post your book title, how people can buy your book, your name, and your testimonial on our website and in Ginie's seminars. This not only helps Ginie's readers; but it also helps you by making others aware of your book and how to buy it.

DVDs on the *How To Write A Book In 3 Weeks – Or Less!* seminar are available at the giniesayles.com website.